Drugs, Victims and Race

THE POLITICS OF DRUG CONTROL

Anita Kalunta-Crumpton is a Senior Lecturer in Criminology at Roehampton University, London, UK. She is the author of *Race and Drug Trials. The Social Construction of Guilt and Innocence* (1999), editor (with Biko Agozino) of *Pan-African Issues in Crime and Justice* (2004) and guest editor of *Race, Ethnicity and Community Safety*, special edition of *Community Safety Journal*, vol. 4, issue 2, April 2005.

Drugs, Victims and Race
The Politics of Drug Control

Published 2006 by
WATERSIDE PRESS
Domum Road
Winchester SO23 9NN
Telephone 01962 855567 UK 0845 2300 733
Fax 01962 855567 UK Low-rate calls 0845 2300 733
E-mail enquiries@watersidepress.co.uk
Web-site www.watersidepress.co.uk

ISBN 1 904 380 18 2

Printing and binding Antony Rowe Ltd, Chippenham and Eastbourne.

North American distributors Sole agents: International Specialised Book Services (ISBS)
920 NE 58th Ave, Suite 300, Portland, Oregon, 97213-3786, USA
Telephone 1 800 944 6190 Fax 1 503 280 8832 orders@isbs.com www.isbs.com

Drugs, Victims and Race

THE POLITICS OF DRUG CONTROL

Anita Kalunta-Crumpton

WATERSIDE PRESS

Acknowledgements

I give my warmest thanks to my father, HRH Dr Ariwodo Kalunta, for his constant appreciation of my published work; to David, for remaining my best friend and my 'rock'; and to my two precious children, Ezinwa and Nkemjika, for coming into my life and for highlighting to me the importance of constructive time management. As always, I give my greatest thanks to God.

Drugs, Victims and Race
The Politics of Drug Control

CONTENTS

List of Tables

Dedication

For

Ezinwa, Nkemjika and David

Select List of Abbreviations and Acronyms

ACMD	Advisory Council on the Misuse of Drugs
AIDS	Acquired Immune Deficiency Syndrome
CARAT	Counselling, Assessment, Referral, Advice, Throughcare
CEECs	Central and Eastern European Countries
CIA	Central Intelligence Agency (US)
DAT	Drug Action Team
DRR	Drug Rehabilitation Requirement
DIP	Drug Interventions Programme
DPAS	Drugs Prevention Advisory Service
DPI	Drugs Prevention Initiative
DTOA	Drug Trafficking Offences Act 1986
DTTO	Drug Treatment and Testing Order
EC	European Community
EDU	Europol Drugs Unit
EEA	European Economic Area
EMCDDA	European Monitoring Centre for Drugs and Drug Addiction
EUFD	European Union Framework Decision
GDP	Gross Domestic Product
HIV	Human Immune Virus
HRT	Habitual Residence Test
MPD	Metropolitan Police District
NCIS	National Criminal Intelligence Service
NCS	National Crime Squad
NDTMS	National Drug Treatment Monitoring System
NDLEA	National Drug Law Enforcement Agency (Nigeria)
NEW-ADAM	New English and Welsh Arrestee Drug Abuse Monitoring
NTA	National Treatment Agency
NTORS	National Treatment Outcomes Research Study
RDMDs	Regional Drug Misuse Databases
SECI	Southeast European Cooperative Initiative
UNDCP	United Nations International Drug Control Programme

Introduction

Drugs, Victims and Race is not so much a dedicated attempt to rehearse the workings of the racialised strategies in Britain's or the West's war on drugs. Instead its underlying aim is to present the drug problem as a cancerous disease that has claimed and is still claiming many victims across the globe regardless of geographical location, race, ethnicity, class, gender and age. In so doing, this book pinpoints the usefulness of a critically constructive approach to addressing not only Britain's drug problem but also the problem as it affects the rest of the world. Fundamental to this approach is a call for a bias-free mechanism in discourse, policy and practice, which shifts from its emphasised assignment of blame on the drug trafficking angle of the problem to genuinely balancing the roles of both drugs supply and demand on the agenda of drug control strategies.

This book highlights that directly or indirectly, everyone is either an actual or a potential victim of the drug problem, whether it is in terms of drug demand or drug supply. In other words, the problem moves beyond its direct impact on the drug user to affect others including those strangers who are robbed or whose homes are burgled by a user in order to finance a habit, those whose run-down neighbourhoods are partly a consequence of drug using and dealing activities in the area and the taxpayers whose hard earned incomes are partly diverted to treatment and rehabilitation services for the drug user. The same taxpayers make financial contributions to the war on drugs including the running of the prisons where drug offenders are housed during their term of imprisonment.

Across the globe, drug offences form one of the categories of offences that attract the most severe penalties. Thailand's death penalty approach to drug trafficking has not been exceptional since Nigeria once adopted that strategy. In the West, the ultimate punitive attack against drug trafficking is demonstrated in lengthy prison sentences with a maximum of life imprisonment and asset confiscation. Despite the key message gleaned from such forms of crusade, which is that drug trafficking has become a global enemy, it is nevertheless an activity that has continued to be sustained by drug demand, and consequently has continued to be attacked by the western-led war on drugs. In this war, drug production sources fall victims to western attack, like the poor farmers whose impoverished economic circumstances have resulted in their engagement in coca bush, opium poppy and cannabis cultivation. At the point of drug trafficking, direct victims of the drug war are often drawn from non-western nationalities that have acquired the stereotype of the drug trafficker, despite their low-level involvement in the drug trade (Green 1998). Thus, West Africans, Caribbeans, South Americans and Asians are prime targets of *indiscriminate* western law enforcement drug controls at both external and internal borders.

Above I have used and italicised the word 'indiscriminate' to draw attention to my own experiences of victimisation in the face of the drug war frenzy. These experiences took place at both London Heathrow and Gatwick airports where on three separate occasions my return trips from Nigeria and the US were interrupted by custom officials searching for drug trafficking arrestees. On two of these occasions, I presumably fitted the criteria used in the so-called drugs intelligence to determine an international drug trafficker: a black woman travelling alone from Nigeria or other countries where race is significant in defining drug trafficking and, in this case, the US. I was released after my luggage had been thoroughly ransacked in full view of other passengers leaving the terminal. The other occasion of my experience with customs was quite interesting. I was returning from Nigeria with my husband who is Caucasian and who had knowledge of my previous experiences at the airport. After lengthy discussions with my husband who was sceptical, we decided to put my theory to the test. We agreed to act as individual travellers. As he walked ahead of me past custom officials, suddenly I heard that familiar phrase, 'Excuse me, Madam' as I was beckoned to the side for probably another luggage search. At that point I attracted my husband's attention and as soon as he turned round I was asked, 'Are you with him?' My reply was, 'Yes' and I was allowed to carry on with my journey, to my relief, without further interruption. However I was astonished by that incident principally because of what seemed to be the forces of race and gender performing individually or collectively to determine who might or who might not be a drug trafficker. My husband could have been carrying a large amount of drugs in his suitcase, but was exempted from customs stop and search practices because he was a white male. Interestingly again, it seemed that being in the company of a white male gave me 'protection' against a search yet on this occasion, I could have been in possession of drugs.

Whilst my own experiences give credence to what we may already know about the biased tactics of the drug war, they simultaneously illustrate that despite the prominent roles of social factors such as race, gender and class in the war on drugs, the problem continues unabated. From this standpoint, the chapters of this book are introduced. Each of the chapters aims to illustrate that the starting point in addressing the drug problem should be to adopt an approach that refrains from measures that are subjectively biased and myopic. Doing so would very importantly require taking an unbiased, critical look at how the drug problem and the war on it claim their victims at both the levels of drug use and supply, with a view to determining how best to tackle the problem in an effective manner. Without using this space to argue theoretical victimology, it is however worth mentioning that various aspects of victimological theoretical framework will find suitable examples drawn from the implicit or explicit accounts of drug victimisation shown in this book.

The primary precipitator of this book was the author's research study of race and drug trials, which essentially looked at how drug offence cases involving black and white defendants were socially constructed by the prosecution (and the police), the defence and the judiciary at a London Crown Court culminating in final decisions over a defendant's guilt or innocence (see Kalunta-Crumpton 1999 for details). The research study entailed a seven-month systematic observation of court proceedings during which 40 drug offences cases (concerning 23 black defendants and 17 white defendants) were observed. Although the research itself, conducted in 1991, is now 14 years old, the findings were and are still crucial in highlighting the practical illustration of racial demarcation in criminal justice conceptions and contextualisations of drugs supply and demand, with the former portrayed as the cause of the latter.

Chapter 1 presents this study, focusing on the role of the prosecution (and the police) in differentiating between 'the drug trafficker' and 'the drug user' along the lines of race. In the legal rhetoric of court proceedings relating to drug offences, black drug use was undermined by associating black defendants with drug trafficking. It was by far more likely for the prosecution to relate problem drug use to white defendants than to their black counterparts in similar cases where both groups claimed to be problem drug users in order to protest their innocence against allegations of drug trafficking. The racial disparity was most evident in prosecutorial response to the two count charge of 'possession of a controlled drug with intent to supply unlawfully', which was the most common drug trafficking charge brought against the defendants and in particular the black defendants. Often both black and white defendants charged with the above offence pleaded guilty to 'unlawful possession of a controlled drug' whilst claiming that the drug in question was for their own personal consumption. In contrast, they pleaded not guilty to allegations that they had intentions to supply drugs.

Nevertheless, prosecutorial presentations of similar drug trafficking cases involving black and white defendants varied. It seemed the racially-based variations were rooted in the prosecution's utilisation of knowledge which had as its important ingredients elements of racial awareness of the characteristics of drug users and drug traffickers. The roots of the racially-underlined knowledge of drug use and drug trafficking are captured in *Chapters* 2 and 3 respectively. *Chapter* 2 goes back through history to look at discursive and policy developments in concerns about drug use. And what seems clear from the trail is that those concerns, particularly in the area of problem drug use, have focused on the white population as the victims of the drug problem. The heroin epidemic of the 1980s is probably one of the most glaring illustrations of how problem drug use and whiteness are intertwined in political and policy interventions. In the opposite direction is drugs supply which, as shown in *Chapter 3*, has been constructed as an alien invention largely responsible for the UK's drug problem. Hence, certain racial groups and black people in particular have secured a prominent place in the political, media and law enforcement reactions to drug trafficking. Popularly portrayed as perpetrators of drug trafficking, these groups invariably fall victim to the law enforcement measures geared toward waging a war on drugs. The seemingly ongoing over-representation of black people in the prison figures for drug offences attests to this.

While years of attack on drugs have constructed a straightforward image of the drug trafficker as foreign and often of African-Caribbean origins, what has been buried under this established notion is the question of problem drug use among such groups. On the basis of the findings from my 1991 study, I was led to ask if the black community was in reality free of problematic drug use. Is the black community far removed from the effects of problem drug use on users, those close to them and the wider community? To date there are still ongoing debates about the nature and extent of problem drug use amongst minority ethnic groups, especially within the black and Asian communities. Such debates are discussed in *Chapter 4*. Despite the complexities surrounding the discussions about visible minority ethnic drug use, one thing that is clear is that people from visible minority ethnic communities are not immune to problem drug use. To add strength to this last point, I refer to my own research study of race, ethnicity and problem drug use, which was conducted in collaboration with a London drug treatment service in 2000/1. The study aimed to look at the impact of drugs on the problem drug using populations from minority ethnic communities and in doing so it prioritised the place of heroin consumption in the lives of those problem drug users. The findings of the study as they relate to the black community are detailed in *Chapter 4.*

The 2000/1 research study moved beyond the drug using experiences of the black community to incorporate the experiences of problem drug users from white minority ethnic communities. Given the traditional all-embracing contextualisation of white drug use in drugs research and policy, the incorporation of minority ethnic groups in my research is to highlight experiences and needs specific to them as problem drug users. This is demonstrated in *Chapter 5* where the primary focus is on Italian and Portuguese problem drug users.

Chapter 6 takes a look at the globalised nature of the drug problem. There it underlines how the demand for drugs and their supply are activities which complement each other; they co-exist and inevitably need each other for survival. Both function globally. Drug demand cuts across nations around the world including drug producing and transit nations. In similar vein, drugs production is not only confined to drug producing nations outside the West; drugs supply itself operates in a complex network intersecting nations on each side of the world. This globalised relationship in drugs production and supply does not function in a vacuum but requires a human labour force to sustain its existence. Invariably, therefore, it must cut across race/ethnic, class and gender boundaries in order to maintain this crucial relationship. In the discussion in *Chapter 6* the key message is that drug demand is not a problem that is restricted to the West and likewise drug supply is not simply a non-western activity.

This book is concluded in *Chapter 7.* While reflecting on the previous chapters, this last chapter argues out a range of suggestions for a way forward in the war on drugs in the UK. The options, which are by no means exhaustive however, encapsulate some of the key debates that have surrounded the drug problem. They are a critical examination of ways of addressing drug demand and drugs supply.

CHAPTER 1

Race and the Prosecution of Drug Offences in Crown Court Trials

The drug trial begins. The prosecutor outlines the case concerning a black male defendant who has been arrested and charged with the two-count offence of being in possession of 6.2 grams of cocaine with intent to supply unlawfully. The prosecutor argues that a crucial reason why the two-count charge is justified is because the quantity of the drug in question is 'large'. The defendant has pleaded guilty to 'unlawful possession' of the said drug and not guilty to 'intent to supply' the drug 'unlawfully'. In justifying his plea status the defendant claims that he is a problem drug user and that the drug found in his possession was for his own personal use. In relation to this issue, part of the prosecutor's interrogation follows thus:

Prosecutor:	Mr L, do you still use cocaine?
Defendant:	(pause) No.
Prosecutor:	When did you stop using cocaine?
Defendant:	When? About six months ago.
Prosecutor:	After you had been arrested and charged for this offence?
Defendant:	Yes. I tried several times to give it up.
Prosecutor:	And that was not possible, you had to have 6.2 grams of cocaine in your home for your own personal use?
Defendant:	(Silence)
Prosecutor:	Mr L, do you really want us to believe that amount of drugs was for your own consumption and not for sale?
Defendant:	It was not for sale. It was for my own use. I have told you that.
Prosecutor:	6.2 grams?
Defendant:	Yes.
Prosecutor:	... For how long were you using cocaine?
Defendant:	Up to six years.
Prosecutor:	I believe that you were using it every day?
Defendant:	Yes.
Prosecutor:	How much were you using in a day?
Defendant:	A quarter of a gram.
Prosecutor:	If you used a quarter of a gram of cocaine a day, why did you have 6.2 grams in your home on the day that you were arrested?
Defendant:	I needed it, that was why I had it.
Prosecutor:	You mean you needed 6.2 grams of the drug on that day?
Defendant:	No. I only used a quarter a day.
Prosecutor:	And what did you intend doing with the rest, sell it?
Defendant:	No. It was all for my use. I shared with my friends sometimes.

Prosecutor: Did these friends you supplied pay you for the drugs?
Defendant: No. They are my friends, you know! We shared.
Prosecutor: Considering the price of the drug, why would you freely give it away?
Defendant: I never said I gave all I bought to my friends. I didn't say that. I bought for my own use and sometimes gave to my friends.
Prosecutor: Did you intend sharing the 6.2 grams with your friends?
Defendant: Perhaps.
Prosecutor: That does not explain why a person that uses a quarter of a gram of cocaine a day should have 6.2 grams, does it, Mr L? I suggest you had the drugs for commercial reasons ...

In the above verbal exchange between the prosecutor and the defendant, the bone of contention centred on what the prosecutor considered to be a 'large' amount of drugs and how that amount could or could not be meant for personal use.

From the prosecutor's point of view the quantity of drugs associated with a defendant was crucial in determining whether or not the defendant was a drug trafficker. In fact this viewpoint was shared by other criminal justice participants in the courtroom—the police, defence and the judiciary. As was made clear during drug trials, there were four evidential criteria agreed by criminal justice agents to be individually or jointly essential to the institution of the two-count offence of 'possession of a controlled drug with intent to supply unlawfully' in particular. These were:

- the amount of drug found in the person's possession or control, which in the terms of the prosecutor and the police must be 'a saleable quantity' or 'a large quantity' or 'a substantial quantity';
- if the drug found in the person's possession or control was separated into two or more portions, in which case it would be believed to be for sale;
- if the suspect had sums of money (especially if considered 'large' or 'substantial') or assets (particularly if considered 'huge') identified to be the proceeds of drug trafficking; and
- if drug-related paraphernalia identified to be for the production and distribution of drugs were found in the suspect's possession or control.

Any of the above criteria made a suspect eligible for incurring the aforementioned 'supply' charge. These criteria were also relevant to other drug trafficking offence charges and they applied irrespective of the class of drug.

In my interviews and discussions with police officers, they were asked what the bases were for charging a suspect with 'possession of a controlled drug with intent to supply unlawfully'. The explanations below, as given by two police officers from the drugs squad, are the *sine qua non* for instituting the charge against a suspect. One of the police officers claimed:

> The quantity of drug in the person's possession is strong incriminating evidence. Another thing is how the drug was broken up. For instance, if a person is in possession of several separate amounts of drugs separately wrapped, it will be fair to assume that that person is a pusher, especially, if he or she has a pocket full of money as well.

My question (to the police officer) as to what quantity of drug would constitute evidence of 'intent to supply unlawfully' received the answer 'a saleable quantity'. On the basis of this answer, a saleable quantity could be any quantity. The second officer's version read thus:

> It depends on a lot of things. If someone is caught on the street with a pocket full of dope, it's obvious that he is a trafficker, after all junkies don't often walk about the streets carrying large quantities of the stuff on them, only the pushers. On the other hand, if you raid a suspect's flat, certain items in that flat can give you a good idea of whether you have got a pusher or not. These dealers have usually got plenty of, you know: little plastic bags, cling film and sometimes you may be lucky and find a set of scales.

These two quotations indicate the existence of objective or factual evidence reasonably believed by the police to be relevant to the institution of the aforementioned drug offence charge; they also show the existence of conjectural and discretional influences in police decisions to press a prosecution for a particular drug offence.

Any or all of the four criteria, upheld by the prosecutor and acknowledged by the defence and the judiciary, indicate what criminal justice officials consider to be relevant to drug trafficking offence charges. Each criterion, although deemed crucial to a drug trafficking allegation, lacked precise definition in the sense that there appeared to be no clear distinction drawn as to how they were determined as evidence of drug trafficking. The splitting of drugs into separately packaged portions (irrespective of the number) was an act construed by the prosecutor as being cognisant with drug trafficking in some cases. There were however other cases where the existence of separate packages of drugs attracted the charge of simple possession, while drugs packaged in one lump warranted a drug trafficking offence charge in yet others. Similar responses were applied to the identification of items as drug-related paraphernalia and the interpretation of assets as proceeds of drug trafficking.

The quantity of drug was another factor that indicated shifts in the imputation of meanings to drug trafficking by the prosecutor. In some drug trafficking cases, quantities of drugs described by the prosecutor as 'large' or 'substantial' were classed by them as an indication of trafficking, and in some other cases similar amounts justified a simple possession charge. Despite the lack of precision as to how quantities of drugs were defined as representing drug trafficking or drug possession, the prosecutor however found it more justifiable to refer to the quantity of drug if the amount involved was believed to be large. Even at that, such references were made in ways which were essentially relative in nature. In the absence of a universal consensus over a relationship between a specified amount of drug and drug trafficking, what tended to be presented was a scenario which harboured the potential to lead to an automatic designation of some defendants, but not others, as drug traffickers. There were variations in definitions given to similar situations, which suggested an intrusion of the prosecutor's own frame of reference with regard to drugs issues. Essentially the discrepancies were intrinsically imbued with racial overtones.

There were two racially underlined dimensions in the prosecutor's description of the link between drug trafficking and the quantity of drugs. For black defendants, the main premise of the 'drug trafficking and quantity of drug' argument was that the amounts of drugs found in the defendants' possession or control could only be explained in terms of drug trafficking. At this end of the spectrum were definitions that described this group of defendants as the drug trafficking class, the real criminals whose principal reason for being in possession of what was notably described by the prosecutor as 'substantial' amounts of drugs, was to sell them in order to make a financial gain. No other explanation was portrayed as rational by the prosecutor. At the other end of the spectrum, we witness the prosecutor seeming to assign or assigning a non-drug trafficking definition to a drug trafficking offence charge brought against white defendants linked to 'large' quantities of drugs. In five white defendants' cases where the issue of the quantity of drug was raised, the drug trafficking offence charges brought against them were however dropped. Although the prosecutor acknowledged the presence of 'large' amounts of drugs in those cases, alternative explanations were given for their existence. For example:

> A white male defendant charged with the two-count charge of 'possession of a controlled drug with intent to supply unlawfully' was associated with 13.04 grams of a class B drug which was described by the prosecutor as 'a substantial quantity of drug'. Whilst dropping the drug trafficking offence charge, the prosecutor stated that 'the defendant said that he had that amount of drug because he intended sharing it with his friends who are known drug users. He said that he did not intend making any financial profit'. (Kalunta-Crumpton 1999)

Claiming drug use or addiction in order to reduce the possibility of a conviction or to avoid a severe penalty was common amongst defendants who pleaded guilty to unlawful possession of a controlled drug but disputed a drug trafficking allegation. This occurred irrespective of race and the amount of drug involved. For the prosecutor this explanation, along with that which portrayed a defendant as a non-drug trafficker who merely supplied to friends on a social basis, justified dropping drug trafficking offence charges against some white defendants linked to 'large' amounts of drugs, thereby exempting them from a trial by jury. In the case of those white defendants who went through a contested trial for drug trafficking, the quantity of drug even when construed as large did not receive a significant negative attention. The defendants' explanations that the 'large' quantities of drugs in question were for their own use failed to give rise to the type of interrogation aimed at creating the image of an 'evil' drug trafficker. The case of a white female defendant charged with possession of 14.6 grams of cannabis with intent to supply unlawfully provides an illustration of this type. In trying to refute the defendant's explanation that the 14.6 grams of cannabis was not meant for sale, the prosecutor asked:

Prosecutor:	In your statement made at the police station, you said that the 14.6 grams of cannabis found in your flat was for your own personal use?
Defendant:	Yes.
Prosecutor:	Did you intend using that amount of drug in one day?
Defendant:	No. That could have lasted me about two weeks unless I gave some to friends.
Prosecutor:	Could those friends have paid you?
Defendant:	No. I wouldn't have paid them if they gave me some.
Prosecutor:	Why would you buy two weeks supply?
Defendant:	I don't like running out. I buy enough to last me till I get my giro.

Because there is a lesser degree of seriousness ascribed to illicit drug use (Young 1971; Dorn *et al.* 1992), defendants found it a favourable explanation to give in order to contest allegations of possession for the principal purpose of trafficking. The 'personal use' or 'sharing with friends on a social basis' explanation however did not always receive a relatively 'minimal' form of questioning, as illustrated in the earlier case above involving a black male defendant. The prosecutor did not place black defendants within the ranks of helpless drug users/addicts—in a way that could advantage them. The image of the problem drug user who falls victim to the 'cruel' drug trafficker did not incorporate black defendants, accused of drug trafficking but who claimed drug use/addiction. As shown in *Chapter 2*, the problem drug user is primarily white, as studies on drug abuse (particularly 'hard' drugs such as heroin) have served to highlight. In contrast, the drug trafficker is popularly portrayed as black (see *Chapter 3*). Whilst the drug user/addict is viewed primarily as a sick person and presented as an object of pity who needs societal help, the drug trafficker is considered morally culpable and a threat to society; whilst preventative and rehabilitative measures move towards helping the drug user/addict, law enforcement strategies are directed towards attacking and penalising the trafficker.

In the courtroom it therefore appeared more logical for an alleged white drug trafficker to claim drug use or addiction even when the amount of drug involved was described as 'large'. On the contrary, the language that the prosecutor used when presenting a case concerning a black drug user or addict aimed at overshadowing the drug use/addiction explanation offered for being in possession of a quantity of drug. In fact, the 'larger' the amount of drug involved, the more justifiable it was for the prosecutor to apply the drug trafficker label. Invariably, a black defendant who related the 'same' personal use or sharing with friends explanations for the supposed large quantity of drugs found in his or her possession or control was fixed with the image of an undisputable drug trafficker.

PROCEEDS OF DRUG TRAFFICKING

In order to prove that a defendant is engaged in drug trafficking, it is important for the prosecutor to establish *inter alia* that the defendant was trafficking in drugs for commercial reasons and as such did profit economically from such action. This line of argument is based on legalistic considerations in the sense that the law is determining of such prosecution practice. In the Drugs Trafficking Offences Act 1986 (upon which this prosecution was based), provisions are made for the confiscation of drug traffickers' assets identified as proceeds of drug trafficking.[1] This Act does not specifically and clearly map out criteria for determining actual proceeds of drug trafficking and in effect a wide door is opened for the use of legally-provided discretion by the prosecutor to identify what he or she consider to be the proceeds of drug trafficking and to impute meanings to a defendant's alleged involvement in drug trafficking. Consequently, differing interpretations can be given to similar items as proceeds of drug trafficking which in turn can influence the imputation of meanings to drug trafficking allegations.

The most significant issue that the prosecutor raised to determine whether or not a defendant benefited economically from drug trafficking was his or her socio-economic condition. This factor was vital in the prosecution process in that it enabled the prosecutor to assess a defendant's account of the sources of his or her assets by weighing the alleged proceeds against the socio-economic status of the defendant. Nevertheless, the utilisation of this factor in evaluating a defendant's accountability was discretionary. Apparently, the majority of the defendants belonged to the lower class: they were mostly unemployed or self-employed (irregular), and the majority of them claimed state benefits. Only a few of the defendants claimed to have regular employment. This fact seemed to coincide very much with the ideology that economic deprivation and illicit drug use/drug trafficking among the lower class are intertwined, with the former leading to the latter (Parker *et al.* 1986; Burr 1987; Pearson 1987a, b; Gilroy 1987). Whether or not the defendants committed the alleged drug trafficking offence due to their socio-economic condition is another issue altogether. The fact remains that their socio-economic standing in society—depending on the definition given to it by the prosecutor—was used by the prosecutor to pursue his or her claim, either for or against the defendants. The black defendants made up a group who found their socio-economic circumstances dysfunctional to them in the trial process but functional and valuable to the prosecutors who drew upon them to enhance or boost their complaint against black defendants in relation to the issue of proceeds of drug trafficking. In spite of the similarities in the socio-economic conditions of black

[1] See also now the Proceeds of Crime Act 2002 mentioned at p. 69.

and white defendants, black defendants' cases were specifically described and highlighted in terms of the significance of a deprived socio-economic context.

The image of the black community as socio-economically deprived and consequently criminally minded is widely acknowledged; it is a belief commonly shared by those in authority (John 1981). The low socio-economic status ascribed to the black community appeared to form a solid ideological construction that permeated the prosecution and created a bedrock upon which was based the prosecution justification process regarding proceeds of drug trafficking. In addressing the relationship between black defendants' economic conditions, alleged proceeds of drug trafficking and their alleged involvement in drug trafficking, the prosecutor's representations had a clear resonance with academic, official and media accounts of black people, deprivation, crime and drug trafficking. Indeed, no consensus existed in the pattern of how black and white defendants' material conditions were portrayed in relation to the subject of proceeds. Interrogations aimed at establishing that defendants benefited economically from drug trafficking were 'detailed' and 'emphasised' in cases involving black defendants. Also negative comments and suggestions (embedded in the interrogations) made about the relationship between defendants' economic circumstances and drug trafficking were apparently confined to black defendants.

The prosecutor's allegations against unemployed black defendants were supported by intricately hammering on the ideological link between 'blackness' and unemployment, and 'black unemployment' and crime. What was subtly presented by the prosecutor to the judge and jury was that an unemployed black defendant dealt in drugs because he or she was constrained by economic circumstances.

On presenting defendants' possessions to the court as evidence of proceeds of drug trafficking, the question ultimately rested on the source of personal possessions and apparently on the defendants' private lives. In relation to the black defendants, once the source of their personal possessions was located in drug trafficking, the very notion of unemployment being consistent with drug trafficking reared its head. The fact that a black defendant was unemployed was presented by the prosecutor as a justifiable argument; in addition, reliance on welfare benefit was defined as unable legitimately to provide for the defendant's possessions, the argument being that it is inconceivable for a defendant whose economic dependence is wholly on state welfare to acquire what the prosecutor considered to be luxurious possessions unless that defendant was into some sort of crime—in this case, drug trafficking. In my observations, cash (no matter the amount), clothes, jewellery and cars (irrespective of their age) were construed as luxurious assets acquired through no other source but drug trafficking.

Even when the supposed proceeds were 'accounted for' by the defendants, such accounts were disputed and subsequently interpreted to suit the prosecutor's version. The picture of an unemployed black defendant created for the judge and jury was one of typical economic deprivation. In the bid to explain logically to the judge and jury that an unemployed black defendant, because of his or her 'poor' economic condition, did resort to drug trafficking in order to make ends meet, the prosecutor ensured that the defendant accounted for each and every one of the items presumed to be the proceeds of drug trafficking – as shown in the following instance:

Prosecutor: Mr X, you are unemployed and on social security of £54 per fortnight?
Defendant: Yes, sir.
Prosecutor: You have four children and I suppose you contribute to their upkeep?
Defendant: Yes, sir.
Prosecutor: ... On the day of your arrest, you had £104 in your possession. For someone that is unemployed, where did the money come from?
Defendant: Actually, I had £160 on that day. Part of the money was my social security which I collected the previous day and money that I borrowed from a girlfriend to help decorate my kids' bedroom. I had spent some of the money on wallpaper before I was arrested.
Prosecutor: How much did you spend on wallpaper?
Defendant: About £50.
Prosecutor: ... When you were arrested, you were wearing three pairs of trousers, two jumpers and the police told you that they were quite new and asked you where you got the money to buy them. What did you tell them?
Defendant: I told them that I get money from my relatives and girlfriends and that I share clothes sometimes with friends.
Prosecutor: ... Did you pay for this jumper yourself [referring to one of the jumpers that the defendant wore on the day of his arrest]?
Defendant: Yes, sir.
Prosecutor: How much did you pay for it?
Defendant: About £10. I bought it from a street market.
Prosecutor: ... What about your car? How were you able to afford a car and maintain it on £54?
Defendant: I don't have the car now. I paid £280 for it and I bought it when my girlfriend was pregnant to make life easier for her, like take her to the hospital and shop, you know!
Prosecutor: You must have paid to fuel the car?
Defendant: I never drove it anytime I didn't have money for fuel.
Prosecutor: And maintenance?
Defendant: I did a lot of repairs myself.

To add validity and strength to its logic about unemployment and crime, the prosecutor searched for 'accuracy' in black defendants' evidence. With the advantage that the prosecutor has for obtaining evidence, it is easier for them to have access to 'incriminating' information although the extent that they want to go in the process of collecting what they consider evidence is discretionary. In the above case, the prosecutor had some of the defendant's alleged proceeds of drug trafficking valued and presented to the judge and jury, and the defendant was interrogated in relation to that:

Prosecutor:	If you are not a drug dealer, from where did you get the money to pay for all the jewellery you were wearing on the evening that you were arrested? You do not expect us to believe that your benefit covered the cost of the jewellery, do you?
Defendant:	I got them from America. I bought some and my relatives and friends gave me some.
Prosecutor:	That was what you told the police. The jewels are estimated to be worth $600. They are quite expensive gifts, are they not?
Defendant:	They were not up to $600 dollars at the time.
Prosecutor:	You have told us that you paid for some of the jewels, how much did you pay for them?
Defendant:	About $200 [some of which he said was given to him by a girlfriend].
Prosecutor:	Can you produce the receipts for the jewels you paid for?
Defendant:	I have receipts for some of them. [The receipts were presented to the jury.]
Prosecutor:	You presumably paid $200 dollars for some of the jewels. Why would your relatives and friends give you jewellery worth $400?
Defendant:	They were not that value at the time, sir. They know I am crazy about jewellery, they form part of my collection.
Prosecutor:	In that case you can do anything to have them, like selling drugs.
Defendant:	No, sir. I am not a drug dealer.
Prosecutor:	Mr X, do you use drugs?
Defendant:	I used to smoke cannabis.
Prosecutor:	…How much did you spend on cannabis a week?
Defendant:	Not more than £10.
Prosecutor:	Meaning £20 out of £54 every fortnight. How did you survive on the remaining £34 if you were not dealing in drugs?
Defendant:	I did not smoke cannabis every week sir. I sometimes got from friends.

Whilst unemployment was portrayed as a convenient explanation for drug trafficking in relation to the black defendants, it was not made a crucial issue in the prosecution of cases involving unemployed white defendants. It appeared unimaginable for an unemployed black defendant to own assets through legal means, yet in contrast it seemed normal for an unemployed white defendant legitimately to have possessions. Questions regarding the source of possessions were in white defendants' cases not emphasised when compared to black defendants' cases. Below is an interrogation of an unemployed white defendant accused of drug trafficking. He was on state benefit, had two children and lived in council accommodation. It was alleged by the prosecutor that the defendant made a profit of £96 from drug trafficking:

Prosecutor:	... When did your girlfriend give you the money? [The defendant claimed that he borrowed £100 from his girlfriend]
Defendant:	Same day I was arrested by the police, in the morning. It's a loan.
Prosecutor:	Why is it taking you a long time to pay back the money that you owe?
Defendant:	mean to pay her back when I start work soon. She's not in a hurry for the money. She knows I'll pay her back

In the above case, interrogation regarding the alleged proceeds was 'minimal' and did not seem to be aimed at refuting the defendant's story; there was no question about the defendant's economic background. The fact that he was unemployed was in no way related to the supposed proceeds of drug trafficking. This was a common prosecution practice in white defendants' cases that were observed.

In the five white defendants' cases where the drug trafficking offence charges brought against them were dropped, three of the defendants who had never been employed since they left school were associated with money believed by the prosecutor to be their proceeds from drug trafficking. The drug trafficking offence charges against these three defendants were dropped on the principal ground that they changed their plea from not guilty to guilty to the less serious charge of 'unlawful possession'. Obviously, they must have satisfied the prosecutor with their explanation regarding the source of the respective sums of £220, £46 and £150 found on them on arrest. According to their defence barristers, the monies were accounted for: the £220 was money that the first defendant borrowed from his girlfriend who was self-employed; the £46 was part of the second defendant's social security benefit; and the £150 was lent to the third defendant by a close friend. In the fourth case, the unemployed defendant, according to the prosecutor, was seen trafficking in drugs by the police and when he was searched, drugs and £53.20 were found on him. The money was believed to be his proceeds from drug trafficking. However, the drug trafficking offence charge was dropped and what the prosecutor previously believed to be his proceeds from drug trafficking was afterwards not considered as such. When the judge asked, 'What about the money found on him when he was arrested?'

The prosecutor replied:

> He accounted for the money, your Honour. The defendant said that the money was part of his pocket money from his mother. He lives with his mother and sister. In fact the police went to his residential address to enquire about his belongings and nothing worthwhile belonged to him ... Your Honour, he does not seem to have made any profit from drugs.

The defendant in the fifth case was charged with two drug trafficking offences and three charges of 'unlawful possession'. It was after a brief submission by the prosecutor that a negotiation ensued leading to the dropping of the drug trafficking offence charges:

Defence:	Your Honour, the defendant has pleaded guilty to being in possession of all the mentioned drugs but he has maintained that he never supplied nor intended to supply drugs for financial gain ... He uses drugs but does not sell them.
Judge:	What have you got to say about this, Mr B? [That is, the prosecutor.] Is there any evidence that he sells drugs?
Prosecutor:	[Pause] No, your Honour. The police found £170 at his residence. He lives with his parents and the money was jointly owned and was meant for domestic use.
Judge:	Did he have money on him at the time of his arrest?
Prosecutor:	Not much. I think it was about £12 ...The defendant told the police that he only supplied drugs to friends who also gave to him when he had none and that it was entirely on a social basis. No sale was involved.
Judge:	I would like to know about his background.
Prosecutor:	... and he left school without qualification. At the moment, he is unemployed and in receipt of unemployment benefit. He is hoping to get a job soon.
Judge:	[interrupting] You do not wish to pursue the charges on supplying?
Prosecutor:	No, your Honour, I agree with my learned friend that he did not make any financial gain from drugs.
Judge:	I that case I will disregard the charges. We do not have any need for a jury. I would like to have a social inquiry report on the defendant.

These cases exemplify Cooney's (1994: 840, 841) observation that:

> legal officials often cite lack of evidence as a reason for the attrition of criminal cases ... That evidence is uncovered is no guarantee that it will be useful or important. A considerable amount of legal strategy revolves around excluding or suppressing information that is available to at least one party.

If we look at how 'trivial' assets are brought into the limelight as proceeds of drug trafficking, albeit in relation to black defendants' cases, we may understand how the dominant image of race, poverty and crime/drug trafficking has become internalised to be invaluable prosecution evidence. A black male was alleged by the prosecutor to have made £14.50 from drug trafficking. The prosecutor's interrogation in relation to this included the following:

Prosecutor:	You have told us that you are unemployed and that you only receive £28 unemployment benefit a week?
Defendant:	Yes.

Prosecutor: I believe that you spend money on at least food?
Defendant: Yes.
Prosecutor: You have told the court that you are a heroin addict and that on the day you were arrested, you were buying drugs?
Defendant: Yes.
Prosecutor: You had £14.50 in your possession when you were arrested. Am I right?
Defendant: Yes.
Prosecutor: And you have also told us that you had £40 on that day and that you gave £25 to the dealer?
Defendant: Yes.
Prosecutor: ... Could you tell the court how you came to have £40 on the day that you were arrested when you claim £28 unemployment benefit a week?
Defendant: My grandma gave me some money plus my social security.
Prosecutor: How much did your grandmother give to you?
Defendant: [pause] I can't remember.
Prosecutor: Did she give it to you on the day you were arrested?
Defendant: No. About two or three days before but I collected my social security on that day.
Prosecutor: ... If you had £40 on you on that day and you paid £25 to the dealer, you should have had £15 on you on arrest but you had £14.50. Why was that?
Defendant: I paid 50p for a bus ride.
Prosecutor: From which area did you catch the bus?
Defendant: From Y road. I walked to that road from where I live to avoid paying more bus fare.
Prosecutor: ... What quantity of heroin do you use in a day?
Defendant: Half a gram.
Prosecutor: And how much does half a gram of heroin cost?
Defendant: About 50 quid street price.
Prosecutor: You spend £50 on heroin alone. On £28 a week, how could you possibly afford to pay £50 daily on heroin that you must have? I suggest it to you that you sell drugs to make profits in order to meet your habit and that on the day that you were arrested, you were dealing in drugs.
Defendant: I was there to buy 'gear'[that is, heroin]. I don't sell drugs.
Prosecutor: Then how do you afford to spend £50 on heroin everyday?
Defendant: I get money from my grandma.
Prosecutor: Always?
Defendant: [pause] No. Sometimes.
Prosecutor: If you are not a drug dealer, how else do you raise money for drugs?
Defendant: [pause] Theft and burglary. I don't always pay £50.
Prosecutor: Oh, you steal from people and burgle buildings and homes to raise money to buy drugs. Is that right?
Defendant: [pause] Yes.

We may understand at this point how the ownership of a 'trivial' amount of money reputed to be the proceeds of drug trafficking can be constructed into the criminalisation of a black defendant. With this method of interrogation, the objective to prove the drug trafficking offence charge resolved in subjectively creating an additional form of criminality as shown in the way that a negative highlight on the defendant's background was produced from the prosecutor's incessant questioning. Emphasis was placed on the relationship between the defendant's drug habit and drug-related criminal behaviour, not with a view to empathise with his drug problem but rather to strengthen the criminalisation process around drug trafficking. The interrogation on this issue continued thus:

Prosecutor:	If you use £50 worth of heroin a day, why did you spend £25 on the drug when you had £39.50?
Defendant:	The 40 quid right! was all I had. I needed some money for food, transportation and other things. All I wanted was a small amount of 'gear' to keep me stable for some hours.
Prosecutor:	I would have thought that a desperate addict would forego such things as food and transportation for drugs. Since £25 worth of heroin would not have sustained you throughout the day, how did you intend paying for the remaining quantity that you needed for that day?
Defendant:	[pause] Thieving.
Prosecutor:	Could you please speak up so that the jury can hear you?
Defendant:	Thieving. I only needed a small amount to keep me stable for some time.
Prosecutor:	How many hours would that quantity have lasted you?
Defendant:	About 12 hours.
Prosecutor:	Enough time for you to steal to raise money for more drugs?
Defendant:	[pause] Yes.

Being self-employed did not exonerate black defendants from prosecutorial scrutiny of their socio-economic condition and the subsequent racialised interpretation of a link between assets and drug trafficking. Black defendants who claimed that they were self-employed and related their alleged proceeds of drug trafficking to their employment had their claim construed by the prosecutor as ill-founded and unimaginable. A negative picture of their employment was painted and doubts and suspicion were cast on their self-employment. And in so doing, the defendants were presented as people who did not fit into the image of the economically productive by way of legitimate self-employment, and whose means of achieving success through self-employment were unacceptable and deviant. In order to logically and conveniently dispose of the defendants' claim of a relationship between their possessions and self-employment, their economic circumstances were screened over and over by the prosecutor to effect the application of a drug trafficking offence label. This contrasted very much with the presentation of similar white defendants' cases where there was an absence of a prosecution inquiry that linked economic aspects to drug trafficking. Thus what was seemingly indicated was normality and acceptability of self-employment as a legitimate access to income and wealth amongst white people (for instances of case studies see Kalunta-Crumpton 1999).

DRUG-RELATED PARAPHERNALIA AND DRUG TRAFFICKING

Drug paraphernalia relating to the production and distribution of drugs constituted a further instrument that the prosecutor used to justify its assertions about drug trafficking. Items such as a set of weighing-scales, cling film, tin foil, bicarbonate of soda, vitamin C and baking powder were identified by the prosecutor as drug-related paraphernalia associated with drug trafficking. A radio pager is another item that was thus classified in as much as it was believed by the prosecutor to have a direct link to the drug trafficking business. A set of weighing-scales was associated with one black and one white defendant; the presence of a radio pager was evident in two black defendants' cases although it was in one of these cases that its supposed link to drug trafficking was made an issue in the sense that all the messages received on the pager were questioned and subsequently related to trafficking. The other noted drug trafficking items were most commonly identified with black defendants.

Each defendant refuted the prosecutor's allegation about drug trafficking paraphernalia. Except for a set of weighing-scales for which there occurred a disparity in the explanations given by the two defendants regarding its presence, domestic use was a common explanation given by the defendants for having an alleged drug-related item; in very few cases, personal use was another reason cited. In some cases, the alleged drug-related items were clearly or intricately portrayed by the prosecutor to be for domestic use or personal use. In others, the 'same' items were exclusively defined as drug trafficking accessories. This finding coincides with Holzner's (1972: 7) view that:

> one can incorporate the same given actuality into a variety of possible value perspectives ... The value perspectives may incorporate the same actuality into different contexts and thus give it quite different specific meanings, even though there is no doubt that it is the same actuality.

Despite the differential imputation of meanings to identical objects by the prosecutor, one factor remained specific—race. It seemed clear that the significance in the disparate definitions given to the 'same' items remained in the perpetuation of the notion of a racial difference located within the context of culture. Counter-claims made by black defendants, relating alleged drug-related items to domestic use, triggered disbelief on the part of the prosecutor. The interrogation of a black male defendant associated with a tin of baking powder, identified as a drug trafficking item, illuminates this point:

Prosecutor:	... I suggest you used baking powder to mix with heroin to produce a larger quantity to sell?
Defendant:	That is untrue.
Prosecutor:	And that explains why a tin of baking powder was found by the police in one of your kitchen cupboards.
Defendant:	[In temper) Untrue!
Prosecutor:	If you say that the tin of baking powder found in your kitchen was not for the purpose of drug dealing, why would you have it?
Defendant:	My Mrs must have kept it there.
Prosecutor:	What did she need it for?
Defendant:	It was in the kitchen. For cooking I suppose. She does the cooking.
Prosecutor:	Do you know exactly what she used it for?
Defendant:	I don't know.
Prosecutor:	Have you ever seen her using baking powder?
Defendant:	Maybe, maybe not. I don't nose around to see what she uses when cooking.
Prosecutor:	Did you know that a tin of baking powder was in that cupboard?
Defendant:	I didn't have any need for it so I can't remember noticing it.
Prosecutor:	You used that cupboard, did you not?
Defendant:	Yes. It's my home in't.
Prosecutor:	Mr C, I do suggest you knew perfectly well that tin of baking powder was in that cupboard and you used it to adulterate heroin to produce a larger saleable quantity.
Defendant:	I don't know what you are talking about.
Prosecutor:	That your common-law wife used it for domestic purposes is a story you have made up to hide your drug dealing activities ...

In this case and others, the black defendants found themselves at complete variance with the prosecutor's perception of the purpose of what the defendants considered as household items—a situation not experienced by their white counterparts. Whilst there was reluctance on the side of the prosecutor to view certain supposed drug-related paraphernalia in terms of their domestic value in black defendants' cases, the 'same' items appeared, in contrast, to be recognised as acceptable culinary apparatus in English households. This was reflected in the relatively minimal attention focused on the relationship between white defendants and drug trafficking on the basis of the presence of drug-related paraphernalia.

As already indicated, five white defendants had the drug trafficking offence charges brought against them dropped by the prosecution. In four of those cases, the defendants were linked to drug-related paraphernalia namely tin foil, cling film, bicarbonate of soda and baking powder. However, the prosecution, the defence and the judge shared a common understanding of the acceptability of these items as domestic items rather than drug trafficking objects. For instance, in one of the five cases, the judge and the defence agreed with the prosecutor's assertion that 'the tins of baking powder and bicarbonate of soda that the police found in the defendant's home were claimed by his mother to be purely for domestic use'. Other white defendants' cases showed that a brief interrogation like the following finalised the claims and counter-claims making activities between the prosecutor and the defendant regarding drug trafficking and drug-related paraphernalia:

Prosecutor:	The police found a quantity of cling film and tin foil in your flat which we suggest was used to wrap drugs prior to their sale?
Defendant:	[Smiling) It's not true. Everybody has got cling film and tin foil in their homes. They are for cooking in't?

The above illustrations have shown how the justification process was meant to work in the prosecutor's favour to the disadvantage of black defendants. The discrepancy in definitions of, and emphasis placed on, objects termed as drug-related, appeared to be a product of cultural variations; it was symptomatic of the prosecutor's affirmation about cultural differences between black and white communities. And as was made to appear, it is from this cultural framework that the link between race and drug trafficking derives part of its strength. By portraying the 'domestic use' explanation for a 'domestic' item as un-cultural for black defendants and cultural for their white counterparts, a logical understanding was anticipated to arise in the minds of the judge and the jury as the prosecutor gradually reproduced the picture of race and drug trafficking.

SEPARATE WRAPS OF DRUGS AND DRUG TRAFFICKING

Splitting a quantity of drug into separately wrapped portions was an act construed by the prosecutor as being fully cognisant with drug trafficking. It was an issue raised by the police during cross-examination to oppose the defence's claim that allegations of drug trafficking on the individual or collective grounds of quantity of drugs, drug-related paraphernalia and proceeds of drug trafficking were hypothetically-based and therefore unwarranted. This police/prosecution line of logic surfaced regardless of the racial background of the defendants. The amount of drug involved was of no relevance in the pursuance of this argument, instead, the greater the number of separately wrapped drugs involved, the more convincing the prosecutor expected the drug trafficking claim to be. The prosecutor's confidence was premised on concepts of why an individual would have a quantity of drug in separately packaged portions. Nevertheless, counter-claims were made by the defendants regarding this issue.

The plea status of defendants influenced the degree of attention that the prosecutor focused on this piece of evidence. In cases where defendants pleaded not guilty to both the two-count charge of 'possession with intent to supply unlawfully', it appeared rather problematic for the prosecutor in the trial-by-jury process to peddle 'rationally' the 'separately wrapped drugs' claim to the court, and this was because the prosecutor faced a twin responsibility for establishing firstly that a defendant actually had the separate wraps of drugs in his or her possession or control, and secondly that he or she had them for the purpose of drug trafficking. Defendants who agreed to being in possession of separately wrapped drugs but refuted the drug trafficking allegation made it convenient for the prosecutor to locate the act of having separate packages of drugs in drug trafficking in the sense that a way was paved for such questions as 'why was the drug in separate packages' to arise. This sort of question was generated by the 'the drug was for my own use' type of explanation that was given by defendants for having drugs in their possession, and from there progressed into a pattern of interrogation that provided two different images of black and white defendants even though the prosecutor's general form of argument relied on the belief that drugs meant for personal use would not be split into separately wrapped portions.

The two cases below illustrate how differential treatment by race was created from the disparate emphasis that was placed on the question of separate wraps of drugs in the prosecutor's claim about drug trafficking. In the first case concerning a black defendant, four wraps of cocaine were involved; in the second case, it was seven wraps of cannabis and the defendant involved was white. In the black defendant's case, the following shows part of the competing claims regarding the issue of 'separate wraps':

Prosecutor:	... If the drug found in your flat was for your own use as you try to make us believe, why was it split into separate wraps?
Defendant:	I bought them like that.
Prosecutor:	You mean you purchased the drug in the state it was found hidden away in your jacket pocket, in four wraps?
Defendant:	Yes.
Prosecutor:	You are not telling us the truth, Mr E, are you?
Defendant:	I am.
Prosecutor:	Why did you not buy the drug in one portion? Why did it have to be in four separately wrapped portions?
Defendant:	That was all the dealer had at the time
Prosecutor:	But it is possible to buy the same quantity of drug in one lump?
Defendant:	Yes.
Prosecutor:	Mr E, it is hard to believe that you were not dealing in drugs. The drug that we are talking about has only a purity of 36 per cent. Am I right to say that you had adulterated cocaine with another substance and then separated it into four wraps ready to be sold for other people's consumption?
Defendant:	They were in wraps when I bought them.

Prosecutor:	Did you know that the wraps contained a substance that was highly impure?
Defendant:	You can't buy drugs with 100 per cent purity on the streets.
Prosecutor:	But you wouldn't buy drugs with that little purity for your own consumption, would you?
Defendant:	I was supposed to use it.
Prosecutor:	Have you ever bought drugs in one lump?
Defendant:	Yes.
Prosecutor:	And never on one occasion have you split drugs into separate quantities for the purpose of selling them?
Defendant:	No.
Prosecutor:	Tell me, did you always purchase drugs from one source?
Defendant:	Not always.
Prosecutor:	What is the name of the dealer that you claim you bought the four wraps of cocaine from?
Defendant:	I know him as Jigsy.
Prosecutor:	The dealer that you claim sold you the four separate wraps of drugs does not exist.
Defendant:	He does exist.
Prosecutor:	I suggest that you are the dealer and that you produced the four wraps from cocaine that you had adulterated with another substance ...

And in the white defendant's case:

Prosecutor:	... and that you had the drugs in several separate wraps does suggest that you had the intention of selling them?
Defendant:	They were not for sale.
Prosecutor:	Could you then tell the court why the drugs found on you were in seven separate wraps?
Defendant:	They are sold in wraps.
Prosecutor:	Why did you buy seven wraps? You intended to sell them to make a profit, did you not?
Defendant:	No. That is not correct.

The general image that emerged from the subject of 'separate wraps' and its alleged relationship with drug trafficking moved in the direction of making inferences consistent with a definition of drug trafficking in terms of race. The disparate portrayals of black and white defendants by the prosecutor in relation to this issue seemed to draw legitimacy from the overall public concerns over drug trafficking which, through saturation media coverage and other sources, has been linked to the black community (see *Chapter 3*). Evident in the case of the black defendant illustrated above was the image of the 'evil' drug trafficker who exploits and sells deadly substances to helpless and innocent drug users for financial gains. White defendants accused of having separate wraps of drugs for the purpose of drug trafficking received relatively minimal derogatory attention in comparison to their black counterparts. It should also be noted that in the aforementioned five white defendants' cases where drug trafficking offence charges against them were dropped, each of the defendants involved was associated with 'several' separate packages of drugs. Justifying their action in dropping the charges, the prosecutor merely stated that the defendants had the drugs for their own use or to share with friends, and apparently silenced the significance that the prosecution attach to the presence of separate wraps of drugs in contested trials. Clearly, significance lay in the use of this information and not in its existence.

CONCLUDING COMMENTS

This chapter has essentially aimed to draw out the influence of race in popular assumptions about drug supply and demand. By describing some of the racially-underlined prosecution rhetoric in drug trafficking trials, the objective is also to highlight how the deep-seated notions of blackness and drug trafficking can present huge obstacles in the way of policy and practical concerns about drug use within the black community.

The official statistics have continued to show that black people are disproportionately represented in the prison figures for drug offences, particularly drug trafficking offences; furthermore they have also continued to be more likely than their white counterparts to end up in prison for a drug offence (see *Chapter 3*). This current scenario seems to invoke some of the findings from my 1991 study, which also showed that not only were the majority of the defendants who appeared in the courts during the period of observation black but also that a disparity existed in the charges brought against black and white defendants with the former charged with a more serious type of drug offence. What had been anticipated was that a greater part of any racially-based discrepancies would stem from differences in the gravity of the offence, which itself is a legally-provided criterion for variations in charges. However, racially-underlined discrepancy in charges surfaced regardless of similarities in drug offence cases. Whilst white defendants were mostly charged with 'unlawful possession of a controlled drug' and 'unlawful supply of a controlled drug to another', 'possession of a controlled drug with intent to supply unlawfully' was a charge mostly brought against black defendants. Apparently, this latter charge was viewed and dealt with by law enforcers more seriously, and in the prosecution process in court it was used to depict and capture derogatory images of the drug trafficker.

CHAPTER 2

Drug Use: Social Characteristics, Policy and Practice

Unlike the glaring signification of drugs and the black community in contemporary Britain, there was a time in history when black people were clearly not a part of discourses and policies on drugs, whether in terms of usage or supply. As far back as the nineteenth century, during which hashish (cannabis) and opiates had made a visible infiltration into Britain, their use as either a medical or a recreational drug was an activity primarily practised by respectable white literary, artistic, upper-class and middle-class members of society (Berridge 1988). To those involved in the consumption and sale of the drug at the time, the use of opiates was normal and acceptable, and was viewed as neither a medical nor social problem but just a 'bad habit' of the privileged class.

Although black people already had a presence in the Britain, at least in terms of the black population whose residence in Britain as far back as the sixteenth century had been effected by the slave trade, they remained absent from the drug scene even at a time of growing concerns around working class use of opiate towards the latter part of the nineteenth century. Despite expressed concerns about Chinese 'opium dens'—the spread of Chinese opium smoking into white middle-class groups and calls by the anti-opium movement to stop what was considered an 'alien vice' (Berridge ibid.) signify the importance of race at the time—it seemed that class was a more prominent concern.

DRUGS AND CLASS

During the late nineteenth century, the class context of concerns about the use of opiate was that which drew a demarcation in perceptions between white middle-class and white working-class opiate consumption. A different interpretation emerged which viewed working-class opiate addiction as a 'problem' and a 'vice' as opposed to the 'bad habit' thesis that had accompanied middle-class opiate use and addiction. In analysing the former, blame was placed on availability and the ease with which drugs could be procured for recreational purposes, and the solution was focused on the need to curtail supplies. To a significant extent, the recreational use of opiate by the working-class influenced the passing of the Pharmacy Act 1868 (Berridge and Edwards 1981), which placed restrictions on opiate sales through a pharmacy. Opiate controls during the late nineteenth century were concerned with restricting not the possession and use of the drug but its availability and sale. While working-class consumption influenced drug prohibition, drug use amongst their middle-class counterparts influenced treatment. The 'disease' theory developed by the medical profession in the late nineteenth century to explain alcoholism was applied principally to explain middle-class addiction to opiate and its perception as a problem of habituation.

This view called for treatment via maintenance prescribing and gradual withdrawal.

Class was integral to drug policy formulations of the nineteenth century and beyond. As Berridge and Edwards (1981: xxviii) note, 'the problem of opium use was in this sense the outcome of the class bias of Victorian society. It was in part a question of social control'. The class basis for differentials in definitions of drug use and policy response is nicely summed up by Conrad and Schneider (1980: 275) with reference to the US:

> As a particular kind of deviance becomes a middle-class rather than solely a lower-class 'problem', the probability of medicalization increases. There seems to be a historical proclivity to define deviance that is thought endemic to lower-class life as badness, but when it becomes evident that it is also a middle-class phenomenon, it is likely to be defined as sickness ... Similarly, when opiate addiction left the ghetto and became a middle-class problem in the 1960s, there was a rapid increase in medicalization ... In short, as public perceptions move from a lower-class problem to a middle-class problem, deviance designations tend to change from badness to sickness.

Moving into the early twentieth century, class continued to be crucial to concerns about drugs. Despite the commonly ascribed relationship between the social factors of race and class, the former seemed non-existent in discussions about drugs during this period. Cocaine came under a special spotlight during World War I following concerns about the recreational use of the drug among prostitutes, other working-class street users and particularly service personnel (Plant 1987; Tyler 1986). Although cocaine use was significant in aristocratic and middle-class circles (Tyler 1986), media and official reactions to cocaine use were those of anxiety about the negative influence of cocaine use on army efficiency. The perception that the use of the drug was becoming widespread among soldiers gave rise to the criminalisation of cocaine possession under the Defence of the Realm Act 1916 (DORA), regulation 40B. Unless prescribed by a doctor, the possession of cocaine (with the exception of members of the medical, veterinary and pharmaceutical professions) was made illegal. The class effect therein was the vulnerability of the working-class to arrest and prosecution for illicit cocaine use, unlike the middle-class and aristocrats who had the connections to avoid law enforcement.

The penal response to cocaine use was extended to opium and morphine under the Dangerous Drugs Act 1920, which was an extension of DORA. Herein, the possession and supply of these drugs as well as cocaine became an offence. The penal response notwithstanding, treatment was made available for heroin addiction. Based on the recommendations of the Rolleston Committee of 1926, that opiate addiction was a legitimate medical problem requiring legitimate medical treatment, the 'British system' of drug control was established. This system of drug controls involved the treatment of drug addiction through maintenance prescribing in order to effect gradual withdrawal. At the time the number of addicts was relatively limited, with class and age constituting essential characteristics. Drug addiction was generally confined to a certain age group and class of people—middle-aged and middle-class therapeutic and non-therapeutic addicts:

> [M]ost regular opium using customers, those who would now be defined as addicts, were elderly. There was also a morphine using addict population, generally of a higher status, quite often medical and certainly middle class ... The drug subculture hardly existed, consisting mostly of artistic, mystic and aesthetic circles ... who smoked cannabis and opium. (Berridge, 1984: 18)

The 'British system' as argued by some was established to the advantage of the middle-class (Berridge 1984; Stein 1985). Whilst doctors secured the powers in 1926 to treat drug addicts in this way until the 1960s, law enforcers gained more powers under the Dangerous Drugs and Poisons (Amendment) Act 1923 to control illegal possession of drugs within the realm of the criminal law.

THE EMERGENCE OF A NEW DRUG PERSPECTIVE IN POSTWAR BRITAIN

Drug use developed another meaning in the post-war years following the influx of West Indian immigrants into Britain in the late 1940s and in the 1950s. Race was gradually becoming deeply intertwined with class in explanations surrounding the use of a 'new' type of drug—cannabis. As alleged, Britain had her first experience of large numbers of people smoking cannabis following post-war black immigration (Plant 1987). Cannabis had already come under legislative controls under the Dangerous Drugs Act 1925 (Dorn *et al.* 1992), which however came into effect in 1929 (Stimson and Oppenheimer 1982). The sanction on cannabis, like other drug legislation passed between 1920 and 1964, was meant to meet international demands. At the time that cannabis was prohibited, its use was not widespread and neither did it pose any significant problem. Rather, its prohibition coincided with international concerns about drug use, particularly of opiates, and the fear that if uncontrolled drug use would grow out of hand to pose an international menace (Willis 1973).

Despite the criminalisation of cannabis, prosecutions for drug offences between 1929 and 1948 were mainly focused on heroin and cocaine, which may imply that cannabis attracted relatively little attention during this period (Stimson and Oppenheimer 1982). The government, satisfied that cannabis was neither extensively used nor causing any grievous harm, was able to claim in its 1932 report to the League of Nations that 'the illicit use of and traffic in the drug appears to be confined to Arab and Indian seamen'; and in 1935 it also stated that 'such cases of illicit import of drugs as were discovered were individual attempts on the part of seamen, mainly orientals, to bring in small quantities for the use of compatriots in the United Kingdom' (Spear 1969: 249). But a year after World War II, the black community was clearly recognised in the government's annual report on drugs in which it was observed, 'it is known that the traffic in Indian Hemp is practically confined to two negro groups in London and those attempting to import the drugs have generally been coloured seamen' (ibid.).

Towards the latter part of the 1940s and into the 1950s the use of cannabis began to increase (Willis 1973), a transition which reflected itself in the rapid rise in the numbers of prosecutions and convictions for cannabis offences. For example, from 1929 to 1945 there were 93 prosecutions for cannabis offences as against 1,269 prosecutions from 1946 to 1959 (Stimson and Oppenheimer 1982). Where race is located in the numbers of the prosecutions, particularly in the post-war period, is not apparent. But what is clear is that race was prominent in influential discursive representations of drugs, albeit cannabis, following post-war black immigration. Although in the 1950s cannabis was commonly used by jazz musicians and delinquent youths from various social backgrounds (Glatt 1974), and had been used for recreational and medical purposes before and during the nineteenth century, it was in the early 1950s that the Home Office appeared to realise that 'cannabis was a drug with a certain amount of appeal' to the 'indigenous population' (Spear 1969: 249). The media were no exception to the racialisation of cannabis. According to *The Times* (2 July 1955), cannabis was 'largely confined to Africans, Asiatics and West Indians....'

The spotlight on cannabis in the 1950s left heroin and cocaine backstage; heroin and cocaine addiction were relatively uncommon and so were offences relating to both drugs. However, this was also a period when addiction was largely confined to professionals and middle-class non-therapeutic addicts (Willis 1969). But this was to change when the relatively quiet moment enjoyed by other drugs particularly heroin ceased in the 1960s following an escalation in drug use and the recognition of this situation as a problem (Bean 2002). During the late 1960s and 1970s, serious concerns were voiced about the emergence of younger (white) addicts whose drug use was viewed as subcultural, hedonistic and non-therapeutic (Hartnoll 1993; MacGregor 1989a). Thus, the early and mid-twentieth-century impression of the use of addictive drugs as an exclusive privilege enjoyed by middle-aged and middle-class therapeutic or non-therapeutic addicts began to change as soon as addiction was seen significantly to affect other social groups of people. The new pattern of drug consumption, according to MacGregor (1989a: 170) involved 'increasing numbers' of pleasure-seeking 'young people' and to Jamieson *et al.* (1984: 6) also involved 'less respectable characters, more often members of the underclass and petty criminal underworld' who obtained 'their drugs from other addicts' and for whom 'the grip of the medical profession over their care began to loosen'.

The rapid rise in youth drug use was parented by a variety of factors: peer pressure, hedonism, political radicalism, social pressures, curiosity and self-indulgence (Plant 1987; Deedes 1970). On the political agenda, a notable contribution to the increase in illicit drug use among young people was availability of drugs. Large amounts of newly invented domestic drugs and drugs from abroad flooded the country and in consequence attracted more recreational drug users. Amphetamines, for example, were recreationally used due to large amounts of the drug being procured either through prescription or theft. Amphetamines consumption was widespread amongst adolescent delinquents (Bewley 1966). With regard to heroin, about one-third of the registered heroin addicts were in their teens and a significant number of them came from the working-class (King 1969). As with other drugs, the use of cocaine began to increase during the second half of the 1960s and this was largely attributed to the arrival of many Canadian cocaine addicts who hoped to benefit from the 'British system' of drug treatment (Tyler 1986).

These issues of availability were also associated with concerns over the practice of overprescribing by doctors. Plant (1987: 41) notes that the 'upsurge in youth heroin use in the 1960s was aggravated by 'over-casual prescribing so that "spare" supplies could be passed on to others eager to experiment'. An illicit heroin market—sustained by the sale of legitimately prescribed heroin – was in existence in Britain from the mid-1960s. Given the striking change that took place in the nature of the drug scene from the 1960s, calls for a new government response were prompted. In terms of curtailing overprescribing, the government's response as it were was to end the 'British system' in the late 1960s. This decision was reached after the drug situation had been reviewed by an interdepartmental committee under the chairmanship of Sir Russell Brain, firstly in 1961 and secondly in 1965. It was the recommendations of the second Brain Committee which brought the British system to an end. The committee recommended that:

- specialist treatment centres, staffed by specialist doctors with interest in drug addiction be set up;
- the prescribing of heroin and cocaine be restricted to specialist licensed doctors; and
- heroin and cocaine addicts be compulsorily notified to a central register.

The Brain Committee report influenced subsequent legislative response to drug misuse. Under the Dangerous Drugs Act 1967, drug dependence units were set up between 1968 and 1970. Whilst GPs were allowed to prescribe opiates, the prescribing of heroin and cocaine was limited to licensed doctors. The units were mainly in the London area and served the majority of drug users who were concentrated in the inner city.

Despite the restrictions on the drug treatment powers of the medical profession prescribing, the 1970s also witnessed a rapid rise in heroin use and addiction (Dorn *et al.* 1987). After 1968, there gradually grew a black market in illegally imported heroin and 'by the end of the 1970s' according to Lewis (1985: 42), 'there was an established and growing black market in imported heroin in the United Kingdom'. Notwithstanding the increasing numbers of heroin users in the late 1960s and in the 1970s, the attention given to heroin addiction had started to lessen. Heroin use in particular attracted both statutory and non-statutory intervention offering treatment, rehabilitation, counselling and advisory services to both drug addicts and users (Dorn and South 1985). Similarly there were not as many prosecutions and convictions relating to heroin as would have been expected. In 1968 for instance, only 73 people were prosecuted and convicted for heroin offences whereas there were 2,240 registered and 2,232 non-therapeutic heroin addicts known to the Home Office (Stimson and Oppenheimer 1982).

Whilst response to drug use maintained the heroin addict as its major focus, concerns however mounted around the use of cannabis, amphetamines, glue for sniffing and the consumption of alcoholic drinks. This period also witnessed a renewed interest in the class context of drug use, whereby working-class addiction was emphatically researched along the lines of the addict's socio-economic background. Thereafter addiction among this category was attributed to inner-city socio-economic deprivation rather than viewed as a medical problem (Bean 2002). However the disquiet about cannabis use, unlike heroin, was not about health concerns over the ramifications of the drug for the black community. Rather the emphasis placed on the spread of cannabis into the indigenous population unveiled resentment towards the black community for the supposed threat that their involvement in cannabis use and trafficking posed to the white community. Consequently, the connection between black people and cannabis was fundamentally understood in its criminal form and also contextualised in relation to structural patterns of social exclusion suffered by the black community. Law enforcement response to cannabis was relatively severe. Prosecutions and convictions for cannabis offences numbered 3,071 in 1968 (Stimson and Oppenhimer 1982)—a far cry from recorded heroin offences in the same year. By this time, the Dangerous Drugs (Prevention of Misuse) Act 1964, the Dangerous Drugs Act 1965 and the Dangerous Drugs Act 1967 were pieces of legislation in place to deter drug offences through increased penalties. These legislative measures were consolidated by the Misuse of Drugs Act 1971, which has since formed the basis of Britain's drug controls.

WHERE WAS RACE IN THE 1980s HEROIN EPIDEMIC?

With evidence of a high increase in heroin use and its spread in various parts of the country in the 1980s (Haw 1985; Parker *et al.* 1986, 1988), the drug problem became top of Britain's social concerns agenda. The 1980s drug problem, as Gay (1989: 8) observed, became an epidemic that 'was no longer confined to certain localities or defined groups' because 'the problem could clearly affect any family anywhere'. However, the heroin outbreaks of the 1980s were concentrated in deprived urban areas in parts of the country such as London, Manchester, Glasgow, Edinburgh and Merseyside. Of particular concern at both public and official levels was the rapid engagement of young people in illicit heroin use. Studies conducted in parts of the country produced evidence of a widespread use of heroin among young people (see for example Newcombe 1987; Parker *et al.* 1988; Burr 1987). In the two decades earlier, heroin use had been part of a hippie lifestyle involving users in their twenties and thirties. At the time, the majority of UK heroin users were based in London (Stimson and Oppenheimer 1982). In contrast, Pearson (1987a: 4) states that the 1980s 'new heroin users are more likely to be young men and women in their teens and early twenties' who were further described by MacGregor (1989b: 11) as 'that new generation whose integration into the social order would, as ever, be necessary if society was to continue much as it had in the past'. Those new and young heroin users mostly resided in deprived localities, were under-educated, unemployed and had to supplement welfare benefits with acquisitive crime and drug dealing in order to fund their drug habits. For females, reliance on prostitution was another source of generating income for drugs.

In all the debates and questions raised as to the nature of the heroin epidemic, its cause and how best to address the problem, race was insignificant in terms of heroin use and addiction. The centre of interest in discourse, research, policy and practice was the white population and 'white' heroin use. Whilst the concerns instigated a transformation of political and research interests into the epidemiology of heroin use, no visibility was given to any influence that the heroin epidemic might have had on visible minority ethnic groups at both individual and community levels. As Pearson and Patel (1998: 199) clearly observe:

> The 'whiteness' of Britain's heroin epidemic was so much taken for granted ... that social researchers almost invariably did not even bother to use any system of ethnic monitoring when studying local populations.

Even when class once again reared its head as an integral part of the discursive and evidential typification of drug users, race was unnoticed. As already indicated, it was commonly noted in studies of the 1980s drug problem that there were high concentrations of heroin use in deprived localities around the country. Most of the new heroin users experienced high rates of socio-economic deprivation in the form of unemployment, substandard housing, homelessness and poverty (Peck and Plant 1986; Pearson 1987a, b; Pearson *et al.* 1987). For example in their research in the Wirral, Parker et al (1986: 143) described a 'typical heroin user' as 'a young unemployed man or woman, aged between 16 and 24, living in a relatively densely populated town with higher than average levels of socio-economic deprivation'. Although theoretical explanations linking drug use to socio-economic deprivation received popularity in academic, official and public discourses, the obvious indications that drug use does not necessarily reflect marginalised socio-economic experiences were not ignored. In the 1980s, correlations were drawn between middle-class areas and drug use, and low rates of drug use and areas of high levels of deprivation (Pearson *et al.* 1987). In fact race is useful to this contrasting viewpoint. By referring to the place of the black community in the heroin epidemic, Pearson (1992: 286) has reasoned that the causal link between drug use and socio-economic deprivation is not that straightforward:

> It was noticeable, for example, that the heroin epidemic mainly affected white working-class communities in the North of England and Scotland, as well as many areas of working-class London; and that in spite of the higher levels of unemployment, educational disadvantage, housing deprivation, etc., experienced by Britain's black communities, black people were considerably underrepresented among known heroin users.

Why black people were and still are underrepresented in the numbers of known heroin users has been a subject of debate since the 1980s, as detailed in *Chapter 4*. In any case their relative absence—for whatever reasons—from the 1980s concerns about the heroin epidemic invariably meant that drug treatment policies of this period catered to the needs of the growing number of heroin addicts who were known to be mainly white.

The 1980s saw development and growth in drug treatment and rehabilitation services, as well as a new approach to addressing the threat of HIV and other diseases transmitted via the blood. The prevalence of HIV infection was rapidly increasing among injecting drug users as a result of sharing injecting equipment. This problem was clearly recognised by the Advisory Council on the Misuse of Drugs (ACMD) in its twin reports *Aids and Drug Misuse* published in 1988 and 1989. Consequently, the development and promotion of initiatives such as needle/syringe-exchange schemes, outreach work and the provision of information on HIV/AIDS, safer injecting and safer sexual practices formed a fundamental part of the tasks undertaken by drug treatment services. Underlining this strategy was the crucial need to minimise the health-related harm caused by drug misuse to the users and the even greater potential threat that the HIV virus posed to the wider society. This harm-reductionist framework had been added on to a drug policy, which was abstinence-oriented. Abstinence from drug use was aimed at through emphasis on law enforcement and the development of a primary prevention strategy meant to prevent the onset of drug use. Policies on abstinence were also extended to treatment services even though the arrival of the HIV/AIDS problem in the mid-1980s had to call for a harm-minimisation approach to what was considered a greater threat. Since then, there has been a development of a wide range of harm-minimisation and treatment services.

YOUTH DRUG USE AND IMPLICATIONS FOR RACE

Whilst it was feared that the heroin problem was becoming uncontrollable in the 1980s, the 1990s witnessed even more complex drug problems. What seemed to be obvious in the 1990s was the spread in poly-drug misuse, whereby a variety of illegal and legal drugs were consumed by drug users alongside their main drug of choice. In this scenario, the use of illicit drugs among young people continued to give cause for concern. The poly-drug culture followed the emergence of the 'rave' scene among young people in the late 1980s. 'New' drugs such as ecstasy had become fashionable and previously scarce drugs such as cocaine and crack were increasingly becoming available (Mirza *et al.* 1991a); meanwhile cannabis, LSD and amphetamines remained popular. The widespread availability of various types of drugs was a feature of the poly-drug scene.

In general, data from national self-report studies and the police provide evidence of an upward trend in the use of drugs in Britain. Whilst cannabis remained the predominant drug used at this time, it was seconded by ecstasy, amphetamines and LSD. Among adolescents in particular there was an 'unprecedented rise' in drug use regardless of social backgrounds (see Measham *et al.* 1998). To a significant extent, this trend is explained within the context of the youth culture of the time whereby the ready availability of drugs and acceptability of drug use in the youth circle culminated in what Parker *et al.* (1998a) refer to as 'normalisation' of drug use, especially within the framework of the dance culture (Measham *et al.* 1998). Herein, young people view the risk-taking behaviour in illicit drug using as normal. This sense of normality extends to poly-drug use where drugs such as cannabis, ecstasy, amphetamines and LSD are key features of youth normative poly-drug use culture (Parker *et al.* 1998a). That said, there is also recognition that there are vulnerable groups of young people whose drug use can be more problematic. Those who experience forms of social exclusion exemplified in the context of homelessness or local authority care, unemployment, exclusions from school, criminal history and mental health problems are likely to be at a higher risk of drug misuse (see Bamford *et al.* 2000). This is further confirmed by findings from the *Crime and Justice Survey* 2003 (Becker and Roe 2005). The survey identified five categories of vulnerable groups of young people aged 10-24: truants, school excludees, the homeless, serious/frequent offenders and those in care. In comparison to non-vulnerable young people, the vulnerable groups were disproportionately represented in the numbers of drug users including those using class 'A' drugs; they also showed higher levels of drug use.[1] This is particularly so amongst those who experienced more than one form of vulnerability.

It is the possible transition from recreational to problematic drug use that poses the greatest threat, particularly where class 'A' drugs in the form of heroin, cocaine and crack cocaine are concerned.

Although drug use is predominant amongst the white population, both in the youth and adult categories, the actual or potential influence of social exclusion on drug use is recognised as a threat which can transcend racial and ethnic boundaries and which further places younger generations at a greater risk of drug abuse, more so for young people from minority ethnic groups (see Patel and Wibberley 2002). In *Updated Drug Strategy 2002*, this connection between drug use, social exclusion and race/ethnicity is also made:

> Young offenders, homeless young people, school excludees and young people in local authority care, or those living in areas with high levels of drug crime, experience much higher levels of drug-related harm than average. Some minority ethnic communities are disproportionately represented within these groups: for example, the latest statistics show that African-Caribbean boys are around three times more likely than other pupils (including those from other minority ethnic groups) to be excluded from school. These vulnerable young people, who are more at risk of developing drug problems than others, will be a particular focus for government action (Home Office 2002a: 17)

The identification of crack cocaine with the black community does raise worrying concerns as to the risk of crack use for young black people and other visible minority ethnic groups who experience adverse effects of social exclusion. Crack cocaine has been linked to the black community since the late 1980s and at some points the emphasis on heroin has shifted to cocaine, especially 'crack', although both were known to Britain long before this period. Unlike heroin and the disease views of addiction and medical treatment, the issue of crack became a policing problem. This was despite the fact that crack use failed to reach epidemic proportions as was expected in line with the US experience. But by the late 1990s, as shown in the 1998 *British Crime Survey* (BCS), there was a significant increase in cocaine (and also cannabis) use, unlike heroin use, which had not increased since the 1996 BCS. The increase in cocaine use according to the BCS report may have been tantamount to the US experiences of the 1980s and was reflective of the 'era of globalisation'. The cocaine use increase was also presented as worrying. The study also noted that there had been a 'levelling off in the use of "hallucinants" or "dance drugs" '.

Heroin use may not have shown a general increase between the 1996 and 1998 BCS. However, heroin outbreaks amongst youth were to resurface in the 1990s, notably in the latter part. Although drug use at least during the first half of the 1990s is marked as an era of youth recreational use of drugs such as ecstasy, amphetamines and cannabis, the heroin scare retained its trail. A Home Office study by Parker and colleagues reported on the *New Heroin Outbreaks* (1998b: v):

> These outbreaks are not currently occurring in the old heroin areas (e.g. NW England, London) nor in many rural areas but they are colonising in most regions of England, particularly NE England, Yorkshire, West Midlands, Avon and SW England. The first outbreaks began around 1993-4 primarily in large towns/cities with a heroin 'footprint' from the past (e.g. established user/dealer networks). However heroin use is now occurring in completely new areas with no heroin history and the spread pattern suggests many communities will see its arrival during this and next year. Young people in these areas initially have only a limited understanding of heroin's potency and dependency potential ... Most of the new young users taking up heroin can be described as 'socially excluded', coming from the poorest parts of the affected towns and cities'.

Interestingly, the outbreaks were known to affect minority ethnic groups. While there were no clear indications that black people were affected, outbreaks in some towns with significant Asian population were known or believed to have affected this ethnic group. That notwithstanding, the new users of the 1990s were primarily drawn from the white populations (ibid.).

Notwithstanding the steady involvement of young people in 'hard' drug use, the twenty-first century shows so far that cannabis retains its trail as the most regularly used recreational drug amongst those aged 16-24 whilst ecstasy follows suit in the class 'A' category. Despite the recreational nature of illicit drug use amongst this age group, the frequency of use of at least two-three times a month is projected to place a large number of young people at risk of developing a drug problem (Home Office 2002a).

MEASURING THE LEVELS OF PROBLEM DRUG MISUSE

There have been various indirect and direct ways of examining the levels of problem drug use. Costs associated with drug use are one indirect method of measurement. According to estimates drug use related costs are overwhelmingly high. This is particularly applicable to problem drug users. Findings from the Home Office study entitled *The Economic and Social Costs of Class A Drug Use in England and Wales 2000* demonstrate this, based on costs to health care services, the criminal justice system and state benefits (economic), and victim costs of crime and costs of premature deaths. Total economic and social costs of class A drug use in England and Wales in 2000 were estimated at £3.5 billion and £12 billion respectively. Problem drug users accounted for the majority of both economic and social costs (Godfrey *et al.* 2002).

In a direct form, it is difficult to provide an accurate national picture of the extent of problem drug use regardless of social variables; it is even more problematic to try to ascertain the level of problem drug use by race. In both scenarios, a key obstacle is the fact that not all problem drug users make themselves known to drug treatment services, more so for minority ethnic groups for whom a variety of reasons, detailed in *Chapter 4*, preclude access to drug treatment agencies. Until recently, knowledge of levels of problem drug use has relied on national estimates drawn primarily from the Department of Health Regional Drug Misuse Databases (RDMDs).[2]

After the defunct Home Office Addicts Index, more detailed data on trends and patterns of drug misuse, and the use of drug treatment services came to be centrally stored by the Department of Health. The 1997 Home Office publication *Statistics of Drug Addicts Notified to the Home Office, United Kingdom, 1996* marked the end of the Home Office Addicts Index, compiled annually from addict notifications to the Home Office by the clinical populations including general practitioners and hospitals. Based on the recommendations of the Advisory Committee on the Misuse of Drugs in 1989, the central drug misuse data—referred to as the Regional Drug Misuse Databases (RDMDs)—at the Department of Health were to derive their source from new episodes of presentations to specialist and non-specialist drug treatment services by people with problem drug use. A 'new episode' is defined as a presentation to a drug treatment service either for the first time ever or for the first time after a break of at least six months.

These data were initially collected by individual regional health authorities from a wide range of drug treatment agencies in their district, and subsequently submitted to the Department of Health biannually for each six-month period covering 1 April to 30 September and 1 October to 31 March respectively. In England, there are eight regional office areas and in each of these are health authorities providing drug treatment. Although data stored by the Department of Health were primarily relevant to England, they however have included information on Scotland and Wales. The data included the socio-demographic composition of drug users, users' main and secondary drugs of use, and methods of drug administration. For example key statistical findings from the Regional Drug Misuse Databases for the six-month period ending 30 September 2000 (Department of Health 2001) indicated that:

- in England, the number of users who presented to drug treatment agencies increased by four per cent from the previous six-month period. This upward trend in presentations is also evident in past periods. In contrast the figures for Scotland and Wales showed a decrease from the previous six-month period;
- more males presented than females;

- the majority of presentations involved users in their twenties;
- the main drug of use was heroin followed by methadone and cannabis; and
- injecting was the most common route of drug administration for users' main drug.

While these findings replicated familiar characteristics of drug misusers in general, the validity of Regional Drug Misuse Databases as a direct measure of prevalence of problem drugs is questionable. In the main, they only drew on the uptake of drug treatment services, which came mainly from specialist agencies and general practitioners. Even the figures submitted by a service may not represent the accurate workload of that service. Ultimately, the reported drug users are likely to be unrepresentative of the general drug-using population. Furthermore, a notable factor amiss in the central Regional Drug Misuse Databases is the ethnic/racial origins of the users. Although there was no precise picture of the race element in problem drug use as presented by the Department of Health Regional Drug Misuse Databases, the racial formation of presentations can be gleaned from individual regional office drug misuse databases or individual health authorities where overall evidence has tended to present white drug use as more problematic, probably because of its link to heroin. In the 1995 Greater London Drug Misuse Database report, it was observed that:

> [H]igher rates of episodes are recorded in the inner city and in the more deprived areas. The typical drug user presenting to services tends to be a white male heroin user in his mid-twenties accessing the services of a community-based agency. (North and South Thames Regional Database Managers 1995: 37).

Where crack is concerned there does not seem to be an adequate informative national estimate of its problematic use. However, drug misuse data from individual regional offices do offer some insight into the levels of crack use according to race and ethnicity (see Sangster *et al.* 2001). Since the late-1980s when the use of crack cocaine—seemingly in the black communities in particular—in the UK began to be noticed, it has yet to receive primary attention in drug treatment policies and provisions. Like cocaine, which has been a feature of the UK's drug using population for decades, crack although relatively new remains to present proportionate drug addiction treatment caseloads in the UK.

As observed by the National Treatment Agency (NTA) (2002a), reasons for the limited cocaine and crack cocaine use presentations to drug treatment services have included the fact that the traditional focus of such services on opiates has largely precluded efforts by service providers to assess and meet the needs of cocaine/crack users.[3] Also a lack of trust in authorities is another crucial reason, which prevents some groups of problem crack users from seeking help. As such many primary cocaine/crack users may find mainstream services unattractive. Currently, information on cocaine/crack users in treatment services is often deduced from presentations of those whose primary drug of use is opiate but who also use cocaine/crack as a secondary drug. In this scenario, opiate addiction precipitated presentations to treatment providers despite the use or even heavy use of cocaine/crack. This poly-drug use situation harbours problematic implications in terms of treatment provisions. In reference to findings by the National Treatment Outcomes Research Study, the NTA notes that 'a third of methadone patients were using crack at treatment entry, a problem which can be missed by an opiate-focused service and worsen even while heroin problems are successfully addressed' (2002b: 1; see also Turning Point/Conference on Crack and Cocaine (COCA) 2005). The NTA further observes (2002a: 3):

> Even people whose primary drug of misuse is crack often misuse methadone or heroin to handle its unpleasant effects. Unless explicitly probed and documented, the prevalence of serious cocaine misuse in methadone patients can easily be underestimated.

Given that contacts between crack users and drug treatment providers are commonly engineered by presentations prompted by heroin addiction, this has also meant that crack users who have no history of heroin problems/addiction are not only less likely to seek help with treatment but also less likely to receive help (NTA 2002a). Effectively, the proportion of crack users in treatment is likely to be on a decline, which in turn places restrictions on 'the extent to which their needs are recorded in referral or service caseload records' (p.3). The negative ramifications of problematic crack use are severe, more so given the fact that there is no acknowledged pharmaceutical treatment substitute for crack/cocaine dependence as methadone is for opiate dependence. It is in the absence of pharmaceutical intervention that other stimulants such as heroin, methadone and alcohol can stand in to provide alternatives to problem cocaine/crack users in managing the unpleasant psychological effects of the drug (Turning Point 2005). Expectedly, the possibility of multiple addictions to such drugs alongside cocaine/crack poses its own inevitable threat to the health, social and economic situations of individuals, and also of the immediate and wider communities.

Since minority ethnic communities are known to be underrepresented in the numbers of those who present to drug treatment agencies, there is a tendency to draw information from national surveys which have concerned themselves with assessing the levels of recreational drug use rather than problem drug use. Thus what relatively useful national information there is with regard to race and drug use is that which looks at recreational drug use rather than problem drug use in its own right. Some evidence has been gleaned from data sources relating to trends in drug use. National self-report surveys and police arrests show that the levels of drug use are higher among whites than ethnic minority communities. In specific racial/ethnic comparisons of prevalence of drug use, whilst white drug use is shown to be either higher (Ramsay and Spiller 1997) or comparable (Ramsay and Percy 1996; Leitner *et al.* 1993)) to black drug use, both racial groups have higher levels of drug use than Asians. Whilst there tends to be a general observation of a higher white drug use than ethnic minority drug use, it does not necessarily still hold where individual drug types are considered. For instance, findings from a Home Office study of drug testing of arrestees showed that non-white arrestees were significantly more likely than their white counterparts to test positive for cocaine and cannabis, while white arrestees were more likely to test positive for opiates, methadone, amphetamines and benzodiazepines (Bennett 1998). National self-report studies also present such variations in drug type. For example, Graham and Bowling's (1995: 15) findings show that:

> Amongst males, whites are significantly more likely to use cannabis and ecstasy than other ethnic groups and, along with Indians, are more likely to use acid/LSD, amphetamines and magic mushrooms. Amongst females, whites and Afro-Caribbeans are significantly more likely to [use] cannabis than Asian females and, as with males, white females are more likely to use acid/LSD, amphetamines and magic mushrooms than other ethnic groups.

Ramsay and Percy's (1996) Home Office study shows the rate of crack use to be slightly higher among blacks than whites although its use ran at low levels among the two groups. In general Asian drug use was by far lower than that for whites and blacks but the use of heroin and crack was higher among Pakistanis/Bangledeshis than other groups including Indians. Unfortunately, this comparative finding about Pakistani/Bangleshi drug use was based on small samples, a limitation which has precluded such surveys from drawing meaningful conclusions on the prevalence of minority ethnic drug use (see Sangster *et al.* 2002). Although a booster sample of ethnic minority respondents was included in the 2000 BCS survey (Ramsay *et al.* 2001) to address this limitation, the findings reiterated those from previous surveys, which showed that overall levels of minority ethnic drug use were lower than those for whites. In the recent 2001/2 BCS study, a booster sample of black and minority ethnic respondents was included and for which a 50 per cent response rate was received (Aust and Smith 2003). Findings show that drug use was significantly higher amongst those of mixed-race backgrounds.[4] Class 'A' drug use was also higher for this group than other groups, followed by the white group. For all groups, cannabis was the most commonly used drug.

FROM THE 1990s ONWARDS: POLICY DEVELOPMENTS ON DRUG MISUSE

The 1990s marked an era of drug policy transitions with regard to illicit drug use, principally in the multi-agency ideals underpinning the contemporary approach to drug use. The multi-agency approach was set in motion by the government publication, *Tackling Drugs Together: A Strategy for England 1995-8* (Home Office 1995). The idea was to fit together the three strands of present British drugs policy – prevention, treatment and law enforcement – in a coordinated approach to illicit drug use. This strategic mechanism was based on the principles of both national and local partnerships involving agencies and local communities in tackling drug misuse.

Until very recently, the identification of race in responses and national policy relating to drug treatment and prevention was seemingly non-existent. National policies in previous decades made little or no reference to race but age was prioritised in relation to young people. Concerns about youth drug use were centralised in the government's drugs strategies in the 1990s. First was the publication of *Tackling Drugs Together: A Strategy for England 1995-8* (for strategies for Scotland and Wales, see Ministerial Drugs Task Force 1995, and Welsh Office 1998 respectively). This strategy, which failed to recognise racial and ethnic diversity, mapped out three aims:

- to increase the safety of communities from drug-related crime;
- to reduce the acceptability and availability of drugs to young people; and
- to reduce the health risks and other damage caused by drug misuse.

These objectives were to be addressed via 'vigorous law enforcement, accessible treatment and a new emphasis on education and prevention'. In 1998, the UK's Anti-Drugs Coordinator introduced the government's ten-year national drugs strategy, *Tackling Drugs to Build a Better Britain: The Government's Ten Year Strategy for Tackling Drug Misuse'* was published (Home Office 1998). It had four main aims, in which concerns about young people were reiterated as a priority:

- to help young people resist drug misuse in order to achieve their full potential in society;
- to protect our communities from drug-related anti-social and criminal behaviour;
- to enable people with drug problems to overcome them and live healthy and crime-free lives; and
- to stifle the availability of illegal drugs on our streets.

Again the emphasis on law enforcement, treatment, prevention and education underlay the way forward for action. Whilst law enforcement clearly has an indirect objective of reducing drugs supply to young people, the main focus of the drug strategy for young people was and has continued to be more on education and prevention. However, no specific recognition was given to young people from minority ethnic groups, whose drug using needs may be compounded by their experience of higher levels of social exclusion, their different cultural backgrounds and differing patterns of drug use. Instead the strategy acknowledged race and ethnicity in a generic context and even at that, merely reiterated what was already known about the reluctance of problem drug users from minority ethnic groups to access white-run mainstream drug services. Moreover recommendations in principle revolved around the need for racial equality to be practised in service provision and delivery.

In the *Updated Drug Strategy 2002*, the key purpose of prevention is clarified:

> Success for the Drug Strategy means preventing today's young people from becoming tomorrow's problematic drug users ... That is why prevention and early intervention with young people, before problems escalate, is the only way to make a long-term difference. (Home Office 2002a: pp 14 and 15)

Prevention was part of the government's drug control policy of the 1980s, although it occupied a secondary position to the law enforcement approach that was top priority on the agenda. The government's drug strategy publication, *Tackling Drug Misuse: A Summary of the Government's Strategy* (Home Office 1985) made the order of priorities clear. Law enforcement efforts toward the control of drug trafficking were the central focus. Whilst the strategy had planned for the development and proliferation of drug prevention measures through health education and information campaigns, local community action and the training of professional groups who came into contact with drug users, controlling drug supply via law enforcement was also integrated in principle as part of drug prevention strategy. The argument behind the connection between prevention and law enforcement was that by restricting the availability of drugs, opportunities for experimentation and continued drug use would invariably be restricted. However, in the early 1990s drug policy attitudes towards supporting prevention in its own right began to gain in importance and in 1995 and 1998, the respective governments' strategies *Tackling Drugs Together* and *Tackling Drugs to Build a Better Britain* made the new emphasis on prevention more explicit.

By 1995, the Home Office Drugs Prevention Initiative (DPI) had supported 2,000 projects in its first term. First set up in Hove and Brighton in 1990, DPI aimed at drug prevention work with local communities by ensuring that 'communities were properly informed, encouraged and supported in their resistance to drugs misuse' (Drugs Prevention Initiative 1999: 3). This mission put in place a wide range of community-based drugs prevention projects across England. Drugs prevention programmes included drugs education projects for young people and those in vulnerable groups such as the homeless; awareness sessions and prevention work with parents of young people; supporting local community development and coordination of drug prevention strategies; and interventions at the point of criminal justice through schemes such as arrest referrals for offenders with drug problems.

Such initiatives were expanded over a wider area and a new range of partnerships under the 1995 government drug strategy and its 'new emphasis on education and prevention'. Despite what seemed to be a growing practice, drug prevention encountered difficulties in reaching minority ethnic groups. In a Home Office DPI paper entitled *Dealing with Diversity*, it was clearly stated that minority ethnic groups were 'not being reached adequately by drug preventive services and health promotional facilities' (Johnson and Carroll 1995: 13). With particular reference to the black and Asian communities, these findings were attributed to factors which on the one hand preclude minority ethnic group use of services, and on the other pose problems for service providers in reaching clientele from minority ethnic groups. For the former, factors restricting access to services include language barriers, distrust of white agencies, inaccessible service provision, and the lack of black and Asian imagery in drug prevention and health promotion materials and locations. In the latter scenario of service provision, barriers include lack of multi-cultural working and ethnically diverse staff composition, service staff ignorance of minority ethnic community issues, lack of resources for positive outreach work, and difficulties in accessing ethnic minority communities (Johnson and Carroll 1995). The acknowledged gap in issues of racial and cultural diversity in prevention work was viewed as an obstacle, which could only be tackled if the often culturally homogenous structuring of drug prevention services began to embrace fully the demands of diversity.

These shortcomings in prevention work were taken on board by the new Drugs Prevention Advisory Service (DPAS). DPAS succeeded DPI in 1999, a move initiated by the 1998 drug strategy, *Tackling Drugs to Build a Better Britain*. The new service was to cover the whole of England, functioning at local, regional and national levels in drugs prevention work (Drugs Prevention Initiative 1999). Functions at the local level were to include:

- support for Drug Action Teams[5] in developing their drugs prevention strategies;
- encouraging the adoption of good drugs prevention practice; and
- promotion of effective and purposeful local partnerships.

At the regional level, they included:

- providing help in establishing and maintaining effective prevention resourcing; and
- creating supportive links between Drug Action Teams.

At the national level, DPAS was to contribute to 'consistent and coherent prevention policy across government' and provide 'evidence of effective drugs prevention' as part of its function.

In these preventive endeavours, the most vulnerable groups of young people are the ones most targeted. This is in recognition of the association of social and economic deprivation with higher risks of drug misuse. Initiatives such as Positive Futures[6] and Connexions Services are instances of twenty-first century developments aimed at channelling vulnerable young people away from drugs and into engaging in productive skilled activities. On a broader level, drug prevention strategy since 1998 has included substance misuse education as part of the National Curriculum and an increase in the numbers of secondary and primary schools with drug policies in place (Home Office 2002a). Drugs educational programmes have since been improved (Home Office 2004a). For example, many young people and their families have access to better information and advice about drugs through FRANK, launched in 2003 as an information campaign aimed at improving drugs awareness through its website and telephone helpline.

In relation to race and ethnicity, addressing some of these barriers to collaborative drugs prevention work in minority ethnic communities, especially black and Asian communities, has also been recognised by the DPAS. In its publication, *Delivering Drug Services to Black and Minority Ethnic Communities* (Sangster *et al.* 2001) recommendations mapped out how best to tackle some of the problems that emerge from work with drug users from minority ethnic communities.

Criminal justice and drug treatment

Interestingly, whilst contacts between cocaine/crack users and drug treatment agencies have been relatively uncommon, their presence is significantly felt at the point of criminal justice where schemes such as arrest referrals and more recently the drug treatment and testing orders (DTTOs) are available as unconventional routes to drug treatment services.[7] According to the NTA (2002b), a snapshot of drug users in treatment in Britain in the mid-1990s showed that black people made up approximately half of the cocaine clients. Furthermore, the NTA (2002a: 5) states, 'arrest and conviction' are 'among the crisis which could prompt crack misusers to seek help and make crack misusers visible to services' (see also NTA 2005).

One of the products of the multi-agency strategy established in the 1990s was the involvement of criminal agencies in drug treatment via such schemes as mentioned above. Arrest referral schemes have entailed the involvement of dedicated drugs workers in a proactive information provision about drug treatment services to drug using arrestees. In the Brighton and Hove arrest referral scheme, project workers contacted over 80 per cent of the sample of 250 clients in police cells while the remainder were contacted at court. White males made up the vast majority of the clients. Although the average age of the clients was 30, those in the 20-25 age group were most commonly contacted. The majority were intravenous drug users, with acquisitive crime constituting the most common offence type for which the clients were held in the police station or appeared before the court (Turnbull *et al.* 1996). All police forces in England and Wales have arrest referral schemes, which aim to refer identified problem drug users at the point of arrest to treatment agencies with the view to breaking the relationship between drug use and acquisitive crime. Here, police officers work in partnership with local drug treatment services and local drug action teams (DATs) to this effect (Home Office 2002a).

Part of the coupling of criminal justice and drug treatment was the start of a number of pilot schemes involving coerced drug treatment initiatives around the country. Examples are the Plymouth and Torbay Fast-Track project established in September 1995, and the Substance Misuse Treatment Enforcement Programme (STEP) established in West Yorkshire in November 1997. Both were coerced treatment schemes for drug using offenders involved in acquisitive crime to finance their drug habits. The schemes facilitated access to drug treatment agencies in order to stabilise offenders' drug use habits and thence curtail their involvement in crime. The multi-agency ethos of these projects was in its plan to fuse the efforts of criminal justice and medical professionals to break the cycle of drug use and offending behaviour. Two approaches underlined this strategy according to Barton (1999) in his evaluation of the Fast-Track scheme:

> firstly by purchasing fast access to treatment agencies (health) and secondly by ensuring adherence to treatment by making it a condition of a probation order (criminal justice). (ibid.: 146)

The latter strategy, permitted under the Powers of the Criminal Courts Act 1973, was boosted under provisions in the Criminal Justice Act 1991, which allow courts to stipulate drug treatment as part of a community sentence, whether a probation or a combination order. According to Hough (1996), this practice is underlined by coercion which can take place at several points in the criminal justice process:

- at sentence, offenders may often be faced with an 'offer they cannot refuse', in that failure to agree to treatment as part of a community sentence may well trigger a prison sentence;
- where treatment is accepted as a condition of probation, defaulting on the condition may well result in breach proceedings (and imprisonment); and
- even if treatment is not a formal condition of probation, continued drug misuse or offending could result in breach, as could results from drug testing.

These criminal justice-based treatment services were rarely used in the ordinary workings of a traditional court for several reasons, which have included reluctance on the part of both drug treatment service providers and the probation service to accept coercive tactics as an appropriate and effective way of addressing problem drug use (see Bean 2002, 2004). The introduction of the Drug Treatment and Testing Order (DTTO) under the Crime and Disorder Act 1998 was meant to address such barriers to coercive drug treatment. This order superseded treatment provisions by the Criminal Justice Act 1991. First made available to the courts in England and Wales in October 2000, the primary aim of the DTTO was to break the drug/crime cycle (see Holloway *et al.* 2005 for a summarised review of evaluative research on the effectiveness of criminal justice programmes in reducing drug-related crime).

Unlike past treatment conditions imposed as part of a community sentence, the DTTO required courts to conduct a regular review of an offender's progress, and provides for compulsory regular drug testing (Turnbull *et al.* 2000). This order was imposed only on certain grounds:

> Before it makes an order, the court must be satisfied that the offender 'is dependent on or has a propensity to misuse drugs', and that the offender would benefit from treatment. The assessment of whether an offender is appropriate for a DTTO is presented in the form of a Pre-sentence Report (PSR) to the court. The offender has to consent to a DTTO being proposed and made. (ibid.: 2)

Like the Fast-Track and STEP projects, the DTTO seemed to be modelled on the US drug courts although there is not much of a resemblance between the two systems (see Bean 2002, 2004 for a comparison of the DTTO and the drug courts). Since their birth in Miami in 1989, drug courts have shown a rapid growth in all US states. Their central features revolve around the integration of alcohol and other drug treatment services with criminal justice case processing. Clients considered suitable for a drug court referral are identified early in the criminal justice process, and upon referral both the prosecution and the defence counsels adopt a non-adversarial approach not only to promote public safety but also to protect the clients' rights. Frequent alcohol and drug testing, ongoing judicial interaction with clients, monitoring and evaluation of programme goals, and partnership building form an integral part of the process.

Although Bean's comparative assessment of the DTTO and the US drug courts unveiled a significant number of pitfalls in the workings of the DTTO, it is however worth noting that as a relatively new development, it was likely to experience teething problems.[8] Likewise the extent to which this scheme has made significant positive impact on minority ethnic groups, particularly the black community, is yet to be determined. As indicated above, the implications of these developments for race have seemed promising. This is further evidenced in *Chapter 4* where the author's 2000/2001 research study of race and problem drug use highlights the importance of the DTTO in channelling otherwise 'hard-to-reach' problem drug users to treatment services. An evaluation of the DTTO by Turnbull *et al.* (2000) provides some insights into its usefulness, at least to the extent that drug using offenders who pass through the criminal justice process can be successfully coerced into drug treatment. There is also evidence of reductions in drug use and drug-related criminal activity. This mark of success is however tempered with the high levels of DTTO breach (also see National Audit Office 2004; Hough *et al.* 2003). Improvements in the area of drug treatment via the criminal justice route have been expected following the introduction of the Drug Interventions Programme (DIP)[9] in April 2003. The DIP is in operation in 66 areas with the highest rates of drug-related crime. This programme, the Home Office (2004a: 17) informs us: 'takes advantage of every opportunity in the criminal justice system to direct drug-misusing out of crime and into treatment'. This includes providing through-care (for those drug misusers passing through the criminal justice system and beyond) and after-care (following sentence/treatment completion) services to drug misusers. Under the DIP, there is evidence of an increase in the numbers of those entering drug treatment. The DTTO, which comes under the DIP, is acknowledged as a key achievement in its significant role in effecting entry into drug treatment (Home Office 2004a). Like the DTTO, arrest referrals[10] have their own advantages in addressing drug treatment.

According to findings by the DPAS, the schemes can make a positive impact in terms of reducing levels of drug use and offending (Edmunds *et al.* 1999). Recently, the success of arrest referral schemes in targeting problem drug using offenders, particularly crack/cocaine and opiate users, is shown in a DPAS publication based on data from the national arrest referral monitoring and evaluation programme (Sondhi *et al.* 2002). The publication also notes that black and Asian problem drug using offenders and young male crack using offenders are among the four groups[11] that fail to engage in drug treatment following an arrest referral. It may be the case that accessing such 'hard-to-reach' groups of problem drug users will be less problematic under the Drugs Act 2005, which makes provisions for drug offenders to be tested on arrest rather than on charge, and for those who test positive to undergo an assessment by a drugs worker.

Prison

Amongst the policy developments of the 1990s was the introduction of mandatory drug testing (MDT) in prisons under the Criminal Justice and Public

Order Act 1994. This policy, influenced by the Government White Paper *Tackling Drugs Together* (Home Office 1995) and the Prison Service Drugs Strategy (HM Prison Service 1995), requires prisoners to undergo a programme of mandatory urine testing for illicit drugs. The primary objectives of MDT were to measure the extent, trends and patterns of drug use in prisons, deter prisoners from drug taking, and identify those who needed help to address their drug problem. These objectives were balanced with a disciplinary measure for those prisoners who tested positive following MDT. In such cases punishment involved additional days of imprisonment and possibly included loss of privileges or closed visits (with no physical contact allowed).

These developments followed revelations in the 1990s that a significant percentage of prisoners had a drug dependency before entering prison and that drugs were easily available within the prison system (HM Inspector of Prisons 1992; Turnbull *et al.* 1991). These observations were also linked to concerns about the levels of intravenous drug use, the sharing of drug using paraphernalia and the consequent health risks which such practices posed to the general population within and outside the prison (Turnbull *et al.* 1991, 1994). As the Home Office (2002a:39) observed, the Prison Service houses the 'biggest simultaneous concentration of drug misusers to be found either in the criminal justice system or the healthcare system'. Since the publication of the 1998 government drug strategy *Tackling Drugs to Build a Better Britain*, drug treatment programmes in prisons have included the CARAT[12] programme involving the provision of Counselling, Assessment, Referral, Advice and Throughcare services to prisoners. Voluntary drug testing has also been introduced alongside the mandatory drug testing programme, to allow prisoners to commit to a drug-free life and to undergo regular drug testing (Home Office 2001).

Such facilities are aimed at addressing problematic drug use in prison with a view to reducing drug use and reoffending when prisoners are back in the community. But how successful are they in addressing problem drug use? A publication by The Federation (2002) refers to a report published by the Social Exclusion Unit of the Home Office, in which it was noted that the majority of prisoners who use drugs do not have access to the treatment services that they need. Prisoners with co-morbidity problems of mental health and drug/alcohol addiction are amongst those most affected. Other obstacles precluding drug treatment have included transfers of inmates to another prison where they have to 'join the back of another treatment queue in the next prison', a situation which also affects prisoners post-release. Thus in the midst of signs of success in drugs interventions services in prison (Ramsay 2003), there are also huge gaps in service provision and delivery in meeting the demands of certain types of drug user and treatment needs of certain groups of prisoners. This is a limitation that has drastic implications for minority ethnic groups and in particular black people who have continued to be disproportionately represented in the prison population, but whose drug needs in prison have been traditionally overshadowed by the research and policy focus on the drug of most concern—heroin. In a Home Office report (2003) on *The Substance Misuse Treatment Needs of Minority Prisoner Groups*, crack was identified as a drug on which both male and female minority ethnic prisoners, particularly black prisoners, were most often dependent unlike their white counterparts whose dependence was mostly on opiates. However, the treatment needs of crack users in prison are yet to be adequately met. Some of the difficulties which preclude appropriate treatment services for black prisoners were also noted in the report:

> It was noted rehabilitation services were not necessarily attracting ethnic minority men into treatment. Practitioners interviewed felt this may in part be due to a lack of ethnic minority practitioners and a perceived lack of cultural understanding from white staff. (p.2)

It adds:

> A further point concerns approaches to detoxification and treatment of crack users. Practitioners saw the management of crack misuse as less straightforward than the treatment of opiate dependence. Unlike cases involving opiates, no substitute medication is available to manage the symptoms of withdrawal from crack. Crack users are less likely to access services because of this and also because they are less likely than opiate users to perceive their substance use as warranting treatment. Further effective treatment for primary crack users requires a different approach from that effective with opiate users. Given this, in conjunction with the high prevalence of crack use among the female prison population, it is vital to employ drug workers specialising in the treatment of crack misuse. (p.3)[13]

Evidently crack occupies a 'special' position in the treatment agenda for a number of reasons. In the absence of a 'substitute medication', the report claims, alcohol is commonly used by problem crack users as 'a sedative to soothe the "come down" effects of the drug'. This is a problem observed with regard to crack using prisoners whose dependence on the drug is significantly accompanied by damaging amounts of alcohol consumption, particularly with the minority ethnic male prisoners. Furthermore, there was also the issue of 'psychotic and manic experiences' as a serious health ramification of drug use found especially amongst crack/alcohol using prisoners. For female prisoners of black and mixed race origins, deliberate self-harm was a symptom of drug dependence specific to them, although there was evidence of 'manic and psychotic experiences' amongst both this group and their white counterparts. These drug dependency problems are compounded by experiences of social exclusion which can render any successful treatment programme in prison useless if reduction in levels of drug use or abstinence after leaving prison is not sustained due to, for example, the stresses of unemployment and/or homelessness. The complications surrounding the role of the prison in addressing drug dependency are further illustrated in the case study below.

A case study: crack use in prison

At the 'Tackling Crack in Lambeth' conference held on 16 April 2004 at the Royal Festival Hall, John Podmore, the Governor of HMP Brixton presented a paper entitled *Crack Users in Prison*. His presentation, which focused on Brixton prison, highlighted not only the increasing 'popularity' of crack use in our communities but also the growing challenges facing both policy makers and practitioners in the field of drugs. In a prison establishment with a population of 800 inmates, a very high proportion of the prisoners from Lambeth reported using crack. Interestingly though, there was no record of the racial/ethnic composition of the crack users. (As a member of the audience, I had asked Podmore for this information and whilst the information couldn't be provided purely because it did not exist, it was an issue which the Governor agreed was worth looking into). A very worrying observation made in the presentation was that many of the crack users were not using or even had no knowledge of community-based treatment facilities available to them. Only a small proportion of crack users were registered with a GP, despite the fact that characteristics of problem crack use were evidently displayed amongst the general population of crack users. The number of those who used crack as the drug of choice far outweighed that for those engaged in poly-drug use. With an average weekly spend of £1,000 on crack, a significant evidence of daily crack use, previous custody for drug-related offences, high incidence of psychotic episodes exemplified in depression, self-harm and suicide attempts, and a significant proportion sectioned under the Mental Health Act, Podmore reported that treatment services were imperative.

The usefulness of prison in terms of drug treatment provisions, as Podmore stressed, is that prisons with rehabilitation facilities provide awareness of and easy access to treatment services, which even though they are also available outside the prison boundaries may not be easily accessible or even known to drug users for a variety of reasons. Within HMP Brixton, for instance, there are drug use intervention programmes such as CARAT, a detoxification programme by the substance misuse team composed of nurses and GPs, mental health outreach and a clinic for sexual health issues. These services notwithstanding, their effectiveness in creating positive results is fraught with problems. For one, effective treatments are not easy to evaluate given that measures are made on outputs rather than inputs, which invariably renders programmes such as one-to-one counselling difficult to assess in quantity terms. Other concerns voiced by Podmore included inconsistencies in detoxification delivery, a situation largely generated by the fact that the substance misuse team is not made up of a specific medical team permanently dedicated to this line of drug treatment. Instead nurses and GPs work part-time and in particular they vary from day to day or week to week; as such no set strategy within this team is in place and neither is familiarity with prison needs developed. Crack use has its own specific problems with regard to treatment provision. As it stands, what is in existence in prison drug services is opiate-based, which means that no drug-related funding is crack specific. In this respect, the prison system is yet to modernise its drug services in order to engage with the crack problem and meet the needs of crack users.

It was apparent from Podmore's presentation that drug use in prison has continued to make a huge negative impact on prison life. Mental health issues constitute one of the major problems linked to drug use. According to Podmore, an average of one suicide attempt a week was evident in HMP Brixton. Self-harm associated with drug withdrawal was significant. Juxtaposed to these medical symptoms of drug use were the many problems of social exclusion—in the form of housing and employment needs—experienced by drug users before entry into the prison system. Hence co-morbidity is a common diagnosis of drug use in prison. A significant proportion of the HMP Brixton drug using inmates had no fixed abode on release from prison and as such instances of prisoners who wished to remain in prison at least for the food and lodging that it provided were not unheard of.

In an even more threatening form, Podmore adds, drug use in prison poses a threat to discipline. Intimidation, violence and gang culture are integral features of drug using lifestyles of inmates. These characteristics, central to the dealing, wheeling and using nature of the drug scene on the streets outside of the prison walls, do not disappear on entering prison. Rather they are retained and practised in custody, where the street gang culture is translated into a prison gang culture. Similarly, despite the ongoing implementation of security measures to combat drugs importation into prison, they continue to find various ways in. Already in place to stifle drugs supply in prisons are measures such as mandatory drug testing, CCTV in visiting areas and border security. Yet drugs continue to be smuggled in through various means. They may be hidden in the anus on entry: a method which, two weeks before Podmore's presentation, took the life of an inmate as the result of a heroin overdose. For those already in prison, visitors play a notable role in drugs supply. An intimate kiss from a female visitor can simply be a way of transferring drugs. In a comical but also worrying story of methods through which drugs are supplied to inmates, Podmore tells of occasions where balls containing drugs have been thrown over the HMP Brixton fence. The balls were not footballs. They were relatively small and sized more like snooker or table tennis balls. On these occasions, the story goes, the balls were thrown for a dog to retrieve. Apparently, a dog owner walking his or her dog near HMP Brixton appeared to be throwing the ball for the dog and what seemed to be an accidental throw which catapulted the ball over the prison fence was in fact a calculated effort to deliver drugs on to the prison grounds.

Podmore's presentation presents a useful insight into some of the pitfalls in the government's Prison Service drug strategy, not only in terms of drug treatment provision, delivery and drugs supply controls in prison but also in terms of the wider social context underpinning some of the difficulties surrounding attempts to achieve drug use reduction or abstinence, and prevent reoffending. (See Penfold *et al.* (2005) for a study of drugs supply and markets in prison.)

CONCLUDING OVERVIEW: DRUG TREATMENT STRATEGY AND WHAT IS NEW FOR RACE

Tackling Drugs to Build a Better Britain: The Government's Ten Year Strategy for Tackling Drug Misuse (Home Office 1998) underlines the drugs agenda for 1998-2008. This strategy which fuses treatment, prevention and education, and tackling drugs supply, was updated in 2002 (Home Office 2002a) with details of what has been achieved and lessons that have been learned. The wide-ranging damage caused by drug misuse and problem drug use in particular continues to front justifications for the Government's drug strategy. In the updated strategy, approximately four million people were known to have used at least one illicit drug in a year and approximately one million had used one of the class 'A' drugs. Problematic drug use was identified with roughly 250,000 drug users in England and Wales, of whom about half were in treatment. Although recreational illicit drug use presents concerns, the greatest threat is posed by problematic drug use. Drug-related crime continues to be an integral feature of problematic drug use, as reflected in approximately three-quarters of heroin and crack cocaine users who claimed to fund their drug habit via crime. Consequently, crimes committed by drug using arrestees were about ten times more than those committed by non-drug using arrestees. Invariably the social and economic costs of drug misuse are virtually accounted for by problematic drug use. The *Updated Drug Strategy 2002* indicated that the annual social and economic costs of drug misuse amount to between £10 billion and £18 billion of which 99 per cent is generated by problem drug use.

Tackling problematic drug use through treatment is therefore an inevitable strategy. 'Treatment works' states the Government in the *Updated Drug Strategy 2002*. Since 1998, there has been an increase in the allocation of funds to drug treatment with the primary objective to increase the numbers of those in treatment regardless of the social characteristics of, and the drug type used by, the drug user. From March 1999 to March 2002, there was a yearly average increase of eight per cent in the number of people presenting to drug treatment services. Whether this increase and treatment itself make a positive impact in achieving permanent abstinence is difficult to ascertain. However the notion that 'treatment works' does draw upon some national evidence of abstinence, albeit periodic, following treatment, which of course has health improvement and crime reduction consequences. The most notable evidence is in the findings from the National Treatment Outcomes Research Study (NTORS) (Gossop *et al.* 2003). This study, which assessed abstinence rates in drug use and the effects on health and crime for five years following entry into treatment, found an increase in abstinence rates, a reduction in the frequency of illicit drug use (with the exception of crack and alcohol), an improvement in health and a reduction in drug-related crime after treatment.

This shift towards an improved drugs treatment system was marked by a number of developments. One was the relaunching of the Regional Drug Misuse Databases as the National Drug Treatment Monitoring System for substance misuse (NDTMS) in 2001 and a subsequent move beyond recording episodes to reviewing client drug treatment. Another development was the creation of the National Treatment Agency (NTA) in 2001. Its aim was to 'oversee the development of drug treatment in England and to ensure that those who need it receive effective, high-quality services regardless of where they live or their source of referral' (Home Office 2002a: 52). Scotland, Wales and Northern Ireland embrace the UK's drug strategy although tailored to suit their differing domestic needs. *Tackling Drugs in Scotland* was a strategy launched in 1999 and supported in 2000 by the Scottish *Executive's Action Plan*. Northern Ireland launched her strategy in 1999, and in 2000, Wales launched the drug strategy *Tackling Substance Misuse in Wales: A Partnership Approach*. As in England, the multi-agency philosophy of drug treatment, prevention and law enforcement is significant across the rest of the UK. In line with the overall aims of the 1998 UK drug strategy relating to the community, young people, treatment and drugs supply reduction, Scotland, Wales and Northern Ireland have since developed and worked towards improving their own strategies which focus on drug misuse.

The relatively higher priority given to drug treatment in England since the latter part of the 1990s also culminated in the improvement of existing treatment and support services, a move towards developing new ones and improved access to treatment through the community and other new criminal justice channels such as the Drug Abstinence Order and the Street Crime Initiative[14] under the umbrella of the criminal justice system. The 'treatment works' notion has also been extended to young people with drug problems. Hence, recent developments have included an increase in the proportion of treatment services for young people, the development of Young People's Substance Misuse Plans by all DATs, and the recruitment of a drug worker to every youth offending team since 2002. Given the acknowledged relationship between drugs and crime, extending the criminal justice route to drug treatment—in the form of drug testing (originally provided for under the Criminal Justice and Court Services Act 2000), arrest referral schemes and drug treatment community sentencing orders—to the youth justice system is in the pipeline.

For race, despite recommendations in the 1998 Government drug strategy for drugs service providers to give considerations to racial and ethnic diversity, the extent to which treatment interventions for minority ethnic groups in general were effectively embraced by mainstream generic services received little or no review. Invariably, it has continued to be unclear in terms of 'what works' in the drug strategy for actual and potential drug users from minority ethnic groups. Key achievements for these communities, albeit relatively minimal, were recorded in the *United Kingdom Anti-Drugs Co-ordinator's Annual Report 2000/1* (Home Office 2001):

- training developed for 47 black and minority ethnic communities throughout England to conduct drugs needs assessments;
- approximately £1 million to be shared between research on drug services for women and for black and minority ethnic groups;
- a £3,880 grant to the African Swahilphone Project in Islington for drugs awareness schemes amongst the African Swahili-speaking community in London; and
- a drugs education project set up in Haringey, aimed at Turkish-speaking people.

The following year, the familiar instances of discourses surrounding ethnic minority drug use and drug treatment provisions and delivery resurfaced in the updated Government drug strategy (Home Office 2002a: 51-2):

> There is now more drug treatment and support available than ever before ... But there are still not enough services of the right type in the right place for all problematic drug users. In recent years, changes in the pattern of drug misuse have also placed additional pressures on services. For example, there is insufficient provision for crack users; and not all who might benefit from prescribed heroin and other interventions at present have access to it ... opiate users from minority ethnic groups are less likely to engage in drug treatment than white opiate users ... there are significant shortcomings in ... specific provision for minority ethnic women.

Services are also criticised for failing to meet the needs of minority ethnic communities. This failure is partly due to the way the services developed. Many emerged out of the heroin epidemics of the mid-1980s and were particularly concerned with the way in which injecting provided a potential route for HIV transmission. Many services, therefore, have developed largely around the needs of the white males who tend to dominate this category of drug misuse. Ethnic differences in patterns of drug misuse suggest that the needs of some minority ethnic groups are marginalised by existing services, which tend to focus on injecting rather than smoking.

Drug use has continued to be predominant amongst the white population regardless of age (Home Office 2002a). The debates which have surrounded drug treatment for black and other minority ethnic groups since the late 1980s (see details in *Chapter* 4) remain integral to concerns about how to facilitate their access to drug treatment. Despite the fact that the presence of crack misuse, often associated with the black community, has been known since the late 1980s, it has only recently begun to gain recognition at governmental level (Weekes 2002), as marked by the Home Office (2002b) publication *Tackling Crack: A National Plan.* This publication is the product of a national conference on crack held in 2002 and it embodies a national action plan for tackling the drug. As demonstrated in the summary tabled below, it is an agenda that has as some of its main objectives treatment, prevention and education, and as one of its anticipated results to meet the 'needs of ethnic minority users ... more effectively' (p.4). The specific reference to minority ethnic users in this sense is linked to observations that African-Caribbeans tend to use crack as a primary drug and are less likely to use heroin either on its own or alongside crack. Asian crack use in contrast is relatively insignificant as little evidence exists in this respect. Although the above publication observes that various data sources such as the NDTMS, the *British Crime Survey* (BCS) and arrest referral systems show that the vast majority of crack users are white, this racial group are more likely to be poly-drug users whose primary drug is more likely to be heroin (p.9). The implication of these racially-based differentials in the nature of crack use is that primary crack users as opposed to secondary crack users are more likely to attract the more acute forms of problems associated with its use. Invariably crack use and its problems are more likely to have a damaging impact on African-Caribbean communities, which according to the Home Office (2002b: 10) are 'more likely to be located in the poorest and most deprived inner city neighbourhoods where crack houses tend to be found'. In the recent progress report on the Government's drug strategy, the Home Office (2004a: 14) identifies as a key achievement the provision of 'better and more accessible treatment for crack cocaine users' effected 'as a result of improved guidance, dedicated training and the promotion of good practice'.

***Table 2.1:* National Crack Action Plan: Objectives**

Action on trafficking	Middle market supply	Street supply	Young people	Criminal justice	Treatment	Effect on communities
Reduce the amount of cocaine reaching the UK.	Interrupt middle-market distribution in the UK.	Close local crack markets and make selling crack very difficult.	Reduce the desire to use crack.	Speedy referral of crack-related offenders into treatment.	Availability of flexible, appropriate treatment for primary crack users.	A reduction in all the indicators of crack-related harm in the community.

Source: Home Office 2002b—*Crack Plan*

The recent approach to crack, according to the publication, stems from a recognition of the fact that crack use is steadily increasing across Britain and its link to acquisitive crime, violent crime and sex work renders it a serious threat to community order, particularly in London. It demonstrates an overt recognition that the relative neglect of crack has also meant that there have been gaps in treatment service provision for crack users, unlike their heroin using counterparts who are predominantly white and whose drug using needs have shaped the development of mainstream services. Even in recent years, heroin users, according to the Home Office (2002a: 54) are 'still by far the biggest group of problematic drug users' and treatment provisions continue to be increased and improved to cater to their needs. For problem crack users there exists as part of the National Crack Action Plan a provision for treatment services provided by specialist programmes, particularly in high crack areas, as well as efforts to improve access to and treatment in generic services (see also Home Office 2004a). Barriers which have precluded ethnic minority access treatment are recognised by the National Treatment Agency (2002c) in its publication *Models of Care for Treatment of Adult Drug Misusers,* in which recommendations are made to address the issue of racial/ethnic diversity in models of care by service providers.

ENDNOTES for *Chapter 2*

1 According to the Home Office (2005a) twice as many vulnerable young people use crack than heroin.

2 In April 2001, RDMDs were relaunched as the National Drug Treatment Monitoring System (NDTMS) and since April 2003 the NDTMS has been managed by the NTA.

3 Crack use has since 2001 become more widespread than heroin use (Home Office 2005b). In spite of this changing trend in patterns of drug use, heroin use by far remains the primary focus of drug treatment service provisions and delivery, resulting in a greater number of heroin users (NTA 2005) and a lesser number of crack users accessing treatment (Turning Point 2005; Turning

Point/Conference on Cocaine and Crack (COCA) 2005). The hidden population of crack users far outweighs the number known to official agencies (Home Office 2005b).

4 Composed of: white and black Caribbean; white and black African; white and Asian; any other mixed-race – these categories are in line with the classifications used by the Office of National Statistics in collecting the 2001 census data.

5 Alongside such drug prevention initiatives was the establishment of Drug Action Teams (DATs) in 1995. Their mission was to implement the national strategy at local level, including drugs prevention work. Membership of DATs draws upon senior representatives from criminal justice agencies, education, health and local authorities. Since their inception, their work has carried on into the twenty-first century, diversifying their local-level foci to embrace a wide range of prevention, treatment and harm-reduction initiatives.

6 A joint partnership between Sport England, Britain Anti-Drugs Co-ordination Unit and the Youth Justice Board. Since its launch in 2000, it has attracted the participation of more than 50,000 young people (Home Office 2004a).

7 Other criminal justice drug treatment schemes include the drug abstinence order (a community sentence introduced under the Criminal Justice and Court Services Act 2000, which allows courts to attach such a requirement to a community punishment/rehabilitation order) and community abstinence requirements attached to community supervision. The DTTO has since April 2005 been embraced within a new generic community order. This order, allowed under the Criminal Justice Act 2003, empowers courts to impose any of a wide range of drug rehabilitation requirements (DRRs), of which DTTO conditions form a part, with one or more community sentences. The replacement of DTTOs with DRRs is meant to provide sentencers with more flexibility to impose drug treatment options in order to meet the needs of individual offenders. What this new criminal justice policy approach to drug treatment holds for race is yet to be determined.

8 As the main criminal justice avenue to drug treatment, the government's intentions were to increase the number of DTTO drug users from an annual uptake of approximately 5,000 in 2001 to 16,000 by 2006 (Turning Point 2004).

9 Formerly known as the Criminal Justice Drug Interventions Programme.

10 The arrest referral scheme has become part of the Drug Interventions Programme.

11 The other two are female crack-using sex workers, and long-term heroin and crack users aged 31 and over who had extensive prison and drug treatment records. For further information on the relationship between sex work and crack use see for example Lindsell 2003; Mainliners 2003.

12 In 1999, CARAT was established in all prison establishments in England and Wales. Other treatment services in prison include detoxification, and rehabilitation programmes including the 'cognitive-behavioural' model.

13 A Home Office report (May 2005) further provides some evidence that the CARAT services are less likely to be used by non-whites.

14 A fast-track access to treatment for street crime offenders with drug problems.

CHAPTER 3

Drugs Supply: Representations in Discourse, Policy and Practice

Post-war black immigration into Britain laid the foundation for what was to become a visible presence of race in the UK's drug problem. That presence has not necessarily been expressed in terms of drug use but rather it has been fully felt in relation to drugs supply. In the post-war period of disquiet about cannabis, the expressed concerns were not about the health implications of the drug on the black community. Instead the emphasis placed on the spread of cannabis use into the indigenous population unveiled resentment towards the black community for the supposed threat that their involvement in cannabis use and dealing posed to the white community. Invariably, the connection drawn between cannabis and the black community was fundamentally understood in its criminal context. For one, there were discursive representations of cannabis dealing as main areas of concern in the political and media arenas (Howe 1973; Gilroy 1987). Juxtaposed to this was a law enforcement response, resulting in a rapid increase in prosecutions and convictions for cannabis offences following black post-war immigration. It was common for the police, particularly in the 1960s, to conduct drug raids in black communities (Roach Family Support Committee 1989). The Chinese community had a similar experience in the 1920s in relation to opium use and trafficking and in consequence attracted significant media attention and law enforcement measures.

By the 1970s, black localities had become popularly noted for drug dealing. Writing about Rastafarianism and criminality, Dodd (1978: 600) referred to 'the emergence of a black street sub-culture in the working class slums' in which 'there is meaning in music, there is meaning in ganja and there is meaning in crime'. Cashmore and Troyna (1982: 12) drew attention to the characterisation of Rastafarianism as a 'mafia-style organization dealing in prostitution and dope ...'. Unemployed West Indians, according to Rex (1982: 65), were believed to 'live by pimping, by cheating and thieving, and by peddling "ganja"'.

Such typifications of black people and drug dealing were illustrated in law enforcement practice amounting to the concentration of policing, police drug raids and arrests in deprived inner-city areas where most black people resided. Police powers to control drugs had been increased under the Dangerous Drugs (Prevention of Misuse) Act 1964, and consequently the police acquired the authority to arrest without a warrant a person who was committing or was 'reasonably suspected' of having committed a drug offence (Deedes 1970), and to search premises if there was evidence that a drug offence was being committed (Plant 1987). Greater powers were accorded the police under the Dangerous

Drugs Act 1965 and the Dangerous Drugs (Prevention of Misuse) Act 1964 (Deedes 1970; Plant 1987). Humphrey and John (1971: 36) observe how these drug laws were allegedly utilised by the police to discriminate against the black community:

> In Moss Side the police had upset the blacks by making a drive on illicit drugs and using their powers under the Dangerous Drugs Act 1965 to stop and search people in the street or at house parties. Black people felt that they were being singled out for these searches and some retaliated leading to charges of assault on the police.

In Handsworth, similar feelings were voiced in the black community:

> Youths and their parents complain ... of men being put against the walls of the police station and searched, at the same time being asked, 'Where are the drugs, you dirty black bastard?', 'You don't work, you scum' ... (ibid. p.7)

Many black people interviewed by Humphrey and John (ibid.) in Handsworth held that black people in some cases were planted with drugs and dangerous weapons. Humphrey (1972) cited cases of alleged police drug planting. The passing of the Dangerous Drugs Act 1967 further exacerbated the subjection of the black community to systematic police harassment (Humphrey, ibid.), a scenario which seemingly continued under the Misuse of Drugs Act 1971 and subsequent legislation.

THE VISIBLITY OF RACE IN THE HEROIN EPIDEMIC

A very strong account voiced in political debates as to the cause of the 1980s heroin epidemic alluded to the plentiful supply and greater availability of modestly priced heroin in many cities and towns. The primary focus of drug policy on the treatment model of maintenance prescribing—ranging from long-term to short-term treatment practices—was to witness a paradigm shift in the mid-1980s. The shift in focus was towards law enforcement. Despite the fact that law enforcement had long been a part of drug control strategy, its role had not been as central as it was in the 1980s. It was during this period that the notion of drug 'dealing' or 'pushing' transformed into drug 'trafficking' to mirror the increased seriousness attached to drugs supply (Dorn *et al.* 1992). It was also in the 1980s that drug trafficking became racialised (ibid.). The treatment and harm-reduction drug policy models, which accompanied the increase and spread in heroin use, and the arrival of and escalation in HIV/AIDS became secondary to the law enforcement approach. This distinction clearly reveals itself in the five-pronged approach outlined in the government's 1985 UK-wide drug strategy, *Tackling Drug Misuse: A Summary of the Government's Strategy* (Home Office 1985):

- reducing supplies from abroad;
- tightening controls on drugs produced and prescribed here;

- making policing even more effective;
- strengthening deterrence; and
- improving prevention, treatment and rehabilitation.

The overt emphasis on controlling drugs supply and thence drug trafficking was clarified in the strategy's aim to:

- support international efforts to curb the production and trafficking of drugs;
- strengthen customs and police enforcement;
- tighten the controls on drugs produced and prescribed in this country so that there is no 'leakage' to the illicit market; and
- deter drug traffickers and dealers by high maximum penalties and by depriving them of the proceeds of their crimes.

These supply-oriented policy measures had been preceded or at least placed alongside political and media discourses which successfully constructed the drug trafficker as one of Britain's No. 1 public enemies. Drug traffickers were viewed in the same light as terrorists by the government and law enforcement officials (Green 1991). Dorn and South (1987: 122) described the 1980s Conservative government's representation of drug traffickers as 'serious criminals akin to terrorists, and drug users ... as helpless victims reduced to moronic garbage'. Green (1991: 18) cites Baroness Cox's description of drug traffickers as 'merchants of death' and as 'despicable people who exploit and profit handsomely from the misery of drug addiction'. At both local and national levels, the press played a prominent role in giving drug trafficking activity prime exposure by presenting a criminal and deadly image of the drug trafficker, alerting the public to the supposed dangerous existence of drug trafficking, and furthermore reporting on an ongoing war on it.

Thus despite the barrage of conflicting debates uttered at the political level relating to the cause of the heroin epidemic, the supply, as opposed to the demand, aspect of its existence was to dominate drugs policy intervention. Such discourses popularised drug trafficking as an imported phenomenon, locating its roots—both in terms of drug production and distribution—in foreign countries and nationalities. From the late 1970s, the increase in heroin use was significantly associated with an increase in the supply of the drug from south Asia. Pakistan, according to MacGregor (1989b: 7) had for some time 'borne the brunt of criticism because of its "lawless frontiers" which were thought to have contributed to the supply of heroin to the west'. A similar point was raised in relation to cocaine. Douglas Hurd was quoted in *The Times* (19 May 1989) as stating:

> The evidence is plain: the North American market having been saturated, the cocaine barons of Latin America are now driving their product into Europe.

Cannabis was no exception to the foreigner status occupied by heroin and cocaine. Most of the cannabis consumed in the UK is illegally imported. As the Home Office (1985: 4) stated, cannabis 'is grown in many areas including the "Golden Crescent" (Pakistan, Afghanistan and Iran), the Middle East and North Africa'. Illicit drugs such as LSD and amphetamines, whilst illegally produced in the UK and abroad, are like other drugs such as barbiturates, 'mainly obtained by diversion from the licit market in this country' (ibid.).

However, the concerns about drugs supply in the 1980s rendered LSD, amphetamines and similar drugs insignificant against the manifest discursive, policy and practical prioritisation of certain class 'A' drugs and to a significant extent, cannabis. Related to that, portrayals of the whole process through which these prioritised drugs found their way to the UK market represented accusations against non-western nations. These included the externalisation of transit points for drugs heading for the UK with reference to, for example, nations and nationalities in Africa and the Caribbean. Following the top priority gained by drug trafficking in the 1980s war on drugs, both international and domestic levels of drug control narratives familiarised and constantly reminded us of the trafficking role of Jamaican 'yardies', Nigerian drug couriers, Colombian cartels, inner-city black males and so forth. Whilst drugs supply was externalised as a foreign invention principally piloted by non-whites, demand was internalised inasmuch as drug addiction was evidenced as a phenomenon threatening the UK white population. This line of distinction drawn between drug supply and drug use is noted by Green (1991: 21) as she argues that the 'constructed drugs "crisis" is seen as a principally imported crisis—imported by West Africans, Asians or South American, fuelled by Third World supplies rather than domestic demand'. Domestically, the racial demarcation in the supply of and demand for drugs was also evident, as exemplified in Gilman's (2000: 205) account of the 1980s heroin markets in Greater Manchester:

> Predominantly white users now bought their heroin from black strangers. These strangers did not use heroin; they did not like heroin and saw it as a 'dirty' drug that was used by 'dirty' white junkies who had no self-respect and therefore deserved no respect.

The discursive externalisation of drug trafficking was to be translated into drug control policy and practice through which the alien threat characterisation of drug trafficking justified stringent law enforcement and repressive punitive measures against certain groups of people. Publicised calls from politicians and government officials were made for the enactment of stringent punitive measures on drug trafficking, including the death penalty. Justifications for such a punitive approach were made clear by Leon Brittan (then Home Secretary) who observed that it was imperative to 'deter and punish very severely those whose trade is in other people's misery' (*News of the World*, 15 January 1984). Subsequently there came the Controlled Drugs (Penalties) Act 1985 and the Drug

Trafficking Offences Act 1986. The former increased the penalty for trafficking in a class 'A' drug from a 14-year prison sentence to life imprisonment while the latter introduced the powers of asset confiscation.[1] In providing justifications for this additional penalty of asset confiscation, the government stated:

> Lengthy sentences of imprisonment may not in themselves be an adequate deterrent. Many drug traffickers make vast profits from their illicit activities. Because of shortcomings in the existing law, they are often able to enjoy these illegal profits on their release from prison. The Home Secretary has decided to introduce legislation in this parliament to make it easier to trace, seize and confiscate the profits of drug trafficking. (Home Office 1985: 15)

Default of payment or refusal to comply with a confiscation order incurred an additional prison sentence commensurate with the assessed value of the proceeds from drug trafficking. The implications of these stringent measures for race were demonstrated in official prison statistics for drug offences for which black people were not only over-represented but were also serving long sentences (Home Office 1986). This was more evident in the female prison population where the highest proportion of blacks received under sentence was for drug offences (ibid.). Since the 1980s, the disproportionate presence of black people in UK prison establishments has been significantly influenced by the high numbers of foreign nationals—from West Africa and the Caribbean—charged or convicted for importing illegal drugs (Green 1991; Richards *et al.* 1995; Harper and Murphy 1999).

The overhaul of drugs law enforcement in the 1980s also reached the police forces. During this period drugs policing witnessed a new organizational structure, based largely on the recommendations of the 1985 Broome Report. Three broad levels of drugs policing were devised (Advisory Council on the Misuse of Drugs (ACMD) 1994; Dorn *et al.* 1992; Foy 1996). They consisted of: (1) regional crime squads to focus on major drug trafficking business involving a network of importers and distributors at both national and international levels; (2) force drug squads to address mid-level traffickers in the drug distribution chain; and (3) divisional-level enforcement involving the policing of localities by police officers in the normal course of their duty.

Out of these three forms of drugs policing, it was the divisional level that attracted emphasis as a vital pattern of drugs law enforcement due to its demand and harm reduction approach to drug misuse. Policing drugs at this level has involved the concentration of street-level police surveillance, and police stop and search practices in specific areas such as council estates, public houses, rented flats and streets. Top-level drugs policing has been known to be problematic (Dorn *et al.* 1992) amidst complexities involved in intercepting drug traffickers at the upper reaches of the drugs economy, thereby rendering this level of policing limited in its cost effectiveness. Although this does not imply ineffectiveness at the higher levels of police operational response to drugs, it does however highlight at least one reason why divisional-level policing in the 1980s and beyond remained prominent in the domestic war on drug trafficking via its focus on drug traffickers, buyers and users in selected areas, usually deprived inner-city areas, with the aim to disrupt low-level drug transactions and in turn reduce the availability of, and demand for, drugs.

This grade of drug trafficking has since received widespread publicity, not only through the prominence accorded it by way of stringent law enforcement measures but also via the media which in their prime and sensational exposure of drug trafficking activities in inner-city neighbourhoods, accompanied by the image of the deadly drug trafficker, constructed and perpetuated a connection between drug trafficking and race. Black men were defined as the drug traffickers and represented in the image of professionals in drug trafficking activities. Accompanying such activities was gun-related violence, which was to escalate in the later part of the 1980s following the arrival of crack cocaine. Black men in effect remained key targets in drugs policing practices. Indeed as Cashmore and McLaughlin (1991: 11) describe:

> Throughout the 1970s and the 1980s the concern about black youth and their supposed 'heritage of violence' as 'muggers', 'drug barons', 'steamers', 'Yardies' and 'posses' has been handled in such a way as to engender public support for police strategies, especially as most of the stereotypes have been uncritically accepted and, at times, supported by politicians and the mass media.

Over-policing operations, including military-style tactics in drug raids and surveillance, in black residential areas had long been justified. In the name of divisional-level policing, the consequences have included violent encounters between the police and the black community as instanced in the 1985 urban disorder in Handsworth (Birmingham) and Broadwater Farm Estate (London). Regardless, it was a form of drugs policing considered necessary, warranting its survival beyond the 1980s.

BEYOND THE 1980s: POLICY, PRACTICE AND RACE

The five main foci of drug control policy established in the 1985 government strategy and referred to earlier were maintained and carried into the 1990s as detailed in the government publication *UK Action Plan on Drug Misuse: The Government's Strategy* (Home Office 1990). Again the priority placed on drugs supply was clear in the strategies to improve international cooperation in order to reduce supplies from abroad, increase the effectiveness of police and customs enforcement, and maintain effective deterrents and tight domestic controls. Furthermore, to many it may seem that the government's 'new' emphasis on preventive and treatment approaches to drug misuse—outlined in the White Paper, *Tackling Drugs Together: A Strategy for England 1995-1998*—demonstrated a clear shift in drug control strategy from supply to demand reduction. But according to Green (1998: 122-3) this was simply not the case. She argues:

> Its Statement of Purpose, 'To take action by vigorous law enforcement and a new emphasis on education and prevention', might superficially have implied a changed emphasis on the direction of demand reduction but a closer reading of the body of the text reveals an undiluted and primary commitment to a punitive crime-control model. Prevention and treatment strategies became the domain of law enforcement, so that the police forces were the primary 'deliverers' of prevention initiatives.

The emphasised participation of the criminal justice system, albeit in a punitive context, in a multi-agency approach to drug prevention and treatment from the 1990s, has not been aimed at subordinating drug trafficking in the war on drugs agenda. As drug traffickers continued to be characterised as evil and unscrupulous, so have law enforcement responses toward them continued to be tougher. One of the most symbolic demonstrations of what was an ongoing war on drugs in the 1990s was Tony Blair's appointment of a 'drugs czar' in 1997.[2] This appointment was celebrated as a visual declaration of intense political and law enforcement intolerance of drug trafficking.

Likewise, the targeting of drug trafficking and traffickers culminated in more legislative attack. Like the 1980s policy developments on trafficking, the emphases continued to be placed on deterrence through increased penalties and more stringent confiscation provisions relating to proceeds of drug trafficking. For example, section 2 Crime (Sentences) Act 1997 introduced mandatory sentences of a minimum of seven years for repeat drug trafficking offenders involved in a class 'A' drug. One of the most significant recent law enforcement policy developments is the increase in the penalty for trafficking in a class 'C' drug from five years to 14 in conjunction with the reclassification of cannabis. Following years of debates over whether or not to decriminalise cannabis, the issue was at that stage resolved by reclassifying it from a class 'B' to a class 'C' drug. A central reason for what was a cannabis policy transition is summarised in the government's *Updated Drug Strategy 2002*:

> to free up the considerable amount of police time currently spent in dealing with minor cannabis possession offences. Most of these offences lead to small financial penalties – in 2000, 19,000 cannabis possession offences were prosecuted resulting in fines averaging £80 ... Police time saved as a result can then be redeployed, supporting the wider strategy objective of refocusing efforts – including enforcement action – on the drugs that cause the most harm, i.e. heroin and cocaine'. (Home Office 2002a: 36)

Consequently the overall law enforcement agenda for cannabis revolves around the reduction of the maximum prison sentence for cannabis possession from five years' imprisonment to two, and the reservation of police warning and drug confiscation for most first offences of cannabis possession, that is only those first offences which are devoid of aggravating circumstances such as an obvious indifference to the law. In other words the police discretion and powers to make an arrest for cannabis possession remain intact. The above government publication cites the impact of the London borough of Lambeth Cannabis Warning Pilot Scheme, introduced and run by the Metropolitan Police Service in July 2001, on the overall drugs law enforcement in Lambeth. The scheme, which had the objective to divert police attention to more serious crime including a focus on class 'A' drugs, involved the use of on-street police warnings in cases where small quantities of cannabis were possessed for personal consumption. The outcome showed, alongside police time saving and reduced arrest rates for cannabis possession, an increase in police law enforcement efforts and arrests in connection with trafficking in a class 'A' drug. In England, arrests for cannabis decreased by 30 per cent following the reclassification of this drug and the renewed emphasis on the policing of class 'A' drugs (Home Office 2004a).

In reality, the reclassification of cannabis only applied to possession cases since no alterations were made in relation to laws governing cannabis supply. With the penalty for trafficking in a class 'C' drug increased from five to 14 years, trafficking in cannabis has retained its original maximum penalty of 14 years. In fact 'C' drugs are the disadvantaged class of drugs in this form of attack on trafficking. However, it reiterates the Government's ongoing and persistent fight against drug trafficking and in particular class 'A' drug trafficking. According to the Home Office (2002a: 32), there is a new focus in the war against trafficking in a class 'A' drug. This new focus aims to reduce 'the supply of class A drugs rather than their availability, with the overall aim of reducing the amount of class A drugs reaching the UK streets'. Herein, the focus is on curtailing heroin and cocaine exportation and transportation from source and transit countries, and also to ensure that these drugs are increasingly seized at the UK border and within.

Asset confiscation constitutes another important preventive measure against drug trafficking. The Criminal Justice (International Cooperation) Act 1990 authorised the forfeiture of drug trafficking money being exported from or imported into the UK, and the Drug Trafficking Act 1994 (DTA) consolidated the Drug Trafficking Offences Act 1986 (DTOA) and the confiscation provisions of the Criminal Justice Act 1993. Under the DTA, a convicted drug trafficker serves a default prison sentence where he or she fails to comply with the confiscation order but unlike the DTOA, this sentence runs consecutively with the term of imprisonment for drug trafficking. In the past, failure to surrender proceeds of drug trafficking was punished by a default prison sentence which thereafter erased the confiscation order. This practice allowed by the DTOA changed under the DTA which not only removes a confiscation order as a determining factor in the prison sentencing decision but also stipulates that a confiscation order still stands even after a prison sentence has been served. The DTA also allows HM Customs or police officers to seize drug trafficking money being imported into or exported out of The UK. Targeting assets as a deterrent measure against drug trafficking continued into the twenty-first century. New legislation, the Proceeds of Crime Act 2002, has attracted weightier law enforcement operations. The establishment of an Assets Recovery Agency under this Act allows law enforcement agencies greater powers of asset confiscation, which moves beyond powers of criminal confiscation to incorporate powers of civil recovery. To act as the operational lead in support of the asset recovery approach to crime proceeds is the Concerted Inter-agency Criminal Finances Action Group established in 2002. The group includes representatives from the Metropolitan Police, HM Customs and Excise (now Revenue and Customs) and the Association of Chief Police Officers (Home Office 2001). As the Home Office (2002a: 34-35) states:

> The strategy includes a target of doubling the amount of criminal assets recovered from £29.4 million in 1999/2000 to £60 million by 2004/5 ... The Act introduces new civil recovery, cash forfeiture and tax powers aimed at criminal proceeds and applies equally to local drug dealers and drug cartels. Where there has been a successful criminal conviction, the Director will be able to exercise powers of criminal confiscation. Where there has been no conviction, civil recovery powers may be used, provided that the total value of recoverable property is not less than the minimum financial threshold, which is to be set at £10,000. If civil recovery is not possible or practicable, and there are reasonable grounds to suspect that income or gain was derived from crime (including drug dealing), a tax assessment may be raised ... The Act provides other powers to police and Customs to seize cash over £10,000 derived from crime or intended for use in crime, and to secure its forfeiture in magistrates' court proceedings. This should result in more effective disruption of criminal enterprises, which continue to rely heavily on cash transactions. There will also be a new power to search for cash.

Such domestic deterrents are juxtaposed alongside the domestic law enforcement activities of HM Customs and Excise, and the police. Both agencies had their drugs law enforcement resources and powers increased during the 1990s. As at the mid-1990s, HM Customs and Excise had 5,100 staff responsible for drugs work and anti-smuggling. Eight hundred of them comprised specialist investigation staff who were based in London and five regional centres. The police had approximately 1,300 officers solely assigned to drugs control work. There were a total of about 345 police officers allocated to the 'drugs wings' of the six regional crime squads in England and Wales (Home Office 1994a)[3] Later developments in police organizational structure saw the amalgamation of the regional crime squads in 1998 to form a National Crime Squad.[4] Furthermore, reliance on information and intelligence was prioritised as very vital to drugs law enforcement and thus access to information was advanced through the formation and expansion of intelligence gathering organizations. An example was the creation of the National Criminal Intelligence Service (NCIS) in 1992, to disseminate collated drugs intelligence to HM Customs and the police. Its staff included personnel from HM Customs and the police (Home Office 1994a). This was in addition to the already existing National Drugs Intelligence Unit, a joint police and customs organization which replaced the Central Drugs Intelligence

Unit that had been set up in 1984. Since the publication of the Government's drug strategy *Tackling Drugs to Build a Better Britain* (Home Office 1998), this interagency response to drugs supply in Britain has further developed into the formation of the Concerted Inter-Agency Drugs Action Group (CIDA), an organization which brings together and coordinates law enforcement and intelligence efforts to tackle drugs supply at every stage (Home Office 2002a).

Drugs law enforcement: evidence of success?

Recorded numbers of drug seizures, police drug arrests and drug offences constitute notable yardsticks for at least assessing whether or not the government's pieces of drug legislation are yielding profit. Depending on the interpretation of the reader, a rise or fall in recorded statistics can appear to indicate that the legislative measures in place are delivering the goods expected of them whether in terms of reducing the amount of drugs in circulation or in reducing the numbers involved in drug trafficking.

HM Customs and National Crime Squad seizures have accounted for a substantial proportion of the total amount of drugs seized although police seizures have been more in number (Corkery 1998, 1999, 2002; see also Corkery and Airs (2003); Ahmad and Mwenda (2004) for updates on drug seizure statistics).

Unlike previous years, the 1999 and 2000 data on drug seizures made by customs, the National Crime Squad and local police forces in the UK show a 12 per cent fall in 1999 and a seven per cent fall in 2000. In contrast there was a 14 per cent and a six per cent rise in drug seizures in 1997 and 1996 respectively (ibid.). During these latter periods, cannabis constituted the majority of the seizures: 77 per cent in 1997 and 75 per cent in 1996, although there were increases in seizures of class 'A' drugs particularly heroin, cocaine and ecstasy-type drugs. But the overall decrease in drug seizures reported in 2000 was largely attributed to a fall in the number of cannabis and amphetamine seizures, despite a rise in class 'A' drug seizures namely cocaine/crack and heroin. As stated in the Home Office Statistical Bulletin *Drug Seizure and Offender Statistics, United Kingdom, 2000*, two reasons can account for this decline in the rate of class 'B' drug seizures. Firstly, recent years have witnessed a shift in the concentration of law enforcement efforts on class 'A' drugs 'in line with the availability targets in the Government's Drugs Strategy' (Corkery 2002: 5). In effect, out of the estimated £789 million (that is, street value) worth of controlled drugs seized by Customs and the police in 2000, £259 million was for cocaine and crack, £237 million for heroin and £218 million for cannabis. In the previous year the figures were £188 million, £152 million and £237 million respectively.

Secondly, the reduction in the numbers of class 'B' drugs seizures, according to the *Home Office Statistical Bulletin* (Corkery 2002), is possibly an after-effect of the Macpherson report on the Stephen Lawrence Inquiry. Following its publication, there has been a continued fall in rates of police stops and searches, particularly in London. Evidently, police stop and search practices play a significant part in arrests for drug offences in the sense that a high proportion of such offences comes to the attention of the police following a stop and search. However, between the periods 1998/1999 and 1999/2000, there was an overall decrease of 24 per cent in rates of drugs stops and searches in England and Wales, and a further fall of 14 per cent in 2000/2001. This fall was particularly evident in the Metropolitan Police District (MPD) where a fall of 43 per cent in the number of drugs stops and searches between 1998/1999 and 1999/2000 represented 71 per cent of the total fall in England and Wales during these periods (Corkery 2002). The MPD figures for 2000/1 show a much-reduced stop and search fall of five per cent and represented 11 per cent of the total fall in England and Wales. Also the numbers of arrests and cautions[5] for drug offences in England and Wales fell between 1998 and 2001. Between 1998/1999 and 1999/2000, the fall rate for drug offence arrests in England and Wales was 15 per cent out of which 55 per cent took place in the MPD, and between 1999/2000 and 2000/2001, the fall in the MPD made-up 28 per cent of the total drop in the number of such arrests in England and Wales which stood at eight per cent.

Similarly, a substantial number of police cautions for cannabis possession dropped in England and Wales, and in particular in the MPD, between 1998 and 2000. The overall decrease in the number of police cautions in England and Wales is reflective of the actual fall rate given that it does not include the number of reprimands and final warnings received by juvenile offenders in 2000. Under the Crime and Disorder Act 1998, police use of Reprimands and Final Warnings was introduced in England and Wales and replaced the use of cautions for juvenile offenders aged ten to 17 years. Where police cautions apply, they have traditionally been mostly reserved for first-time offenders and those charged with illegal possession of class 'B' or 'C' drugs.

Illegal possession of a controlled drug has over the years formed the most common offence for which the majority of offenders are associated with cannabis possession. This is despite the general fall in recent years in the number of known drug offenders in the UK. Since 1998 when the number of drug offenders reached a peak of 130,600, the figure has dropped by seven per cent in 1999 and 14 per cent in 2000 (see Ahmad and Mwenda 2004 for an update on drug offender statistics). The number of illegal drug possession offences fell from 117,710 in 1998 to 108,353 in 1999 and 92,877 in 2000. This recent decline had been preceded by years of an upward trend dating back to the 1980s.[6] A similar scenario applies to drug trafficking offences relating to possession of a controlled drug with intent to supply unlawfully and unlawful supply of a controlled drug, which together continued an upward trend from 1990 to a peak of 16,700 in 1998. This figure dropped to 15,400 in 1999 and 15,000 in 2000.

Table 3.1: Number of persons[1] found guilty, cautioned, given a fiscal fine, or dealt with by compounding for drug offences in the UK, in 1990 and from 1998-2000

Type of drug offence	1990	Year 1998[2]	1999	2000
Unlawful possession				
—cannabis	613	91,153	82,131	70,305
—other drugs	17	33,290	32,387	27,375
Possession with intent to supply unlawfully	2,751	9,480	8,479	7,296
Unlawful supply	2,151	7,210	6,936	5,742
Unlawful import or export	2,478	1,152	1,234	1,490

1 As the same person may be found guilty, cautioned or dealt with by compounding for more than one drugs offence, rows cannot be added together to produce sub-totals. Includes companies.

2 Court appearance data not available for Northern Ireland in 1998 to 2000.
Source: Corkery 2002.

However, a steady increase in the number of possession with intent to supply unlawfully offences in particular had occurred for over a decade before the recent decline. Whilst the number of unlawful supply offences indicates a combination of a rise and fall trend from the 1980s, there was an almost three-fold increase overall between 1990 and 2000. For drug importation and exportation offences (primarily the former), there has been a mixed rise and fall trend between 1990 and 2000. Towards the later part of the 1990s, changes in HM Customs drugs law enforcement policy had meant a shift of focus from small-time drug importers and exporters to major drug smuggling organizations. According to the aforementioned *Home Office Statistical Bulletin* (Corkery 2002), this policy change is reflected in the fall in this offence category of drug trafficking in 1998. However the 1998 decline was subsequently followed by increases in drug importation/exportation offences in 1999 and 2000.[7]

Unlike illegal drug possession, for which cautions and non-custodial penalties constitute the most likely form of criminal justice response, drug trafficking offences more often than not attract an immediate custodial sentence. Such response to drug trafficking was clearly evident in the 1980s. For example in 1986, of those found guilty for the respective offences of possession with intent to supply unlawfully and unlawful supply, 63 per cent of the former and 59 per cent of the latter received an immediate custodial sentence. As *Table 3.2* shows, despite the fact that there has since been a decline in the use of immediate custody for these drug trafficking offences, it has none the less remained significant.

Table 3.2: *Percentage of persons in the UK found guilty, cautioned or dealt with by compounding/fiscal fine for unlawful supply, possession with intent to supply unlawfully, and unlawful import or export by sentence or order[1] given – from 1986-2000.*

Sentence or order				Year				
	1986	1988	1990	1992	1994	1996	1998	2000
Unlawful supply								
Immediate custody	59	49	38	35	39	52	45	53
Fine	13	17	20	15	9	6	6	4
Other found guilty[2]	26	30	35	37	36	32	40	34
Cautioned	2	4	7	13	15	10	9	8
Compounding/fiscal fine	0	0	0	0	0	0	0	0
Possession with intent to supply unlawfully								
Immediate custody	63	56	40	37	44	53	45	49
Fine	11	13	18	16	10	6	5	5
Other found guilty	24	31	40	42	40	35	43	40
Cautioned	1	1	2	5	6	6	6	7
Compounding/fiscal fine	0	0	0	0	0	0	0	0
Unlawful import or export								
Immediate custody	50	36	31	41	40	43	36	N/A
Fine	23	20	17	18	13	12	12	N/A
Other found guilty	6	4	4	5	6	5	3	N/A
Cautioned	-[3]	-[3]	-[3]	0	0	0	0	N/A
Compounding/fiscal fine	21	39	48	35	41	40	49	N/A

1 Where a person is found guilty of two or more drugs offences at the same court appearance, the sentence or order shown is the most severe penalty.
2 Received a community sentence or other non-custodial sentences such as absolute or conditional discharge.
3 Less than half per cent.
Source: Corkery 1998, 2002.

Figures for people received under sentence in prison for drug offences (Corkery 1998, 2002) further demonstrate the prominent position of custodial sentences as a law enforcement response to drug trafficking.

It is worth noting however that not all drug importers or exporters who get apprehended by HM Customs appear before the court. A significant proportion of such arrests are dealt with by compounding.[8] To a notable extent, the decline in the rate of importation/exportation offences in 1998 was offset by the increase in the use of compounding. While there was an increase to 49 per cent in the proportion of those dealt with by compounding in 1998, the number of those found guilty at court dropped to 51 per cent from its 1997 level of 69 per cent. However, the number of drug offenders received under sentence in prison establishments in England and Wales has shown an upward trend since 1993 (Corkery 2002). These increases are particular for drugs supply and importation offences, and are further evidenced by the proportion of female drug offenders in prison in both 1999 and 2000. The figure for female drug offending prisoners, which stood at eleven per cent during these periods, was higher than the total female prison population of five per cent in England and Wales. To a large extent the relatively high rates in the numbers of female drug offenders in prison have been influenced by the number of foreign national female prisoners—mostly from Africa, the Caribbean and South America—imprisoned for drug importation offences. This category of prisoners has often operated at the lower level of the drugs trade as couriers and 'mules' who upon arrest were found with relatively small quantities of drugs (Green 1991, 1998).

Questioning the effectiveness of drugs law enforcement

While legislative and law enforcement developments overtly depict the image of large-scale government operations determined to reach all parameters of drug trafficking activities, success is however questionable. For one thing, the increasing availability and use of controlled drugs raises critical questions around the effectiveness of current drug control strategy. In the Home Office publication, *Sizing the UK Market for Illicit Drugs* (Bramley-Harker 2001), the value of the UK market for illicit drugs in 1998 was estimated at £6.6 billion. The drugs covered in the study on which this publication was based were: cocaine, crack, heroin, ecstasy, amphetamines and cannabis, but with heroin and crack forming the most significant illicit drug types in the British market. Previous estimates made by the Office for National Statistics (Groom *et al.* 1998, cited in Bramley-Harker 2001) had valued the UK market for illicit drugs in 1996 at up to £4.2 billion.[9]

Estimates from the Home Office study were based on data drawn from the 1998/99 NEW-ADAM (New English and Welsh Arrestee Drug Abuse Monitoring) programme. The NEW-ADAM programme involved a survey of arrestees in Liverpool, Nottingham, Sunderland and South Norwood, using structured interviews and collection of urine specimens as data collection methods. Both estimates by the Home Office and the Office for National Statistics present their own methodological flaws (see Bramley-Harker ibid.). However, there are drugs law enforcement control objectives underpinning such estimates. As Bramley-Harker states, the research on which the 1998 estimates were based was

> part of a wider programme of work to examine the dynamics of the market for illicit drugs and to study the interactions between drug markets and law enforcement … it also has potentially wider applications and could be used, for example, to allow HM Customs and Excise to judge their success in intercepting drugs destined for the UK market. (ibid.: 1)

Often drugs law enforcement success has been judged favourably by the government and law enforcers themselves through the use of statistics and rhetoric, which to critics (Green 1998; Kalunta-Crumpton 1998; Murji 1998) are merely symbolic rather than a realistic indication of success in reducing drugs availability and demand. Whereas progress reports on the Government's drug strategy are not hesitant to outline key drugs law enforcement achievements, what has continued to remain unclear in such reports is the direct impact of law enforcement progress in curbing the drug problem. For example, in the Home Office publication, *Tackling Drugs. Changing Lives: Keeping Communities Safe from Drugs*, it is noted that 11,044 kilograms of heroin and 26,079 kilograms of cocaine were seized between April 2002 and December 2003. Also seized during the first nine months of 2003/2004 were 18,456 kilograms of cocaine and heroin targeted at the UK drugs market. The disruption of 121 class 'A' drugs organized criminal groups during this period is also identified as a key achievement. In addition, proceeds from drug trafficking to the amount of £84 million (including street cash) have been seized since December 30 2002. But the relationship between this progress and drug availability on the streets is not stated. Instead it is projected that 'reduced availability of drugs on our streets' will be evident in 2008 (Home Office 2004a).

To a significant extent critical questions that have been raised around the efforts of law enforcement to deal with what seems to be an escalating drug problem are rooted in the practical applications of drugs law enforcement policies at the lower levels of trafficking. Despite the claim (Corkery 2002) that in the latter part of the 1990s, Customs law enforcement policy moved toward focusing on major drug smugglers, resulting in a decline in the number of primarily drug importation offences, it is not clear as to the extent to which this policy change reduced the number of arrests of small-time drug importers, especially those of foreign nationalities. The decline occurred in 1998 after which there were increases in 1999 and 2000 (Corkery 2002). Several studies have drawn attention to the low-level drug trafficking role of drug importers often arrested by HM Customs and Excise (Green 1991; Green 1996). According to Green (1998), the majority of drug seizures by HM Customs and Excise involve relatively small amounts of drugs; cannabis comprises most of the seizures; and often they are from individual air passengers rather than air freight:

> the reality of customs targeting has been defined by an overarching emphasis on one drug, cannabis, and on the lowest level 'trafficker', the individual drug courier originating from the Third World (p.148).

Green (1998) also argues that drug traffickers who appear in court are often at the lower end of the drugs trade. Furthermore, she adds:

> Despite a small number of very large orders, confiscation orders are routinely applied against the bottom-end of drug trafficking defendants and there is no evidence to suggest that they have had any impact at all on the profits of large-scale drug traffickers. Rather, as with the powerful and wealthy in other spheres of capitalist enterprise, major drug traffickers have few problems protecting and concealing their assets. (p.168)

Similarly drugs policing features at the lowest levels of drug offences, namely drug possession where most arrests occur. Also, drug dealing/trafficking has traditionally mostly attracted this level of policing endeavours, which became more apparent in the 1980s.

Since the organizational restructuring of drugs policing in the wake of the 1985 Broome Report, it has seemed that the three components of drugs policing were clearly arranged on the presumption that drug trafficking is structured on a three-tier hierarchical system composed of upper, middle and lower levels. Despite this, it is not certain as to the criteria upon which the varied categories are determined or the actual influence of this classification on drugs policing. Whilst the emphasis on divisional level drugs policing has continued to shine, there is however evidence that there exist inconsistencies at the point of law enforcement in relation to how drug trafficking is graded. In the Home Office research study, *Middle Market Drug Distribution* (Pearson and Hobbs 2001), this inconsistency is acknowledged. The authors' interviews with law enforcement agents of the National Criminal Intelligence Service (NCIS), the National Crime Squad (NCS) and police force drug squads unveiled conflicting definitions of 'middle market' drug distribution as given by the interviewees. This is illustrated in the following responses (ibid.: 14):

> The middle, I suppose, that's the ounce dealers ... That's what I'd call the middle market ... We don't deal with that; drugs enforcement has gone up-stream in recent years. (NCIS in reference to the cocaine market)
>
> Kilo dealers, in both heroin and cocaine, they're the middlemen. (Source: NCS)
>
> In a global market, which is what drugs are, I'd say importation is the middle market. (Source: NCIS)
>
> In terms of heroin, I'd say it was the kilo dealers ... the one and two kilo level people. That's my idea of the middle. (Source: NCIS)
>
> It's all middle. (Source: Metropolitan Police Service)

In the government's *Updated Drug Strategy 2002*, the middle market, described as 'the critical supply link between the illegal importation of drugs into the UK and their sale at street level', typifies 'drugs in quantities of between one and five kg' (Home Office 2002a: 28).

Such variations in definitions shown above may well define how the foci of drugs law enforcement in terms of grades of drug trafficking can be premised on law enforcers' own perceptions and understandings of what forms upper-, middle- or low-level drug trafficking. It is a form of disparity which seems to cut across as well as function within different levels of drugs law enforcement (including HM Customs and Excise), and which may harbour practical implications with regard to who gets arrested for drug trafficking. For example, if an ounce of heroin may be an indication of 'middle market' drug trafficking in one police force drug squad, 'upper market' in another and 'lower market' in yet another, and if such a variation also occurs among individual law enforcement officers within a given organization, it may then follow that such variations and inconsistencies would be reflected at the practical point of drugs law enforcement. Crucial to this scenario is the fact that these law enforcers' judgements are anchored in discretion, meaning that similar events can be viewed and defined differently and consequently result in different outcomes. The ample discretion exercised by the police is well acknowledged (Box 1981; Smith and Gray 1985; Sanders 1994).

To further illustrate this point, the author refers the reader to her 1991 study of drug offence trials at a London Crown Court. As already indicated in *Chapter 1*, the prescribed criteria—proceeds of drug trafficking, quantity of the drug, the number of portions into which the drug is divided and drug-related paraphernalia—were considered by criminal justice officials to be crucial to the allegation of drug trafficking. Nevertheless, these criteria lacked precise definitions in the sense that there seemed to be no clear distinction as to how they were determined as evidence of drug trafficking.

Prior to my observations of drug trafficking trials, what I had not anticipated was the observed fact that the defendants, particularly black defendants, did not represent the popular media and political discursive portrayal of drug trafficking as a mafia-style organization involving large-scale, highly lucrative drug trafficking enterprise. Not only were there no indications, in the author's observations, that the defendants were wealthy or led the sort of luxurious lifestyle associated with the drug trafficking business, but also the defendants appeared before the court for seemingly small-scale drug trafficking. The majority of the defendants belonged to the lower class: they resided in deprived inner city areas, lived in council or rented accommodation, were unemployed or in irregular self-employment and received welfare benefits. The quantities of drugs associated with them shed light on the defendants' level of drug trafficking. Nine defendants were associated with quantities of drugs under one gram; 23 for quantities over one gram and under 50 grams; two for quantities over 50 grams and under 100 grams; and two for quantities over 100 grams and under 150 grams. In relation to alleged proceeds of drug trafficking, the defendants were linked to amounts of monies under £4,000. In one case, a defendant was connected to a building society account of £30,000, which was in a different name. But in spite of what seemed to be a lower grade of drug trafficking, it was primarily evident in black defendants' cases for criminal justice officials to depict them as 'big-time' drug traffickers who deserved severe punitive reaction. The following cases demonstrate this point.

> ***Case 1***: Six police officers in uniform were on general patrol in a police van when they saw a black man running towards and into a public house situated in an inner-city area. According to the police officers, they found that behaviour suspicious and believed that he was running away from them. The police officers decided to go after him inside the public house. He was taken to the police station and searched and drugs were not found on him. A search of his council accommodation was made and 8.5 grams of cocaine, described by the police and the prosecutor as a 'large' quantity

were found. Also found was £210, alleged to be his 'substantial' profit from drug trafficking. The defendant who was self-employed was charged with unlawful possession of a class 'A' drug with intent to supply.

Case 2: A black male defendant was convicted for trafficking in 27.1 grams of cannabis resin, a class 'B' drug at the time. The defendant had pleaded guilty to unlawful possession of the drug and in his defence claimed that the drug was for his own use and that of his friends. In sentencing the defendant, the judge stated: 'You have been found guilty of trafficking in substantial quantities of drugs. Drug trafficking is a serious crime and those people who sell drugs deserve severe punishment'.

Case 3: In this case, it was ascertained that a black male defendant, who was convicted for drug trafficking, had made a profit of £1,455 from the offence. At the sentencing stage, the judge stated: 'I have no doubt in my mind that you benefited enormously from drug trafficking'.

The features of low-level drug trafficking evidenced in the above cases become more highlighted when placed alongside the level of policing which brought the defendants before the court. Arrests for these cases and for the majority of the drug cases in general emerged from police surveillance practices involving the targeting of specific areas identified by the police with drug trafficking. Such police activities have geared toward detecting retail drug markets and despite their implications for race are deemed justifiable. In a report by the Advisory Council on the Misuse of Drugs (1994: 3-4), divisional-level drugs policing strategy and what seems to be its inevitable consequence on race are justified thus:

> An important element of street-level policing is the tactic of stop and search of individuals suspected of involvement in drug offences. A significant amount of activity involving drugs is concentrated in our inner cities, where ethnic minorities are also heavily represented. In turn, this can result in apparently disproportionate numbers of ethnic minorities being stopped and searched compared with the general population.

Notwithstanding the racial and class implications of the emphasis on low-level drugs policing, it is a strategy that has not only remained prominent but has subordinated higher levels of police operational response to drugs. Related to this the punitive consequences for those most affected—the black community—are further mirrored in the disproportionate representation of black people in the prison establishment for drug offences (Home Office 1993, 1994b, 1999, 2000, 2002c, 2004b). In the twenty-first century the emphasis on street-level drugs policing has retained its trail. According to the Home Office (Corkery 2002), drugs seized at this point of police law enforcement 'mostly involve small amounts, typically from users or minor drug dealers'.

However there has been a recent Government pledge to place 'a new emphasis' on 'cross regional, or middle markets' points of the drug trade described as 'one of the most profitable parts of the supply chain' (Home Office 2002a: 33). In November 2004, the Middle Market Drugs Project was launched. It comprised a team of officers from HM Customs and Excise, the National Criminal Intelligence Service, the Metropolitan Police Service and the City of London police. The new unit aims to dismantle class 'A' drug trafficking links between wholesale drug suppliers and street dealers (that is the upper and lower levels). In its 'two month transition period' the unit, according to the Home Office (2004a), is estimated to have 'stopped the equivalent of 200,070[10] class A deals reaching the streets of London' (ibid.: 10). Furthermore, the unit confiscated £35,000 in cash and made a total of 25 arrests leading to 'various drug trafficking-related' offence charges and 'offences under the Proceeds of Crime Act' (ibid.).

Despite the new drugs law enforcement development, it is nevertheless logical to ask why it has taken so long to acknowledge the crucial role of this level of drug trafficking. It is also worth asking: what the implications of this 'new emphasis' are for street-level drugs policing which claims many of its clients from the black community? Does this new move mean that street-level drugs policing will be less prominent than middle market drugs policing or is it a case of merely treating the former as if it were the latter?

Without trying to provide answers to these important critical questions, what is clear is that efforts to disrupt low-level drug trafficking have continued to be strengthened, more evidently in the area of crack cocaine. Since the late 1980s policing crack has been a central aspect of drugs policing in the black community. At a time when the crack presence in the UK was nowhere near the US crack experience, the government, law enforcement and the media joined forces in exaggerating its potentially dangerous combination of guns and violence to mean an imminent threat to law and order in and beyond the black community. The sensational reportage of the dangers of crack intertwined with a new police focus on tracking crack dealers, particularly 'yardies'. Through Operation Lucy set up by the Metropolitan Police Service (MPS) in 1988 and later replaced by Operation Dalehouse, the MPS created its own Crack Intelligence Coordinating Unit to gather intelligence. Although Operation Dalehouse as a specialist unit for crack came to an end in 1992, crack supply was still targeted within the general operational framework of drugs policing. This was to change with resurrected specialist police interest in crack. According to Sudbury (2002: 66) 'the Metropolitan Police received £800,000 in 2000 to carry out Operation Crackdown'. This operation targeted 'low-level dealers of crack and class A drugs on council estates in boroughs with large black populations. The operation led to surveillance of 700 properties, over 80 raids and 1,000 arrests' (ibid.). In 2000 when Operation Trident (*Guardian*, 1 August 2000), an elite unit set up in 1998 (Evans 2002) to focus on all gun crime in London, redirected its focus to wholly concentrate on the so-called drug-related black-on-black killings, it thereby served as another reminder that the police specialist interest in the 'yardies' and crack was not over. According to Evans (ibid.), Lambeth, Southwark, Hackney, Haringey, Brent and Newham make up the six 'hotspot' localities of Operation Trident, and in 2001, the operation made 441 arrests following an increase in the same year in the number of shooting incidents and Operation Trident murders.

More recently, *Tackling Crack: A National Plan* (Home Office 2002b) has underlined crack as a special drug deserving a special attention. Whilst the plan takes on board the need to address treatment and preventive measures for crack cocaine, law enforcement also features as an integral part of the plan (see *Table 3.1* in *Chapter* 2) to tackle the increasing use of crack via a focus on dealing and markets. In the executive summary of the National Crack Action Plan, crack dealing is identified as an activity linked to acquisitive crime, gun crime and commercial sex, and the African-Caribbean community is identified as a group disproportionately affected by crack markets that mostly operate in deprived localities. Law enforcement strategy in this respect has intensively focused on increasing arrests and convictions for crack trafficking, and closing crack houses particularly in areas named as high crack areas, many of which are also high crime areas (NTA 2003). The results from these law enforcement tactics are exemplified in the following excerpt from the executive summary of the *Updated Drug Strategy 2002* (Home Office 2002a: 8) with regard to the London borough of Lambeth, a named high crack area:

LAMBETH – AN EXAMPLE OF WHAT CAN BE ACHIEVED

Lambeth, with the major crack market of Brixton, was an area where crack problems had reached crisis point early in 2002, with open crack markets and 80 plus crack houses. Accompanying the use of crack was open street prostitution and the use of guns. The local community had had enough and wanted action.

In June 2002, the Home Secretary met with local politicians and services to help develop an action plan for crack. This has been put into action and since June, Lambeth has made a major start on tackling its problems. Over 100 crack house raids have taken place. The achievements so far have been:

33 per cent fewer robberies have been reported;
90 plus people arrested;
564 searches made;
148 abandoned vehicles removed; and
118 prostitutes arrested and referred to treatment.

The Lambeth community now knows that selling crack will meet with a swift and decisive police response. Much more action is underway as part of a comprehensive multi-agency plan to tackle the crack problem in the borough and much more is needed to sustain the progress made, but Lambeth shows that community pressure, coupled with a rapid response can make a difference.[11]

In the name of law enforcement achievements such as those illustrated above, the black community continues to see its members drawn into the criminal justice system for drug offences, particularly drug trafficking for which their involvement is often shown at street-level or the lower end of the drugs trade. By June 2002 the percentage of black people imprisoned for drug offences had soared to 30 per cent, from 18 per cent in June 1998. These figures were revealed by Bob Ainsworth[12] in response to Lyne Jones MP's parliamentary question in 2003 about the proportion of black and minority ethnic people in prison for drug offences (Kalunta-Crumpton 2003a). Clearly they are a stark indication of the prominent position that the black community has come to occupy as clients of the criminal justice system for drug offences, and in particular drug trafficking.

Key drugs law enforcement achievements outlined in the Government's drug strategy progress report 2004 have included the closure of approximately 150 crack houses between January and September 2004, a practice effected under new powers given to the police in the Anti-Social Behaviour Act 2003. This piece of legislation allows the police 'to close crack houses within 48 hours', to seize assets and firearms (aimed at tackling gun crime, part of which is associated with drug trafficking) and to target drug dealers. Following the introduction of the Drugs Act 2005, the Anti-Social Behaviour Act 2003 has been amended to enhance police powers to enter premises (using reasonable force where necessary), including crack houses, for the purpose of serving a closure notice.[13] Increased powers given to law enforcement agencies under the Drugs Act 2005 include allowing courts to remand in police custody for up to a further 192 hours those who swallow packaged drugs, in order to increase the likelihood of recovering the evidence; and requiring a court or jury to assume intent to supply where an accused is found in possession of a certain quantity of a controlled drug. The implications of these new legislative developments for race are yet to be determined.

THE UK'S INTERNATIONALISED WAR ON DRUGS

The UK's policy attempts to curb drug trafficking have extended to international levels. The UK's involvement in international cooperation, particularly with member states of the European Community (EC), has at least in principle been tabled as a strong base for the fight against international drug trafficking. At this point of attack on what has been presented as the EC's common enemy, lie xenophobic characteristics of Europe's drug control strategy and its emphasis on drug trafficking. That common enemy found in the drug trafficker is not only perceived as dangerous but also he or she is viewed as foreign and as such constituting an alien threat, not just to the UK but also to Europe and the West in general. Calling on Europe to organize in a greater coordinated fight against drug trafficking, Murji (1998: 143) notes how during the exaggerated concerns about crack in the late 1980s, Douglas Hurd (then Home Secretary) 'likened the threat of crack to a medieval plague' and called it a 'spectre hanging over Europe'.

Since the 1980s, during which drug trafficking was apparently racialised, the war on drugs has, as Dorn *et al.* (1992: 153) have observed, involved a 'combination of drugs intelligence and immigration intelligence', which 'reflected a perception (which recurred in the 1980s) that it was immigrants, legal and/or illegal, who were responsible for much of the importation of illegal drugs into Britain'. This drug control strategy has also been favoured at the European level. According to Green (1998: pp. 16, 17), 'blaming ethnic minorities is central to western strategies of drug control', and drug traffickers are seemingly 'linked, in the lexicon of European policy, with illegal immigrants'. The consequence has been the concentration of European-led drugs law enforcement on select targets often relating to nations in and individuals from Africa, the Caribbean, Asia and South America.

Europe's strategic attack on international drug trafficking, or to be precise on primarily non-western drug traffickers, followed the birth of the European Community in 1957. The relaxation of internal border controls for its member states and the tightening of external border controls for non-members were the product of the European Community. The formation of the EC was based on the Treaty of Rome signed by six countries—France, Belgium, Italy, Luxembourg, Germany and The Netherlands. In 1973, the UK joined the EC. Subsequent developments in the form of the Single European Act and the Treaty of European Union (referred to as the Maastricht Treaty) expanded and solidified the EC (Cook 1999). The former removed frontier controls between member states and the latter *inter alia* strengthened cooperation between them. These developments have since laid a foundation upon which sits comfortably the utilisation of international drug trafficking as a justification in Europe's collective policy efforts to exclude foreign nationalities and immigrants stereotyped as the alien threat.

European drugs policies have been developed and implemented through a range of initiatives and bodies. European drugs policy development and cooperation began with the formation of a number of groups. Two significant groups were the TREVI[14] Group and CELAD.[15] Set up in 1975 by the European Council of Ministers, the TREVI Group drew its membership from representatives of each EC member state, consisting of ministers, senior police officers and civil servants. Its agenda was to formulate greater European cooperation to combat terrorism. This initial agenda was later extended to encompass other organized crime including drug trafficking. Initiatives to tackle drug trafficking included the creation of national drugs intelligence units in member states, a network of drugs liaison officers in member states, drug producer and transit countries, and the development of a European drugs intelligence unit.

CELAD was established in 1989 with the fundamental responsibility to co-ordinate anti-drug trafficking programmes undertaken by member states as well as work carried out by the European Commission. Its membership consisted of the European Commission and government-nominated representatives. From 1990 when CELAD's first pan-European Action Plan was approved by the

European Council, its target areas have prioritised measures to suppress drug trafficking. For example, it created a European Observatory on Drugs to monitor, alongside demand reduction, the production of and trafficking in drugs, and drug control legislation (Cook 1999).

The UK's policy and practical responses to drug trafficking have also been addressed through other long-standing drug-related European groups such as the Pompidou Group established in 1971 by the Council of Europe. Included in the drug trafficking-related work undertaken by the Pompidou Group is the task to design approaches to locate and confiscate financial assets of drug traffickers.

In more recent years, developments in EC drugs policy cooperation to combat drug trafficking have resulted in the creation of the Europol Drugs Unit (EDU) following the ratification of the Maastricht Treaty in 1993. The formation of the EDU was the first phase toward the establishment of a European Police Office (Europol). Both the EDU and Europol convention were formed to perform non-operational tasks of exchanging information. Europol was agreed under Title VI of the Maastricht Treaty. According to the 1994 government Green Paper, *Tackling Drugs Together*, the aim of this aspect of the treaty was 'to enhance cooperation between governments in tackling drug misuse' (Home Office 1994a: 23). The establishment of Europol was aimed at intensifying the exchange of information and intelligence in order to effect improved police cooperation in the fight against international organized crime, including terrorism and drug trafficking. On a specific level, information gathering and exchange on drug trafficking between member states of the European Union has come under the domain of the EDU. Through information collected and collated by each member state's national criminal intelligence service, the EDU facilitates the coordination of law enforcement operations. Since its birth, this unit, which is staffed by police and customs officers from member states, has extended its territory to include illegal immigration networks, illicit trade in radioactive and nuclear materials, money laundering, and vehicle and human trafficking (Cook 1999).

Drug strategies are also set at the European level whereby member states of the EU work closely with each other to deliver *inter alia* strategies to combat drugs supply and demand within and beyond the EU. This is reflected for example in the *2000-2004 EU Drug Strategy* (Home Office 2002a). The emphasis on closer cooperation between member states found a formal platform in the European Union Framework Decision (EUFD) on collaborative criminal investigations in 2002. Effected by Article 13 of the EU Convention on mutual assistance, the EUFD requires adherence to collaborative investigations amongst EU members (ibid). Such collaborative work is instanced in Operation Containment carried out by 13 European countries in June and July 2002. The operation, which was coordinated by the Southeast European Cooperative Initiative (SECI) regional centre in Bucharest involved 'intelligence-sharing and interdiction efforts at land, sea and air border checkpoints' aimed at tackling heroin trafficking along the Balkan route (United Nations (UN) 2002).

In the Home Office publication, *Tackling Drugs. Changing Lives: Keeping Communities Safe from Drugs*, pan-European collaborative efforts and attacks on drug trafficking are summarised thus:

> We are bearing down on the criminals who do not recognise national boundaries, through the partnerships we have established with our international and European counterparts. To support that, we are using the combined strength of Europe: through Europol and EUROJUST; through new European instruments to agree pan-European minimum penalties for drug trafficking; to facilitate action against money laundering; to support joint investigation teams and mutual legal assistance; through joint customs operations and maritime co-operation (Home Office 2004a: 3).

The UK's international cooperation strategy to fight drug trafficking has not been restricted to initiatives at the European level. For one thing, the UK is involved in the United Nations International Drug Control Programme (UNDCP), which was formed in 1991 to act as the UN focal point for coordinating international assistance and action against drugs for the purpose of curbing drug production, trafficking and demand. This UN objective sustained by drugs-related financial contributions by donor countries, including the UK, has amounted to various UNDCP projects such as those geared toward crop eradication and substitution in drug producer countries, and improved law enforcement in both drug producer and transit countries. Afghanistan, a country which has accounted for over 90 per cent of heroin destined for the UK market stands to exemplify the UK's international involvement in tackling drug production in recent years. Since the fall of the Taliban, the British government has embarked on a range of international assistance strategies, including law enforcement and alternative sources of subsistence for poppy farmers in Afghanistan, with an aim to achieving a reduction and elimination of poppy cultivation in Afghanistan by 70 per cent by 2008 and fully by 2013 (Home Office 2002a). Tackling drugs distribution at international level is instanced by the 'Memorandum of Understanding' signed by the UK and Jamaican governments in order to effect law enforcement tactics to intercept cocaine trafficking in the Caribbean before it reaches the UK shores to feed the crack market (Home Office 2001).[16]

Other UK participation in international drug matters beyond Europe has included involvement with the Dublin Group and the Mutual Legal Assistance Treaties (MLATS). The former, whose membership has included countries outside Europe such as the US, Canada and Australia, has served as a meeting point for the coordination of policies relating to drug production, trafficking and demand at global, regional and national levels. In the latter case, the treaties have been US-led. According to Green (1998: 39), they are 'agreements between countries which attempt to overcome national legal impediments in the process of international evidence gathering', including evidence and assistance toward the extradition of drug traffickers and the confiscation of the proceeds of drug trafficking (ibid.).

In all such efforts in globalised drugs policy and practice towards drug trafficking, I conclude by referring to Kushlick's (2004: 5) observation that:

> It is invariably the weakest links in the illegal drug chain (peasant growers, drug 'mules', and problematic users) who feel the greatest impact of drug [law] enforcement. The alarming rise in the UK female prison population of foreign national drug 'mules' from the Caribbean (around 25 per cent in total) has been well documented ... The bigger players have the resources to evade legal consequences and bargaining powers (as informants) if they are caught ... the UK locks up ten times as many black people under the drug laws as it does whites.

ENDNOTES for *Chapter 3*

1 Confiscation orders were introduced in Scotland in 1988 and in Northern Ireland in 1991.

2 The post of 'drugs czar' was abolished in 2001.

3 In Scotland, the Crime Squad, made up of 85 officers, dedicated 60 per cent of their work to drugs. Northern Ireland's Royal Ulster Constabulary allocated over 20 officers to its Drugs Squad.

4 The Scottish Crime Squad together with the Scottish Criminal Intelligence Office and the Scottish Police Technical Support Unit were incorporated under a new organization, the Scottish Drug Enforcement Agency, which was established in 2001.

5 In Scotland, cautioning is not available. Fines and fiscal fines are used instead. Introduced in 1995, fiscal fines involve the imposition of a financial penalty by procurators fiscal in the absence of a formal admission of guilt. Fiscal fines are reserved for relatively minor offences and do not apply in cases involving a class 'A' drug.

6 See Corkery (1998) for mid-1980s figures on drug offences.

7 Information on import/export offences for 2000 were based on police and court data only; HM Customs offender data for 2000 were incomplete.

8 Compounding is an administrative sanction used by HM Customs. It involves financial penalty.

9 The 1996 estimates by the Office for National Statistics relied on secondary data sources: the 1996 British Crime Survey data on recreational drug users; Regional Drug Misuse Databases for data on the number of problematic drug users who presented to drug treatment services; data on drug seizures.

10 Relates to the total number of seizures with each deal calculated as one gram (Home Office 2004a: 10).

11 From August 2002 to March 2003, Crack OUT programme was introduced in the London borough of Lambeth as a Home Office funded initiative to tackle crack supply and use in the borough. Closing down crack houses was prioritised in this initiative (Lindsell 2003).

12 Home Office Drugs Minister.

13 In 2005, 'Operation Crackdown' was launched to target class 'A' drug dealers and drug-related gun crime, and to close crack houses (Turning Point 2005).

14 Terrorism, Radicalism, Extremism, Violence, International.

15 European Committee to Combat Drugs.

16 The memorandum came into effect in 2002 and was signed by the then Cabinet Office Minister Mo Mowlam. It was also signed with Iran and Colombia.

CHAPTER 4

Visible Minority Ethnic Community Issues in Problematic Drug Use

A key concern about minority ethnic communities' drug use has revolved around their level of presentation to drug treatment and related services. As already noted in *Chapter 2*, determining the extent of problem drug use according to race and ethnicity has drawn strength from drug misuse databases at least at regional and health authority levels. Although these sources of information have drawbacks in terms of their degree of reliability in estimating overall levels of problem drug use by race/ethnicity, they do at least shed some light on racial/ethnic variations in types of drugs and route of drug administration based

Table 4.1: *Percentage of presentations to drug services in and outside London by ethnicity.*

Outside London (% of episodes)[3]	**Birmingham**	**Leicestershire**	**Bradford**	**Lancashire**
White	77	92	87	96
African-Caribbean[4]	6	4	3	1
Indian	1	2	2	*
Pakistani or Bangladeshi	9	*	5	1
Chinese	0	0	0	0
Other	7	2	4	1
Total in number	946	531	534	2686
London (% of people)[5]	LSL	EHH		
White	68	65		
Black-Caribbean	20	10		
Black- African	2	1		
Indian, Pakistani or Bangladeshi[6]				
Indian	1	N/A		
Pakistani or	N/A	14		
Bangladeshi	N/A	3		
Chinese	1	*		
Other	8	6		
Total in number	2926	1289		

* = less than 0.5 per cent
LSL = Lewisham, Southwark and Lambeth
EHH = Ealing, Hammersmith and Hounslow
Source: Sangster *et al.* (2001)

Table 4.2: Percentage of primary drug in episodes presented to LSL and EHH services by ethnicity[7]

LSL	Opiates (injected)	Opiates (other)	Crack	Other	Number
White	47	32	7	14	2396
Black-Caribbean	13	24	42	21	666
Black- African	17	29	30	24	77
Indian, Pakistani or Bangladeshi	a	a	a	a	31
Chinese	4	84	4	8	45
Other	29	42	16	13	316
EHH					
White	25	37	11	27	953
Black - African/Caribbean	6	20	52	22	164
Indian	5	80	5	10	212
Pakistani or Bangladeshi	7	73	5	15	44
Other (including Chinese)	10	47	14	29	88

a = insufficient cases
Source: Sangster *et al.* (2001)

on presentations to services. In the Home Office publication *Delivering Drug Services to Black and Minority Ethnic Communities* (Sangster *et al.* 2001), a comparative analysis of presentations to drug services according to ethnicity in six DAT areas[1] not only demonstrated ethnic disparities in drug type and drug administration method but also showed that regional differences impacted on ethnic differences in levels of presentations to services (see *Tables 4.1* and 4.2).

Sangster and colleagues' analysis in *Table 4.1* shows that black and minority ethnic communities[2] were 'well represented' in the London DAT areas and in contrast under-represented in the chosen DAT areas outside London. While there seem to be adequate levels of representation for black and minority ethnic communities in the London areas, these findings begin to lose absoluteness when specific ethnic groups are taken into consideration. In the two London areas, black-Caribbean level of presentation was 'slightly over-represented' while their black-African counterparts were 'consistently under-represented'. A similar scenario applies to south Asians who were under-represented in the LSL area. And in the EHH area, Indians were 'well represented' while their Pakistani and Bangladeshi counterparts were under-represented. *Table 4.2* draws upon data from LSL and EHH areas and focuses on race/ethnic differences in presentations according to the primary drug used and the route of drug administration. In relation to these data, Sangster *et al.* (2001) state:

> African-Caribbean episodes presented to drug services in the London case study areas showed a particular concentration on crack. In LSL, presentations from African-Caribbean users were more than four times as likely to focus on crack as were those made by whites and in EHH they were more than five times as likely to do so ... while white users accounted for 32 per cent of primary crack episodes in LSL and 48

> per cent of such episodes in EHH South Asians accounted for one per cent and five per cent respectively ... Within EHH, South Asian presentations were similar to those of whites in the sense that they focused primarily on opiates. There were, however, striking contrasts in relation to mode of use. While episodes relating to opiate injecting were, by some distance, highest among white clients, those presented by South Asians focused overwhelmingly on non-injectable use ... African-Caribbean communities are affected by opiate use. More than a quarter of episodes presented by users from these communities in LSL and EHH focused primarily on opiates. While these episodes tended to focus on non-injecting use they also provide evidence of injecting. (p.17)

In a nutshell, the findings above depict the complexities that have underpinned issues of race/ethnicity and problem drug use. Why visible minority ethnic groups are generally under-represented in the numbers of presentations to drug services is a key question to which answers have pointed in two broad directions. One is that which assumes that problematic drug use is not an issue in minority ethnic communities. The other presents the existence of minority ethnic problematic drug use but for a variety of reasons it is significantly hidden from official records of known problem drug users. These broad accounts however complement each other. For example, problematic drug use may not be seen as an issue in minority ethnic communities because their use of opiate—the traditional drug of concern—is shown to be relatively limited and for those who use it, non-injecting is often presented as the sole route of administration. For these reasons they may not be known to drug treatment services which are often injecting-opiate-led.

Black and Asian communities constitute the visible minority ethnic groups most affected by these lines of reasoning. To an extent, this may be attributed to the fact that they have a longer historical presence in the UK. These communities have so far attracted the most attention in debates surrounding drug use amongst visible minority ethnic groups. This fact is reflected throughout this chapter, where much of the information refers to black (i.e. African-Caribbean and African) and Asian (i.e. Indian, Pakistani and Bangladeshi) issues, while some information, albeit minimal, is clearly specific in identifying issues relevant to other distinct visible minority ethnic groups more recently-established in the UK. For example, Sangster *et al.* (2001) made reference to Somalis and Vietnamese as groups who are also experiencing problematic drug use in their midst but who are much less likely to make contact with drug services.[8] However, where generic terms such as 'visible minority ethnic' and 'minority ethnic' are used they are also meant to encompass common issues and experiences applicable to non-white minority ethnic groups.

COMMUNITIES WITHOUT A DRUG PROBLEM?

To date, the drug using circumstances of visible minority ethnic communities are yet to gain clarity in studies of problem drug use. Existing major studies have generally aimed at measuring lifetime prevalence rates of drug use in its recreational pattern (Graham and Bowling 1995; Leitner *et al.* 1993; Mott and

Mirrlees-Black 1995; Home Office 1996) rather than engage in attempts to explore the actual harm caused by drug misuse to the users themselves. This is more so with heroin. Whilst heroin has remained the traditional drug of concern in mainstream discourse, policy and practical concerns about drug misuse, very little is known about its impact on the heroin using minority ethnic population. The relative neglect of the role of race or ethnicity in problem heroin use was probably most evident in the 1980s, especially with regard to the heroin epidemic. As noted in *Chapter* 2, that period saw concerns about the effects of heroin misuse at both individual and societal levels amounting to significant transformation of political and research interests into the epidemiology of heroin use. The centre of interest was the white population and 'white' heroin use, and those concerns instigated a relative increase in treatment and rehabilitation services (MacGregor 1989c; Jamieson *et al.* 1984). No visibility was given to any influence that the heroin epidemic might have had on Britain's black and Asian populations—at both individual and community levels.

Questions that emerged around minority ethnic drug use in the 1980s seem to have been motivated by the arrival of the crack cocaine tremor in the late 1980s and its production of a mix of discourses around black drug use of, and trafficking in, crack cocaine (Keith 1993; Murji 1998). Debates about minority ethnic communities' problem drug use prioritised their under-representation in the numbers of those who presented to drug treatment services (Mirza *et al.* 1991a). Whether those communities were relatively drug problem-free (see for example Ruggiero 1992) or whether they had a significant drug using population but were unwilling to turn to treatment services for help (Awiah *et al.* 1990, 1992) were crucial questions raised in the debate.

Despite acknowledging the under-representation of minority ethnic communities as clients of drug services, Mirza *et al.* (1991a) drew attention to the relationship between black drug use and the criminal justice system. They noted that the majority of drug users known to criminal justice agencies were black people who were most likely to be arrested for a drug offence. Relating such arrests to crack cocaine, Mirza *et al.* (1991b) observed that while such police action presented crack and cocaine use as a black problem, white people made up the vast majority of users of these drugs. A similar scenario surfaced in the area of mental health where a high proportion of black drug users were known to be diagnosed as mentally ill (Crowley *et al.* 1992; Chantler 1998) unlike their drug using white counterparts (King *et al.* 1994). In Sangster *et al.*'s (2001) study, the relationship drawn between black drug use and mental health was a concern raised in interviews held with drug workers.

These findings clearly point to the possibility of a significant black drug problem, which is seemingly 'hidden' in institutions outside of drug treatment services. Furthermore, difficulties surrounding efforts to ascertain the extent of black problem drug use have been complicated by the contradictory accounts within which black drug use has been located. Observations, which have implied the existence of a black drug problem at least enough to deserve policy attention, have at the same time condemned the association of drug use with the black community. For example, whilst Awiah *et al.* (1990) identified with the under-representation of black drug users in drug services due to the fact that such services are operated by white staff for white drug (primarily heroin) users, they have simultaneously tended to disassociate black people from extensive drug use. Instead, they have claimed that the conception that many blacks misuse drugs is merely a myth derived from racial stereotypes rather than evidence.

Despite the persistent stereotypical association of drug use and dealing with the black community, there is evidence to the contrary. According to Mirza *et al.* (1991a), the black people-drug use mythical connection has a lot to do with limitations in drawing statistical inference based on the high numbers of a group within an area associated with certain behaviour. They termed this inference 'ecological fallacy' in the sense that because there are high concentrations of black people in areas with high levels of drug use, it is assumed that all black people are likely to be drug users. But in reality, according to the authors, 'the high rates of drug misuse' involved 'white heroin users living in neighbourhoods of black settlement' (p.12). As already established, those areas of high rates of drug use are characterised by social and economic forms of deprivation. Related to this, the majority of black people are resident in those areas of deprivation and drug use, a connection which may explain the racial stereotype.

The Asian community and other minority ethnic groups are no exception to the confusions that have faced minority ethnic community problem drug use. Whilst research findings generally suggest a relatively low Asian drug use, a few indicate that drug use in Asian communities is not to be underestimated and therefore taken for granted. In a BBC2 documentary *East*, aired on 24 July 2000, some worrying aspects of Asian problematic heroin use were documented. The documentary focused on the London borough of Tower Hamlets where a high proportion of Asians reside. At the time the borough had an unemployment rate of 90 per cent, and the overall levels of deprivation were significantly related to problem heroin use within the borough. Drugs were openly used in stairwells of council estates where also drug-related paraphernalia were commonly found littered everywhere. According to ADACTION, a drug treatment service in the borough, 40 per cent of its clientele was Bangladeshi. Criminal activities such as mugging, prostitution and drug dealing formed common sources of feeding drug habits. Ninety per cent of drug dealers in the borough were identified as Asian; Asian women, it was claimed, were increasingly getting into prostitution in order to serve the interests of their drug dealing/using boyfriends. Despite Asian community denunciation of drug use in their community, problem drug use amongst the younger generations was nevertheless acknowledged as a cause for concern.

Patel (2000) also argues that results from drug prevalence studies, which show Asian drug use to be lower than that of blacks and whites are misleading. The findings could have been influenced by poor Asian participation due to factors including the community's suspicion of drug-related studies conducted by white researchers. Such factors have precluded attempts to decipher the extent and nature of drug use amongst the Asian community. As such the common perceptions of Asians and drug use are constantly reflected in the following cited sample of statements made by a range of drug workers and leaders in the Asian community across Britain (ibid.: 127):

- 'If there are Asian drug users, they don't use these [drug] services.'
- 'Asian people don't use drugs.'
- 'The few that do use will never inject.'
- 'Religion prohibits drug taking – therefore it is not a problem.'
- 'It is a white western disease.'
- Our strong religious and cultural values stop us from this behaviour.'

Such views have not only been fuelled by findings from prevalence studies. It is also known that Asians are under-represented in the numbers of problem drug users who present to drug treatment services for reasons which include the tendency within the Asian community to deny that there is a drug problem in its midst (also see DrugScope 2003). Under these circumstances, as Patel (2000) observes, certain aspects of Asian drug use are overlooked. For other visible minority ethnic communities particularly those who have a relatively recent historical presence in the UK, their very limited presence in drugs research and literature is invariably reflected in their even more marginalised position in drugs policy and practice. Sangster *et al.* (2001), for example, reported of low rates of presentations to drug treatment services amongst Somalis and Vietnamese despite evidence of crack and opiate use amongst these communities. Khat (or Qat, Kat)—a traditional stimulant used by Somalis—is known to be popular within this community (Cunningham 1998; Fountain *et al.* 2002) and although it generates problematic drug use, there is a tendency among the Somalis to view its use as non-problematic; hence its presence in service provision is very limited (Sangster *et al.* 2001).

What is seemingly clear from the above instance of conflicting attitudes towards minority ethnic community drug use is that the complexities surrounding their problem drug use owe a great deal to issues of race. For example, those with interest in drug use within the black community are continually torn between unveiling the nature of black problem drug use and avoiding the promotion of racial stereotyping. The vital role of race in perceptions of drug use is demonstrated in other studies. For example, in a study conducted by the Department of Sociology, City University (1997) the racially underlined images of black people (and Asians) and drugs are mirrored thus:

> Notions about drug usage and needs in those communities have been informed more by racist constructions of criminality and assumptions of 'ethnic welfare' than fact. The representation of the cannabis smoking, crack dealing [African-Caribbean] attests to the former, whilst in the latter that of the 'Asians don't do drugs', or '[African-Caribbeans] don't inject' is still prevalent in the approach of agencies towards black communities.

Referring to the racialisation of crack cocaine use, Chantler (1998: 8) notes how the use of the drug is not only 'stereotypically associated almost exclusively with African-Caribbean men' but also that the 'image of a crack user as violent, aggressive and paranoid feeds into existing stereotypes, specifically about young African-Caribbean men'. A major consequence of such racially-based assumptions, Chantler adds, is that they harbour the tendency to preclude 'any mention of drug related activity in Black communities' due to fears of reproducing already existing stereotypical notions of blacks and drugs. Amongst service providers and commissioners, such fears do exist resulting in a lack of acknowledgement of drug use amongst Black and minority ethnic communities. As Fountain *et al.* (2002: 8) state, 'fear of accusations of racism by drawing attention to drug use in these communities, and a desire to avoid increasing stigmatisation of them' in part create such reactions from service commissioners and providers. Ultimately, any drug service needs that these communities might have are undermined by policy makers and practitioners alike (Dorn and Murji 1992; Fountain *et al.* 2002).

There are already years of claims that national drugs policy initiatives have been relatively silent on the needs of problematic drug users among black and other minority ethnic groups (Chantler 1998; Khan 1999; Johnson and Carroll 1995). It is the sort of silence which, as Chantler (1998: 8) states, 'even if well intentioned, ultimately does black communities a disservice as it fails to acknowledge the need for drug services in those communities'. This absence of recognition is, for instance, partly reflected in the limited drug service provisions and deliveries available to visible minority ethnic communities (Nefertari and Ahmun 1999; Dale-Perera and Farrant 1999; Khan 1999; Sangster *et al.* 2001; Home Office 2002a).

FACTORS PRECLUDING NOTIFICATION OF PROBLEM DRUG USE AND ACCESS TO TREATMENT SERVICES

There are a variety of reasons why precise levels of problem drug use amongst visible minority ethnic communities may not be officially recorded. These have ranged from the exclusionary nature of mainstream drug services of problem drug users from minority ethnic communities to the distinct cultural issues within these communities, which prevent drug users from seeking the help of drug treatment services. Over the years, much of the debates on this issue has however emphasised mainstream drug services as a key area where urgent strategic restructuring is needed to effect significant minority ethnic community access.

For one, the focus of the majority of drug services on injecting opiate use has harboured a tendency to exclude the majority of minority ethnic drug users whose primary drug and/or method of administration may require interventions which differ from the conventional models traditionally operated by mainstream services. This is not to claim as studies have shown that opiate use is unfamiliar to drug users from minority ethnic communities. For example, during the 1980s heroin epidemic in the UK, heroin use and injecting showed a rapid growth in many Asian countries, and HIV/AIDS outbreaks were reported in some parts of the continent (Patel 2000). In the UK, Patel (ibid.) further states: an increasing number of Asian youth use drugs; heroin is the first drug of choice for many Asian users especially amongst Pakistani and Bangledeshi males; intravenous drug use is a major issue in Asian heroin use; many Asians, particularly Pakistanis and Bangledeshis, fall into the age profile (birth to 15) predisposed to drug use; and most Asians, especially Pakistanis and

Bangledeshis, experience high levels of poverty and reside in deprived inner city localities—drug use has been associated with areas of social and economic deprivation. These socio-economic factors place these groups at risk of problematic drug use (Patel and Webberly 2002).

Other studies, whilst often ad hoc and piecemeal tend to reveal similarly the nature of south Asian drug use, which is that despite evidence of use of a range of drugs amongst south Asians particularly by young males (Bashford *et al.* 2000, 2001; Sheikh *et al.* 2002), heroin is likely to be their drug of choice (Perera 1996; Chaundery *et al.* 1997; Sheikh *et al.* 2001; Webster 2001; Patel *et al.* 2001). Whilst south Asians seem to have a strong preference for smoking rather than injecting heroin, partly because it reflects their traditional method of drug use, the intravenous mode of administration among them is not to be discounted given that there is evidence of its existence especially in relation to opiate within this community (Pearson and Patel 1998; Sheikh *et al.* 2001; Patel *et al.* 2001; Webster 2001). Like their Asian counterparts, the black community is not unfamiliar with opiate use, including intravenously; opiate has been known to act as a substitute for crack for African-Caribbeans in prison or it has been used for its 'coming down' effect on crack (Sangster *et al.* 2001). Other visible minority ethnic communities such as the Chinese and the Vietnamese have shown evidence of both opiate use and injecting (Patel *et al.* 1998; Whittington 1999; Sangster *et al.* 2001).

Notwithstanding the evidence of opiate use and injecting opiate use among visible minority ethnic communities, the contentious issue around their access to treatment services has continually drawn attention to the supposedly lesser degree to which their involvement in opiate poses a problem to these communities. And as such, associations between Asians, black people and non-injecting opiate use, and black and crack/cannabis use have remained instances of recurring arguments to explain their overall under-representation in mainstream services where opiate and intravenous opiate use underline models of treatment intervention, and where clients are encouraged to switch from injecting to non-injecting as part of a harm reduction approach (Kalunta-Crumpton 2003b). In other words the majority of mainstream services do not have much to offer problem drug users who do not inject opiate or whose sole drug of choice is not opiate. Criticisms of the failure of opiate-based services effectively to diversify their focus in terms of drug type and mode of use to incorporate non-opiate drugs and non-injecting (Home Office 2002a; Sangster *et al.* 2001; Turning Point 2005; Turning Point/COCA 2005) further highlight this common knowledge that links minority ethnic groups with non-opiate and non-intravenous drug use.

Whether or not injecting opiate use is an issue among minority ethnic communities is not a debate that can successfully erase the key question about the extent of problem drug use in such communities and the arguments that drug use is a problem in these communities regardless of drug type. As Sangster *et al.* (2001) have argued, while the under-representation of minority ethnic groups may suggest that they experience relatively lower levels of problematic drug use than their white counterparts, this is not necessarily the case. The tendency for African-Caribbeans to use the services of voluntary-based drug agencies (rather than statutory agencies) with service interests in crack users, the lesser likelihood of visible minority ethnic problem drug users to present to their GPs and the low treatment retention rates for these groups are instances of minority ethnic problematic responses to statutory agencies, a situation which simultaneously raises critical questions around the nature and structure of service provision and delivery. In 1998, the Advisory Council on the Misuse of Drugs noted that, 'the under-representation of black people among populations of drug users known to agencies might, for example, be a consequence of the failure of agencies to make themselves accessible and meaningful to all members of a multi-cultural society' (p.41).

Beyond the notion that the injecting opiate-based structure of mainstream services is an exclusionary mechanism for problem drug users from minority ethnic groups are other barriers which relate to what Sangster *et al.* (2001) refer to as 'institutional failings' and problems of 'cultural competence and cultural appropriateness' of existing drug services. In demonstrating that the under-representation of visible minority ethnic groups to drug treatment services is a problem that has carried into the twenty-first century and once again is demonstrative of the weak relationship between the two parties, they argue that the lapsed relationship not only has a great deal to do with issues of racism and social exclusion but also embodies 'institutional failings' and 'cultural [in]competence and cultural [in]appropriateness' (*emphasis added*) of existing drug services. They outline three areas of 'institutional failings'—noted as particularly evident in specialist residential services—as relating to:

- the image of services and their isolation from the community;
- an inability to respond to distinct patterns of drug use shown by black and minority ethnic communities; and
- a more general inability to respond to different needs.

Where cultural competence and appropriateness are a fundamental part of existing services, they should include the following separate but also interdependent aspects:

- Cultural ownership and leadership (the extent to which race and ethnicity are considered important by a service).
- Symbols of accessibility (something that shows black and minority ethnic people that they are welcomed by a service, for example a newspaper).
- Familiarity with, and ability to meet, the distinct needs of communities.
- Holistic, therapeutic and social help.
- A range of services.
- Black and minority ethnic workers.
- Community attachment and ownership and capacity building (the process through which the skills and structures needed to provide drug services are developed. (p.2)

Examples of 'institutional failings' include the dominate image of 'whiteness' in the staffing, clientele, decoration and scenery of statutory agencies; their focus on injecting opiate use; and their failure to embrace cultural diversity (reflected for example in language, norms and religious needs). When dissected these instances of 'institutional failings' will also point to the above elements of 'cultural [in]competence and cultural [in]appropriateness'.

Without detailing Sangster *et al.*'s (2001) research-based interpretations of these key points, it is however important to note that their findings are not unfamiliar but are a reiteration of issues which have for many years also accompanied concerns over the under-representation of minority ethnic communities in drug treatment services. That statutory agencies are run by whites for white clientele (Awiah *et al.* 1990, 1992; Southwell 1995; Gooden 1999), are not often ethnically representative in terms of staffing (Awiah *et al.* 1990, 1992; Perera *et al.* 1997), do not often operate culturally competent, responsive and sensitive programmes to address the needs (such as linguistic, religious, issues of racism and social exclusion) of problem drug users from minority ethnic groups (Maynard 1994; Bentley and Hanton 1997; Chantler 1998) are instances of recurring concerns. In short, as Matthews (2002: 7) states 'the power base of drug treatment services provision remains within the white majority who lack any real insight into the problems faced by black people'. These factors arguably restrict access to those services for visible minority ethnic groups due to their distrust of services run by whites and, believably, for whites (Awiah *et al.* 1992).

It is a sort of distrust which according to Sangster *et al.* (2001: 20) is mirrored 'within the broader context of racism and social exclusion'. For instance, the tendency for problematic crack and cannabis use amongst black and minority ethnic communities, particularly African-Caribbeans, to be misdiagnosed as mental health cases leads in part to the lack of trust held by these communities in mainstream drug services (Bashford *et al.* 2000; Weekes 2002). The lack of trust extends to GPs where there is evidence of low levels of African- Caribbean presentations for reasons which include fear of being diverted into psychiatric services. Like crack, cannabis, according to Sangster *et al.* (2001: 15), 'provides a particular focus for problematic drug use among African-Caribbeans' as presentations to drug services suggest. Some of those who are not known to treatment services are located in mental health units as a result of the diagnosis of 'cannabis psychosis' and the consequent compulsory hospital admissions that are imposed on them (Harrison *et al.* 1997).

Interestingly, there are suggestions that the minority ethnic distrust of mainstream services is not entirely confined to white service providers. Fears that confidentiality and anonymity may be breached by an Asian service provider regardless of their knowledge and understanding of the cultural background of an Asian problem drug user could create a barrier to drug service access for Asian problem drug users (Bentley and Hanton 1997; DrugScope 2003). Sangster *et al.* (2001: 49) also presented a similar scenario with reference to GPs when they stated that their respondents in Ealing, Hammersmith and Hounslow 'suggested that low levels of south Asian presentation to GPs might reflect concerns about anonymity and confidentiality because a large number of GPs in this area are, themselves, south Asian'. The whole issue of anonymity and confidentiality has always been part of the discourses around how the cultural norms and values of minority ethnic communities harbour implications for their drug use. For fear of attracting unwanted stigma from the community and causing shame to oneself and relatives, problem drug users from minority ethnic communities with strong cultural norms and values are more likely to remain hidden from drug treatment records (Khan and Ditton 1999; Gooden 1999; Sangster *et al.* 2001). This situation calls to mind the aforementioned BBC2 documentary 'East', which also highlighted some of the consequences of stigma attached to drug use within the Asian community. The documentary showed how family reactions toward drug use tended to be negative. Asian drug use can lead to family breakdown as it brings shame to the family. In the documentary, an Asian youth described how he was hit on the head with a baseball bat by his father and kicked out of the house because of his drug addiction. Another Asian male with problem drug use was left by his wife and their six-year-old son. This cultural issue may also explain why Asians are more likely to seek private, inpatient detoxification services, which provide quick treatment (Sangster *et al.* 2001).

CASE STUDY: ANALYSIS OF A SAMPLE OF BLACK[9] PRESENTATIONS TO A LONDON DRUG TREATMENT SERVICE (LDTS)

Here the place of heroin in the lives of black drug users is prioritised principally because this aspect of black drug use is severely under-researched when compared to the extensive research literature on white heroin use. This case study draws upon findings from the author's research study of black problem heroin users registered with an LDTS. The research study aimed to identify the pattern and nature of drug problems experienced by the black clients of the LDTS project. This focus was guided by the definition of problematic drug use by the Advisory Council on the Misuse of Drugs (1982, 1988) – initially in 1982, to mean excessive consumption of drugs on a regular basis and/or dependence on drugs resulting in physical, psychological, social or legal problems, and in 1988 broadened to recognise the spread of HIV/AIDS through intravenous drug use.

Firstly, this objective was grounded on a quantitative examination of clients' files over a six-month period in 2000/2001. This involved a detailed study of 29 files belonging to black problem drug users registered with the LDTS. The selection of files was based on purposive and convenience non-probability sampling techniques because the busy daily operation of the LDTS did not lend itself to systematic random sampling of clients' files. Nevertheless, its working arrangements were such that accessing files on the basis of ethnic groups was made easier. Once the purpose to target the files of black clients was clear, the files studied were ones readily available during the data collection period. The application of non-probability sampling methods is not to claim that the sample size for black clients was unrepresentative of their total number in the LDTS. Despite the fact that no statistical breakdown of the ethnic composition of the LDTS's clientele had been compiled for the period after August 2000, previous statistics can provide a guide to the ethnic make-up of presentations to the LDTS. As at the end of September 1999, the number of black clients was 45 and made-up eleven per cent of the total number of clients, which stood at 422. At the end of August 2000 when the total number of clients was 382, the number of black clients was 39.[10] The LDTS's records of client figures were based on new presentations, closed cases and re-opened cases, and this fact resulted in fluctuations in recorded client figures.

Secondly, a qualitative approach was adopted by conducting a brief open-ended mail questionnaire interview with staff of the LDTS. The interview focused on the social problems of clients' drug use. Thus, questions revolved around how issues of housing, employment, family, race, immigration and criminal justice impact on black drug use. Staff's verbatim answers to the lines of questioning gave more clarity to social issues identified in the clients' files.

The LDTS has a well-established and long-standing history of rendering services to drug users, primarily long-term users of opiate. Its services have included harm reduction programmes such as needle exchange schemes and outreach work; counselling; medical referrals; referrals and advice on housing and welfare benefits; and assistance with legal matters. The LDTS was located in a multi-racial/ethnic part of London and had an ethnic mix of staff members who worked directly with the clients. The author's choice of the LDTS as a research site was significantly influenced by its orientation toward ethnic diversity, and therefore the assumption that it would suit the research objective.

Clients' socio-demographics

Twenty-six of the black clients were male while three were female. This wide gap in the sex composition of the clients is reflective of the traditional make-up of users of drug treatment services: they are often male – although mostly of white racial origin (Department of Health 2001). The extent to which this sex disparity in the use of drug treatment services is indicative of differences in levels of problem drug use is debatable. However, it is known that female drug users are less likely than their male counterparts to contact drug treatment services for help. Reasons for the reluctance have ranged from fear of attracting gendered stereotypical representations and sexist responses to fear of losing their children to the welfare state (Nolan-Trainer 1996; Henderson 1999). For black women, such fears are compounded by their race (Nolan-Trainer 1996).

The age composition of the clients showed that the majority were in their thirties at the time of fieldwork. While this observation shows black problematic drug use to be most common among the more adult population, and especially those in their thirties, it is not a reflection of the actual time length of problematic drug use. One of the inferences that has been drawn from the age profile of drug users has related to age at time of presentation to drug treatment services. This has aimed at ascertaining the ages of those most likely to seek help. According to data from the Regional Drug Misuse Databases (RDMDs) on drug use in England (Department of Health 2001), presentation to drug treatment services is mostly common among drug users in their twenties. To some extent, this observation coincides with the author's research findings inasmuch as a significant number (41 per cent) of the black clients fell into the twenties age range at the time of presentation to the LDTS, although the majority were above twenty-five. An equally significant proportion (38 per cent) of the clients were in their thirties. Sangster *et al.*'s (2001) analysis of age at time of presentation to drug treatment services in their two case study areas of London: EHH (Ealing, Hammersmith and Hounslow) and LSL (Lewisham, Southwark and Lambeth) does show that for the period beginning April 1999 to end September 2000, the 'average age for episodes associated with opiates' was 32 and 30-32 for blacks in EHH and LSL respectively.

The socio-economic characteristics of the clients showed that their unemployment rate was very high. Despite the fact that data on employment were missing on two clients, findings still showed that almost all the clients were unemployed, and many of those were on state benefits. For the very few who were employed, they were in semi-skilled jobs. The marginalised socio-economic position of the clients was also revealed in the area of housing. Although the vast majority of the clients had stable accommodation, they were mostly in local authority housing. There were those who would be classed as having 'no fixed abode' because they were temporarily residing with friends or relatives, or living in squats. Except for the one person who was in prison at the time of fieldwork, all the clients resided in an inner-city locality often in the deprived parts.

Problem drug use: pattern and health problems

All the clients presented heroin as their primary drug and it was consumed on a daily basis at the time of presentation to the LDTS. The amount of heroin used ranged from a quarter of a gram to one-and-half grams a day. The clients were more likely to have had their first taste of heroin later in their adult life, often from their mid-twenties (see *Table 4.3*). Despite that the clients presented with an opiate problem, many were engaged in poly-drug use. Crack cocaine was the most common combination. This finding tallies with Pearson's (1992) observation that crack use is more likely to present as a secondary feature of heroin use. Like heroin, first crack use amongst the clients seemed to have occurred mostly from their twenties. Although this piece of data was available on only 14 clients who reported crack use, it does show that 79 per cent of them were in their twenties, 14 per cent in their teens and seven per cent were in the thirties age range. Other complementary drugs used were cannabis, cocaine, amphetamine, methadone and LSD.

Table 4.3 *Drug using characteristics of the clients (n)*

Drug type (n=29)		**Age at first heroin use (n=26[11])**	
Heroin (main drug)	29	Under 13	1
Crack	24	Teens	7
Cannabis	9	20s	10
Cocaine	1	30s	7
Amphetamines	1	40s	1
Acid [LSD]	1		
Methadone	3		

	Method of administration **Heroin (n=26[11])**	**Crack (n=20[12])**
Intravenous	8	4
Smoke	14	14
Combination (injecting & smoking)	4	2

While most combinations were limited to heroin and crack, over one-third of the clients used another drug alongside those. Found to be rare amongst the clients was the use of tranquillisers; similarly, the use of anti-depressant drugs was seemingly non-existent. Drug users, especially those who use crack or cocaine, have been known to rely on tranquillisers and anti-depressants to tackle problems of anxiety, sleeplessness, depression and suicidal thoughts that accompany certain forms of drug use (Gossop 1993; Brian *et al.* 1998). However, it has been argued that for black people, heroin is more likely to be used as a coping mechanism for crack addiction (Turning Point 2005) and this may explain the clients' seeming lack of interest in tranquillisers and anti-depressants. These drug-induced symptoms, including the more serious instances of self-harm and suicide attempts, were nevertheless exhibited by some of the clients. They administered heroin by intravenous injection or/and by smoking although the most common route of administration involved the smoking method (see *Table 4.3*). A similar scenario occurred in relation to crack use where the available information revealed that the vast majority only smoked. That drug administration by way of smoking was seemingly more favoured by the clients may account for their seemingly low level of injection-related health problems.

The LDTS staff highly commended non-intravenous drug use in health assessments of clients, and in such reports what was highlighted related to concerns over the health risk factor and the importance of harm reduction in drug use. In the UK, the relationship between intravenous drug use and HIV infection has featured uppermost in health concerns about drug use. Such concerns found origin in the 1980s heroin epidemic, during which the spread of HIV was largely attributed to the use of shared drug injecting paraphernalia among injecting drug users (MacGregor 1989c; Stimson and Lart 1991; Gossop 1993). HIV infection was considered as the most serious complication of injecting drug use, and according to the Advisory Council on the Misuse of Drugs (1988: 1), it posed 'a greater threat to public and individual health than drug misuse'. HIV infection was reported on three of the clients. Other serious infections that can be contracted and spread through the sharing of injecting equipment have included types of the hepatitis virus (Gossop 1993). Three of the clients (one of whom was also HIV positive) were diagnosed with hepatitis C. The LDTS staff's concerns about the injecting practices of its clients were not only restricted to the health implications of sharing injecting equipment. The staff drew a distinction between 'good' and 'bad' injecting practices. This was usually related to the state of a client's injecting sites and one notable consequence of a bad-injecting practice identified was the formation of abscesses on injecting sites. More often than not, the clients were reported as presenting no problems relating to bad injecting practices.

Social problematics of black drug use

In various ways, the social contexts within which black problem drug use is located display characteristics of socio-economic deprivation found in problem drug use in general. But according to Chantler (1998), the strong correlation between drug use and socio-economic disadvantage poses major consequences for black communities given their overall deplorable social and economic circumstances.

It is not clear as to the extent to which the drug using habits of the clients in this study were precipitated by socio-economic needs or were the resultant effects of socio-economic deprivation. Evidently, the clients showed a very high level of unemployment and a significant reliance on state benefits, but simultaneously unstable housing was not a common component of their socio-economic needs. Presentations to drug treatment services can be influenced by practical problems—such as housing and employment—associated with drug use rather than any objectives to break the drug using habit. Herein, drug users merely wish to seek advice from drug services on how to tackle such practical problems (Velleman and Rigby 1990). The drug related practical needs of the black clients did not seem significantly to revolve around socio-economic needs relating to housing and employment, and this observation tallied with the following statement made by a staff member of the LDTS:

> They are familiar with the system (that is, welfare system) and therefore need no more help than their English counterparts with housing, employment and/or social security benefits.

Clients' knowledge of how the welfare system works was based on the fact that they were mostly second generation black immigrants, born and bred in the UK. As demonstrated in the statement below, the LDTS staff had very little contact with black clients who had immigration issues and who may have thus needed assistance with accessing public funds:

> We see very few black clients with immigration problems. Many black refugees and economic migrants are non-EC [i.e. European Community] migrants. However, we do have a few linked to our services but they are dealt with on a case by case basis. If they request assistance in applying to the immigration authority, we are happy to give them assistance by pointing them in the right direction. But we do not give advice. It is likely that we would still work very hard at linking them into public health services if they were in need of urgent healthcare'.

As virtually all the clients were UK nationals and were habitually resident in the UK, they had access to welfare services without having to face the restrictions imposed upon persons of non-British nationality (Glover *et al.* 2001).

One of the areas of concern surrounding black problematic drug use relates to gaps in service provision for black drug users and barriers to seeking the help of drug services. As already stated, the under-usage of drug treatment services by black and other minority ethnic drug users has prompted a range of explanations, which have often voiced the perceptions of minority ethnic groups against services dominated by white staff (Awiah *et al.* 1990, 1992; Mirza *et al.* 1999a; Dale-Perera and Farrant 1999; Nefertari and Ahmun 1999). All in all, the reluctance on the part of mainstream services to accommodate and embrace cultural diversity in service provision and delivery—or the failure of national and local policy initiatives to prioritise culturally specific services for minority ethnic groups—underline existing failures to capture clients from minority ethnic groups (Nefertari and Ahmun 1999; Southwell 1995; Dale-Perera and Farrant 1999). Within other institutional spheres with links to drug treatment services, Eurocentric white images and views eclipse policy and practical applications of racial and cultural diversity whilst reinforcing racist stereotyping (Chantler 1998). In the following statement, a staff member of the LDTS reflects on the issue of diversity and how its perceived neglect across a range of institutions such as the social services, the medical and the criminal justice sectors impacts on the needs of black drug users:

> [T]hey are less likely to be aware of their drug treatment options, there is poor communication between professionals and themselves, they have great difficulty with self-expression and getting their points of view across. They are less likely to leave a consultation session having all their concerns voiced. Although they speak English, if it is spoken with an accent or with cultural specific expression it is often misunderstood and often seen as threatening, ignorance or self-pity.

Whilst the above scenario, which describes the apathy of agencies towards black drug users, can account for the reluctance of black drug users to turn to relevant services for help, it may well explain why this racial group of drug users tend to rely on family support for their drug problem, even when drug services are involved. Family members have been known to play a significant part in initiating black referrals to drug services (Pearson 1996). This observation is relevant to the LDTS where self-directed referrals have had input from a family member who has also taken a positive approach towards a client's problem drug use. The role of the family in the drug using lives of black people is well acknowledged by the LDTS staff as very beneficial to addressing the needs of black drug users:

> I find black families are generally much more involved with our black clients. Family members are more likely to attend the service or contact us by phone. They are usually introduced to the service by the client and consent is usually given to discuss care plans or ongoing matters. Generally, the role assumed is one of a buffer between the client and his/her family. This often acts as an important role for communication with someone that understands their cultural values and can provide the family with useful information about drugs that does not conflict and is also mindful of their belief system. This help is usually welcomed and well received by family members. Black families are more likely to remain in contact through thick and thin and see the care of their loved ones as their responsibility.

That said, black problem drug users can also experience a loss of family and community support amounting to a sense of dislocation. Some may lose contact with their family and community, while others may choose to sever links with such 'significant others', or maintain ties with them but keep them uninformed of their drug use. A staff member of LDTS elaborates on such forms of social exclusion and their invariable implications for black problem drug use:

> Our black clients tend to fall into two categories: those who associate within their own black social circles and those who have lost ties with their family and friends and are isolated or may have [an] ethnic-mix of friends. Clients who socialise outside of

their own ethnic group are much more likely to have grown up outside of their own group i.e., in foster-care, adoption or children's homes. However, some black clients who have grown up and lived within their own social circles make informed decisions not to associate within their own ethnic group. This can sometimes be down to isolation through their drug use or a preference to socialise with other drug users. Some black clients remain in their own black social circles and continue to use drugs. This group is most likely to find it difficult to access generic drug services.

A striking feature of the clients' problematic drug use is its relationship with the criminal justice system. Twenty-eight (out of 29) of the clients had a past criminal record, out of which 64 per cent were clearly shown to have served a prison sentence. Offences with which the clients were most commonly associated involved acquisitive crime such as theft, burglary and robbery. The LDTS's reports on the clients showed indications that such offences were committed as a direct consequence of their drug use. Nevertheless, there is nothing new in terms of how acquisitive crime and drug use complement each other, particularly amongst the socio-economically disadvantaged. Any points of controversy over the relationship have broadly revolved around the preceding and succeeding influences of drug use on crime (South 1994; Bennett 1994), rather than on attempts to deny their correlation. In fact, one of the major concerns during the 1980s heroin epidemic was related to the engagement of drug users in acquisitive crime to finance their heroin habit (MacGregor 1989c; Jarvis and Parker 1989). In recent years, this issue has again featured as one of the uppermost concerns on the political agenda (see Home Office 1998; 2002a) and has been charted in academic circles as a major form through which drug users fund their drug habit (Brain *et al.* 1998; Hughes 2000).

It was also obvious that a significant number of the past convictions and prison sentences pertaining to the clients were related to a drug offence. Convictions relating to a drug offence were recorded among 15 clients. Of these, 80 per cent had also served a prison sentence for a drug offence, of which the most common pertained to drugs supply, often in the form of 'unlawful possession of a controlled drug with intent to supply'. In some cases, clients had a long history of (sometimes lengthy) custodial sentences. Dealing in drugs is known to be one of the forms through which drug habits are financed (Brain *et al.* 1998). In some of the clients' files, the LDTS staff clearly identified clients' engagement in a drug offence in general with their drug using habit. Nevertheless, there were overt instances where prosecutions and convictions for drug trafficking were believed to undermine the drug using needs of the clients. In such cases, staff had questioned accusations of drug trafficking by drawing attention to the 'small' quantity of drug over which a client was charged. This was to ascertain that the client's drug consumption rate meant that the drug in question was for personal use rather than for commercial purposes.

The above scenario in which clients' drug use had strong links with the criminal justice system, particularly in relation to drug trafficking, gives some support to findings from the author's 1991 research study of drug offence trials outlined in *Chapter 1*. Like the findings from this study, the black clients of the LDTS were likely to be charged and imprisoned for the serious form of a drug offence—drug trafficking. Although this LDTS finding is a stand-alone observation, which means that it is not compared against another racial group, it does however embrace ingredients similar to those evident in the 1991 study of drug offence trials involving black defendants. The following case study of a black male client of the LDTS exemplifies this:

> The client was arrested by the police for being in unlawful possession of heroin. The quantity of the heroin was one gram, which was in eight separate wraps. The client was charged with 'unlawful possession of a class "A" drug with intent to supply, and he entered a guilty plea to "possession" and a not guilty plea to "intent to supply". He claimed that he had the drug for his own personal use and to share with his girlfriend on a non-commercial basis. The LDTS staff supported this claim in a report to the court in which it was stated that the client and his girlfriend consumed that amount of heroin on a daily basis. Following arrest, the client was remanded in custody pending trial. He was convicted for the drug trafficking charge and sentenced to three years in prison.

Granted, not all the antecedents to this case were available to the author, for example, processes surrounding the prosecution and trial of the case. However, it was apparent in the client's file that he had had many years of substance misuse involving cannabis, heroin and crack; it was also clear that the client had a long history of offending and custodial sentences starting in his teenage years. It was during two of his prison terms that he was first introduced to heroin and crack respectively, and subsequent offending involving acquisitive crime became related to his drug use. That the client was convicted and imprisoned for drug trafficking over a 'small' quantity of heroin may stand to show a strong interface between black drug use and the criminal justice system. Prison terms have had their consequences on the clients: disruption of housing stability was evident, and some clients developed their drug using habit in prison or had been introduced to a 'new' type of drug such as crack. The latter scenario, which illustrates how an offender's drug use can commence on entering prison has been observed in studies concerned with the misuse of drugs in prison (for example, Hucklesby and Wilkinson 2001).

As the LDTS study further reveals, the criminal justice angle of the clients' problematic drug use also showed itself in the number of referrals that had been directed by the probation service. Some of the clients had had a probation-directed referral and the majority of the referrals were made in the year 2000. The recentness of most of the probation-directed referrals is probably reflective of the implementation of the drug treatment and testing order (DTTO). Various provisions have strengthened the involvement of the courts and the probation service in the treatment strategies of problem drug users. The clients whose referrals were directed by the probation service were serving a probation order with treatment as a condition for their community sentence. In some cases the referrals were preceded by periods of past custodial sentences for offences directly or indirectly associated with their drug use.

CONCLUDING REMARKS

Offences of drug trafficking, which catapult a high number of black people towards prison, may well hide the drug using needs of many black people as victims, while they simultaneously reinforce already existing images of race and the perpetration of drug trafficking. Clearly, the involvement of black drug users with the criminal justice system is seemingly a worrying social implication of black drug use as shown in the LDTS study. It is an observation that reiterates images of black people and drugs that have over the years represented black people as drug traffickers whilst clouding concerns that might have been highlighted around black drug use. The stereotype of the black drug trafficker and law enforcement focus on the black community in the war against drug trafficking have culminated in relegating black problem drug use to the bottom of mainstream agenda of drug policies.

On looking at the author's study of black drug users registered with the LDTS, it is clear that problem drug use and in particular heroin use is not unfamiliar to black people, and neither is poly-drug use where the primary drug is heroin. While the 1980s health concerns about heroin failed to embrace racial diversity overtly, the notion in recent years that injecting drug use is not common amongst black drug users constitutes another issue, which also complicates attempts to decipher the nature of black problem drug use. Even though evidence from the LDTS shows smoking to be the most favoured route of drug administration among the clients, there is the need to recognise that intravenous drug use was solely preferred by some of the clients. Some others adopted the combination method of smoking and injecting. Furthermore, there were instances of HIV and hepatitis infections as reported among five clients, of whom 60 per cent used drugs intravenously. These findings are perhaps a far cry from the actual level of intravenous drug use and drug injection-related infection cases among black people, whose cultural orientations also present further obstacles in the way of determining the nature and extent of their problem drug use, and related to that, their health and treatment needs. In the black community, commonly held beliefs about drug use have included perceptions that heroin use, injecting drug use and HIV are a 'white problem'. This has meant that black heroin and injecting drug users tend to deny or hide these patterns of drug use—viewed as 'junkie behaviour'—for fear of being ostracised from other black drug using groups and the wider black community (Perera *et al.* 1993). Invariably, they will tend to form a 'hard to reach' group within the drug using population and consequently any drug injection-related health problems that they may have will go unrecognised.

Although it may still be the case that black heroin users or black drug users in general are under-represented in drug treatment services, the characteristics of those who do present may well enlighten us on the problems associated with black drug use and how best to tackle them.

Since measuring the extent of black problem drug use is known to be largely hampered by users' limited take up of drug treatment services, a great deal of useful information can be deduced from their contacts with the criminal justice system with which they are quick to make contact. The number of probation-directed referrals of the black clients of the LDTS itself shows the unique position of the criminal justice system in a multi-agency approach to the treatment of drug use, not least to the detection and treatment of it amongst those who have the most contact with it. If the recent drug policy emphasis on drug treatment through the criminal justice system continues to function towards drug treatment, it is likely that a criminal justice-directed referral could form a recognised route to treatment services for black problem drug users. However, the extent which they are retained in treatment through to completion is a worrying situation given that the drug with which they are most associated, crack, has no medical treatment substitute as methadone is for heroin. This issue was identified by Sangster *et al.* (2001) as a concern raised by their sample of interviewees (drug workers) who noted that black and ethnic minority drug users were more likely to be in breach of a DTTO given that there was a lack of suitable treatment options available to them. The threat of imprisonment was therefore a reality.

ENDNOTES for *Chapter 4*

1 The six DAT areas are Lewisham, Southwark and Lambeth (LSL); Ealing, Hammersmith and Hounslow (EEH); Birmingham; Leicestershire; Bradford; and Lancashire.

2 Sangster *et al.* (2001) use the term 'black' to refer not only to 'groups which may be considered to be "black"' but also to acknowledge 'diversity within these communities and denotes a greater degree of inclusion'. The term "minority ethnic' recognises the position of groups who may not consider their identity to be characterised as 'black' but who nevertheless constitute a distinct minority ethnic group' (p.11). This definition applies wherever the term 'black and minority ethnic communities/groups' is used in the text.

3 A cautionary note from Sangster *et al.* (2001: 44): the analysis relating to presentations outside London

> must be treated with some degree of caution because of the doubt that surrounds the efficacy of the ethnicity data recorded on the RDMD. This was particularly evident in relation to Birmingham as ethnic information was missing for 28 per cent of all recorded episodes. The situation in Birmingham was further clouded by the high proportion of cases in the RDMD which were recorded as having an 'other' ethnicity. These issues were less evident in relation to the other areas. Ethnicity data was, for example, missing in ten per cent of recorded episodes for Bradford, nine per cent for Leicestershire and 13 per cent for Lancashire. The use of the other category was also less marked in these areas.

4 A cautionary note from Sangster *et al.* (ibid.): in presentations outside London the 'categories of black-Caribbean and black-African have been combined because of the very small numbers of black-Africans living in these areas'

5 A cautionary note from Sangster *et al.* (2001: 45):

> Figures relating to drug services were taken from the RDMD for the period from the beginning of April 1999 to the end of September 2000 and were based on people presenting to services for the first time or doing so after a break of six months or more. It is important to distinguish people from episodes. Where a person presents to more than one agency or presents to the same agency twice with a gap of six months or more between presentations then multiple episodes are recorded by the RDMD. For the analysis presented in this table, multiple presentations were ignored and thus the figures relate to people not episodes.

6 These three ethnic categories are combined in LSL but are separated into 'Indian' and 'Pakistani or Bangladeshi' categories in EHH.

7 A cautionary note from Sangster *et al.* (ibid.: 16):

> although the ethnic classification used in the RDMD was based on the 1991 census classification, the small number of cases in some categories mean that adaptations were required for the analysis presented here. In EHH there were very few black-African episodes and thus this category was combined with that of black-Caribbean. Similarly in LSL there were very few Indian, Pakistani or Bangladeshi episodes and so these categories were combined in to one south Asian category. Although not all episodes included information about injecting, the rate at which this information was missing for primary opiate users showed little variation according to ethnicity of the client. Measures of statistical significance was not applied to the RDMD because it was, in theory, based on a population not a sample.

8 See Turning Point/Home Office 2004 for a study of drug use in Ethiopian, Somali and Yemeni communities.

9 Refers to Caribbeans/Africans. Asians are not included in this study because of their relatively small sample of three. Overall Asian presentation to LDTS was very low in comparison to white and black presentations.

10 It is worth noting that the Office for National Statistics 1999 mid-year estimates show that the total black population of the area of London where the LDTS was situated was 25 per cent, making up the highest proportion of the total ethnic minority population of 34 per cent.

11 Data were missing on three clients.

12 Data were missing on four clients.

CHAPTER 5

Double Invisibility: The Case of Italian and Portuguese Problem Drug Use

Where it exists, race-related information on drugs has been straightforward in underlining the racial composition of its subject groups. An example is shown in Home Office publications on the statistical breakdown of those sentenced and imprisoned for drug offences. Such publications have tended either to adopt a broad categorisation of such statistical data according to 'white', 'black', 'Asian' and 'other' racial groups, or to move towards narrower racially-based groupings as in 'West Indian/Guyanese/African' and Indian/Pakistan/Bangladeshi' for example (Home Office 1986, 1989, 1994b). In studies of drug use, as Chantler (1998) has observed, there are signs of a shift towards acknowledging ethnic diversity. In some recent studies, the use of the term 'black and minority ethnic' is meant to accommodate distinct ethnic groups regardless of their skin colour. But despite what is seemingly an awareness of ethnicity, there is the tendency to concentrate the primary focus of ethnic classifications on the visible minority ethnic groups, primarily black people and people of Asian origin. In contrast, *white* has traditionally tended to retain its unitary form—as instanced in the drugs component of the *British Crime Surveys* (see for example Home Office 1996, 1997).

Similarly, discourses of drug issues have usually identified with black people and Asians when references are made to minority ethnic groups. Despite the nature and extent of problematic drug use amongst blacks and Asians being unclear there has at least been some evidence of concerns and research questions around their involvement in drug use, as shown in *Chapter 4*. Such interests have tended to underline centrally the non-white minority status of these groups as the reference point of analysis. This has usually involved conceptualising and contextualising issues of cultural differences and racism as needing recognition in drug policies and practices, argued to be traditionally tailored to cater to the drug needs of the white population.

Where white minority ethnic groups feature in the often all-inclusive assessment of drug needs along two broadly defined racially-based categories: 'White' and 'minority ethnic groups'—has remained unclear. As already established in the literature, years of researching drug use have had their focus on the white community, particularly during the 1980s heroin epidemic and its significant transformation of political and research interests into the epidemiology of heroin use as well as its link to health and crime. At that time, as Pearson and Patel (1998) made clear, ethnic monitoring systems were insignificant to studies of heroin use. But judging by the tradition of racial and ethnic classifications referred to above, any use of an ethnic monitoring system during the 1980s would probably have been relevant in identifying non-white minority ethnic groups to the exclusion of white minority ethnic groups who seemingly stay invisible under the umbrella of 'white'. Invariably treatment services aimed at homogenous 'whiteness' will not have given specific consideration to non-physical differences such as culture and language. An impression one can glean from what seems to be an absence of adequate recognition of the heterogeneity and diversity of Britain's white population is of well-integrated drug using needs of white minority ethnic groups into mainstream drug treatment services.

Yet, there is abundant evidence to show that like non-white ethnic minorities, white ethnic minorities, albeit to a lesser degree, can for reasons relating to their ethnic backgrounds also be disadvantaged in the dominant white British society. Notions of biological and cultural inferiority have grounded hostile public and political responses towards white immigrants, most notably the Irish and the Jews whose history of immigration into Britain produce illuminating information on English-held anti-Irish and anti-Semitic stereotypes and images, sometimes outwardly exhibited in racial attacks on the Irish and the Jews (Solomos 1989, 1993). With the growing numbers of those European white minority ethnic groups whose establishment in the UK is relatively recent, there has invariably followed a huge ethnic and cultural diversity amongst the white race. In the area of drug use, this issue of ethnic diversity as it cuts across race is acknowledged (Sangster *et al.* 2001; DrugScope 2003), yet the extent to which research has addressed it is limited. The ACMD (1998: 25) notes this point thus:

> The influence of ethnicity on illicit drug use is an under-researched topic. Ethnicity is not a single dimension of experience but a composite of identity, beliefs, expectations, cultural history and language. Many of these components are liable to change over time across successive generations. In addition, there will be degree[s] to which ethnicity overlaps with other variables including, for example, unemployment, so that it becomes very difficult to identify the specific influence of ethnicity on drug use. A necessary first step is to establish accurate information on the extent of drug use within different ethnic groups.

For white minority ethnic groups living in the UK, their nature and pattern of drug use is severely under-researched. Such information is particularly scanty for those from member states of the European Union and recently-arrived asylum seekers and refugees from Europe.

To begin to fill the noted gaps in existing knowledge this chapter provides findings from the author's study of drug using characteristics and social problematic features of drug use among two ethnic groups of white minorities: the Portuguese and the Italians. The concern about these white minority ethnic groups draws upon the study of problem drug use and race/ethnicity (referred to in *Chapter 4* and also see that chapter for more details of the methodological approach), which was conducted at a London drug treatment service (LDTS) in 2000/1. While this chapter focuses on the Portuguese and Italian clientele of the LDTS, it however provides data on a control group of indigenous white[1] clientele of the drug project for comparison. Findings show points of convergence and divergence in drug using patterns and social needs of clients across the three ethnic groups. The findings also point to forms of social exclusion that are seemingly specific to Portuguese and Italians, which can compound their problem drug use.

BACKGROUND INFORMATION

The advent of the single market resulting from the formation of the European Union (EU) has facilitated flows of immigration into Britain from other European countries – outside of Irish immigration – who are member states of the European Community (EC) or the European Economic Area (EEA). These have included migrants from Portugal and Italy. A high proportion of the Portuguese and Italian migrants may be likely to reside in London given that it is a city known for harbouring high concentrations of migrants due to the size of its labour market (Glover *et al.* 2001). The relative newness of the migrant populations from Portugal and Italy is reflected in the seemingly short time which many of the drug using Italians and in particular the Portuguese in the author's study have been resident in the UK. On average, this ranged from a few months to five years. Like many migrants, these drug using groups have concentrated in areas of relative social and economic deprivation, where the relatively cheap housing costs, fluid economy and an already established community of fellow countrymen present huge attraction to such areas.

Whilst they have the free access to reside and work in the UK as EEA migrants, they face the condition of financial independence of the state since nationals of EEA member states who are resident in the UK in a non-economic capacity are expected to have sufficient financial stability not to warrant reliance on public funds (Glover *et al.* 2001). Although claims for public funds can be made in some circumstances, they are determined by proof of habitual residence in the UK. The introduction of the habitual residence test (HRT) in 1994 imposed restrictions on access to social security benefits relating to income support, housing benefit and council tax benefit for EEA nationals who are not habitually resident in the UK. In 1996, the HRT was extended to include the job seeker's allowance. Proof of habitual residence includes the claimant's employment record, length and continuity of residence in another country, reasons for coming to, and intentions in, the UK (Department of Social Security 1998, 2000).

Thus drug use amongst Portuguese and Italians can be compounded by difficulties and problems associated with identifying with, and adjusting to, the demands of a new society. As this chapter makes clear, the socio-economic needs of Portuguese and Italian drug users, their unfamiliarity with the British system, their lack of fluency in the English language, their limited or absent family networks and ties all interact in complex ways to place their problem drug use in a special category.

THE RESEARCH

The primary objectives of the research as it relates to the aforementioned white minority ethnic groups were two-fold:

1. To identify ethnic similarities and disparities in the drug using and socio-economic features of white clients registered with the LDTS; and

2. To pinpoint social problems specific to clientele from white minority ethnic groups particularly the Portuguese and Italian clients. This objective derived from *Objective 1* where specific findings from the files of Portuguese and Italian clientele gave rise to further inquiries into their social needs.

Objective 1 was principally based on a detailed examination of clients' files using quantitative methods. During the period of fieldwork 57 of the files studied belonged to Portuguese clients whilst 30 were related to Italian clients. White UK clients made up 82 of the files studied[2]. These figures were not the total numbers of these groups of clientele of the LDTS but were representative samples. As already indicated in *Chapter 4*, the LDTS had not compiled the statistical breakdown of the ethnic composition of its clientele for the period following August 2000, which meant that information on the ethnic orientations of presentations to the LDTS had to rely on previous statistics. As at the end of September 1999 when the total number of the LDTS clients stood at 422, the recorded number of the Portuguese clients for that period was 44 and 60 for the Italian clients. Both ethnic groups made up 45 per cent of the entire ethnic minority clientele. For the white UK clients, the figure was 190 and made up 45 per cent of the total clientele. As at the end of August 2000 when the total number of the LDTS clients open on formal caseload was 382, the numbers for the Portuguese and Italian clients had increased to 50 and 62 respectively while the number of white UK clients had decreased to 166.

Objective 2 was reached by adopting a qualitative approach, which entailed conducting an open-ended mail questionnaire interview with staff of the LDTS. The questionnaire was composed of five questions relating to Portuguese and Italian clients:

1. The relationship between these ethnic minority clients' employment status and access to the welfare system;
2. The influence of language on housing, employment, medical and criminal justice needs of clients from these minority ethnic groups;
3. The influence of immigration status on the housing and employment needs of the ethnic groups of clients;
4. The involvement of the family in their problematic drug using life; and
5. The social relationship between clients/drug users from these minority ethnic groups and people outside their ethnic groups.

Also useful to the qualitative approach was information drawn from the LDTS's in-house reports on white minority drug use.

Findings

Socio-economic profile

All the clients from the three groups resided in the inner city. The Portuguese and Italian clients in particular often resided in the most deprived parts already associated with high levels of crime and drug abuse. Client unemployment was high for all groups but higher for the Italian group (see *Table 5.1* below). The Portuguese clients in employment were virtually all located in unskilled manual jobs, usually in the catering industry and often on a temporary basis. Seventy-five per cent of the employed white UK clients were either in unskilled or semi-skilled jobs. Unemployed clients who were on state benefits were made up of: 51 per cent Portuguese, 79 per cent Italians and 100 per cent white UK (n=61). Clients' housing status shows the vast majority of the white UK clients to have secure accommodation in local authority housing. A high proportion of the Italian group also had permanent or temporary local authority housing. But the Portuguese clients were less likely than the other ethnic groups to have stable accommodation and more likely to have no fixed abode.

Table 5.1 *Percentage of clients' employment and housing status*

	Portuguese	**Italian**	**White UK**
Employment[3]	(n=56)	(n=30)	(n=81)
Unemployed	66.0	93.3	83.9
Employed	30.3	6.6	14.8
Student	3.5	-	1.2
Housing	(n=57)	(n=30)	(n=82)
No fixed abode	40.3	20	12.1
Local authority housing	29.8	66.6	74.3
Private renting	15.7	10	7.3
Owner occupier	-	-	1
Friends/relatives	12.2	3.3	4.8
Bail hostel	1.7	-	-
Prison	-	-	-

Patterns of drug use

Heroin was the main drug used by clients from all the ethnic groups. At the time of their first contact with the LDTS, the clients were using heroin on a daily basis. The daily intake of heroin by clients of white UK, Portuguese and Italian origins ranged from a quarter of a gram to two grams. Data on first heroin use (see *Table 5.2* below) show that most of the Portuguese and Italian clients reported that they started using heroin in their teens. Nevertheless, significant numbers of the two ethnic groups of clients were in their twenties at first heroin use. For the white UK group, those in their twenties at first heroin only marginally surpassed the figure for clients in their teens. It was amongst the Portuguese group that first heroin use was identified amongst clients below the age of 13: the clients concerned were aged 12.

Table 5.2 Percentage of clients' age at first heroin use[4]

	Portuguese (*n*=48)	Italian (*n*=21)	White UK (*n*=72)
Age-group			
Under 13	4.1	-	-
Teens	47.9	57.1	44.4
20s	39.5	38	45.8
30s	8.3	4.7	9.7
40s	-	-	-

Clients used other drugs alongside heroin (see *Table 5.3* below) and the most popular combination drug was crack cocaine. As shown, except for crack, cannabis, ecstasy and methadone, which featured as complementary drugs across the three groups, other drugs listed on the table were mostly restricted to white UK clients. The most common route of administration of heroin was by intravenous injection (see *Table 5.4* below) and this was particularly the case with the Italian and white UK groups. Almost all the Italian clients practised injection as the sole route of heroin use. The one Italian who practised smoking combined it with injecting. Similar patterns of drug administration appeared in relation to crack use amongst the Italian clients with the vast majority engaging in intravenous crack use while smoking and the combination method was practised by a relatively small number of the clients. Heroin and crack use by smoking was seemingly as popular as injection amongst the Portuguese clients, unlike the Italian clients. With regard to the white UK clients, intravenous drug use started to lose its popularity in the area of crack use although it still remained significant.

Table 5.3 Percentage of types of drugs used by clients

	Portuguese (*n*=57)	Italian (*n*=30)	White UK (*n*=82)
Drug Type			
Heroin (main drug)	100	100	100
Crack	68.4	40	50
Cocaine	-	-	7.3
Cannabis	12.2	16.6	10.9
Ecstasy	1.7	6.6	4.8
Methadone	14.0	20	34.1
Amphetamines	-	-	4.8
LSD	-	-	1.2
Glue	-	-	1.2

Table 5.4 *Percentage of clients' method/s of drug administration*

	Portuguese	Italian	White UK
Heroin[5]	(*n*=55)	(*n*=25)	(*n*=82)
Injection	50.9	96	64.6
Smoke	40	-	21.9
Combination	9.0	4.0	13.4
Crack[6]	(*n*=35)	(*n*=11)	(*n*=38)
Injection	42.8	72.7	31.5
Smoke	40	9.0	52.6
Combination	17.1	18.1	15.7

Clients' drug using characteristics show similarities and variations across ethnic groups. One such similarity is that most of the drug combinations involved the use of heroin and crack. As in *Chapter 4*, this finding is consistent with Pearson's (1992) observation that crack is more likely to be used by known users of heroin as a main drug. Surprisingly, the use of tranquillisers and depressant drugs was found to be rare or non-existent amongst those most likely to use crack: the Portuguese group. These drugs were also rarely used by the Italian group. This was despite the known calming effect of these drugs on drug-induced problems of anxiety, depression and so forth, especially with regard to crack or cocaine use. Some clients from these minority ethnic groups however had these drug use associated problems and some even had a history of self-harm and suicide attempts. These drug-related problems also featured amongst the white UK clients, 28 per cent of whom used anti-depressants and another 28 per cent used tranquillisers. In terms of variations in clients' patterns of drug use, a notable example relates to the method of drug administration. In general, the Italian group stands out in its clear preference for the injection method of drug administration.

As shown in *Chapter 4*, the LDTS also demonstrated concerns about intravenous drug use amongst these three groups of clients by commending non-intravenous drug use as a significant barrier to HIV/AIDS and other blood-transmitted diseases. During the period of the heroin epidemic and the threat of HIV/AIDS in the UK, parts of Europe were experiencing the AIDS epidemic (Aviles *et al.* 2000). In Italy and Spain, the exposure to AIDS was substantial amongst injecting drug users who accounted 'for over 60 per cent of new AIDS cases' in 'the second half of 1989' (Wodak 1994: 127). Amongst the sample of Italian clients of the LDTS, HIV/AIDS infection was significantly evident: 17 per cent were reported to be HIV positive and 13 per cent had AIDS. This finding coincides with the overall trend of drug use involving intravenous injection among the Italian group. There were cases where Italian clients were reported to share or had previously shared injecting equipment. For the Portuguese, some clients had never injected and some had switched to smoking having injected in the past. It also seemed to be the case that Portuguese clients were more likely not to share or never to have shared injecting equipment than their Italian counterparts. HIV infection among the Portuguese group was seemingly rare and was only shown in two per cent of the cases. However, this finding was somewhat contradicted by information gathered from an LDTS in-house report, which claimed that the 'real' extent of HIV infection amongst the Portuguese clients was yet to be determined given that this group was less likely to test for HIV. The level of HIV infection was seemingly very low for the white UK clients: two per cent were shown to be HIV positive (a small number of the clients refused to test for HIV/hepatitis) and one per cent had AIDS. Clients from the three groups and in particular the Italian group were also infected with types of the hepatitis viruses especially hepatitis C. Seventy per cent of the Italian clients, 28 per cent of the Portuguese clients and 30 per cent of the white UK clients had hepatitis.

Clients from the three groups showed signs of a chaotic injecting drug use in their decision to inject in 'unusual' parts of the body such as the veins in the groin, neck, leg and foot. According to Gossop (1993: 131), this form of injecting practice occurs when drug users fail 'to discover any further sites to inject themselves' due to the 'formation of scar tissue and other vein damage' on a vein abused through continuous injection. This 'unconventional' practice was not without its consequences as shown in cases of severe abscesses and deep vein thrombosis. The dangers of drug use for these three ethnic groups of clients were further shown in cases of accidental opiate overdose, which again can be related to how the drug was used – for instance in terms of its level of purity or the effect of an incompatible combination with another drug.

Social needs of Portuguese and Italian problem drug users

This discussion places emphasis on the Portuguese and Italian clients principally because it is at this stage that their drug using life tends to differ in some remarkable ways from those of their white UK counterparts. Patterns of drug use within these two minority ethnic groups can be compounded by certain social problems that are either encountered to a lesser degree or not encountered at all by their white UK counterparts. Such problems include linguistic difficulties and immigration issues.

Already there is a well-established literature to present the various social problems with which drug use is characterised. Out of them all, socio-economic deprivation is seemingly one of the most narrated issues in discussions charting the social ramifications of problem drug use. Its centrality can be traced to the 1980s when concerns around the increasing prevalence of heroin use especially among youths highlighted a relationship between drug use, unemployment, inner city areas and adverse socio-economic deprivation (Burr 1987; Pearson 1987b; Peck and Plant 1986). As recent studies have also shown, the justifications for the deprivation-drug use link are owed principally to the fact that drug-related problems tend to concentrate in the most deprived inner city localities (Home Office 1996; European Monitoring Centre for Drugs and Drug Addiction 2000). The unemployment rate was high for the three groups but higher among the Italians. There were indications that clients from the three ethnic groups suffered financial difficulties exemplified in rent and council tax arrears, and outstanding utility bills. Such financial strain was seemingly most evident among the Italian and white UK clients who were also shown to indulge in heavy drug use. Despite evidence of similarities in the social circumstances of the three groups, the minority ethnic white clients however exhibited attributes of social exclusion consistent with their migrant status and cultural differences. Macgregor's (2000: 122) analysis of the link between social exclusion and migration trend highlights this point. According to her, increased migration gives rise to 'concentrations of refugees, asylum-seekers and economic migrants in certain areas, and a general loss of community and family supports consequent on social and geographical mobility and changed lifestyles'. Social exclusion can also be premised upon other processes outside of poverty, for example, 'discrimination against people with disabilities, refugees, people of other languages, colour or religion, or people with certain health statuses or criminal records' (ibid.: 121).

The challenge of integrating into the mainstream culture forms one of the major problems which minority ethnic white clients have had to face. Culturally, Portuguese and Italians have a strong extended family system upon which members rely for various forms of support including financial. Relating this culture of family to the drug using problems of the Italian clients, the LDTS had this to say:

> Italian families are always aware of their children's drug problem. They tend to be highly colluded. Some 90 per cent of Italian economic migrants were living with their parents in Italy. In some cases they have been asked to leave ... Families back in Italy continue to be involved. *(Response to Question 4).*

The same cannot exactly be said for the Portuguese problem drug users according to the LDTS. Despite the Portuguese system of extended family, their traditional notion of family values is such which gives a strong family and community disapproval to unconventional behaviours such as drug use. For this reason the LDTS states, Portuguese drug users

> tend to sever links with their family members because of shame and they don't want to see them. They do not have a lot of involvement with their families. *(Response to Question 4)*

In the absence of a strong family structure and stable links with family members, many of the Portuguese clients in particular have experienced a strong sense of dislocation amounting to increasing levels of isolation. Information gathered from the minority white clients' files revealed that the intention to abstain from drug use prompted some of the clients to move to the UK, away from the drug scene in their home country. To achieve this objective has proved difficult amidst feelings of alienation and isolation, which themselves have implications for problematic drug use. These minority ethnic groups of clients were clearly shown to be predisposed to associate and socialise with fellow drug users with whom they felt most comfortable. Thus, the chances of breaking the drug using cycle were made less likely under this condition. It is known that the micro-social settings in which drug users operate such as the sharing of living space and socialising with other drug users are key contextual factors with large influences on drug use and risk behaviours. As Aviles *et al.* (2000: 106) state:

> To a large extent, individuals' decisions to share used equipment with others have been shown to be influenced by the nature of the situations and relationships in which sharing occurs, and by the perceived social norms and etiquette with regard to the reciprocal rights and obligations of friendship. Needle sharing has rarely been found to be a random activity, but instead tends to follow lines of kith and kin. Most sharing takes place between IDUs [intravenous drug users] who are either in a sexual relationship with each other or who are friends or family.

For the Portuguese and Italian clients such relationships were often with Portuguese or Italian drug users as the following statements by the LDTS make clear:

> Portuguese drug users almost exclusively associate amongst themselves, and do not socialise outside of that. *(Response to Question 5).*

> Italian drug users associate amongst themselves and also attend services targeting this minority group. *(Response to Question 5).*

The choice by Portuguese and Italian clients to keep within their own ethnic groups also had a great deal to do with their unfamiliarity with the mainstream culture, from which they became increasingly detached as they continually operated within their own communities. More often than not the clients had language problems and did not speak or understand English. Linguistic difficulties pose ramifications for problem drug use. In its direct form, this problem was evidenced in initial reluctance by some clients to seek help with treatment services for fear of a hostile staff response based on language-linked discrimination. Furthermore, as indicated in an LDTS in-house report on Portuguese drug users, this problem was seen to affect relations between ethnic minority white clients and their doctors. Such strained relations are exemplified in situations where a general practitioner exercised no patience in listening or explaining issues clearly to the patient. Notwithstanding the option of using the assistance of an interpreter, it is an alternative that was not always possible to obtain—an interpreter might not turn up at all or decide not to stay for the duration of the appointment. Such communication problems were shown to extend to the pharmacy where pharmacists have been known to show reluctance in dispensing prescription drugs to ethnic minority white drug users owing to the latter's illiteracy on and ignorance of prescription collection procedures. Concerns about this issue were expressed by the LDTS thus:

> Their [that is, Portuguese and Italian drug users] relationship ... with medical professional figures is problematic because of language barriers and cultural prejudice. *(Response to Question 2).*

The lack of English for drug users from the Portuguese and Italian groups can compound other social aspects of their life and ultimately their drug problem as revealed in the following observation made by the LDTS:

> Newly arrived Portuguese and Italian drug users do not speak English. This makes it difficult to access DSS [that is, Department of Social Security] benefits. This has been complicated by the introduction of the HRT [that is, Habitual Residence Test] in the late nineties. As they revolve around small Portuguese and Italian communities, they find themselves isolated and unlikely to access information on the DSS system and entitlement. Almost every one of them will be working in the catering industry due to poor skills and language barriers. They are usually under-employed, under-paid (cash-in-hand), and work long and unsociable hours. They are generally exploited in their workplace. *(Response to Question 1)*

Intertwined with the problem of language for Portuguese and Italian drug users is the crucial role of cultural discrimination in determining employment opportunities. This scenario is described thus by the LDTS:

> Their [that is, Portuguese and Italian drug users] very reduced employment opportunities are also depending on the prejudice of the British culture against South European economic migrants. *(Response to Question 1)*

Alongside the limited awareness and knowledge of how the UK welfare system operates, another major impediment to white minority access to welfare services was the nature of the clients' employment, as highlighted in one of the LDTS's in-house reports. Amongst the Portuguese clients, employment was in the majority of cases on a temporary basis and the form of payment was cash-in-hand, which meant that those employees paid no national insurance contributions. Under the guidelines of the habitual residence test, eligibility for welfare benefits as a result of a job loss requires evidence of previous employment. In cases where clients were unable to produce such evidence, the ramifications of not receiving financial assistance from the state have included homelessness. Not surprisingly, the housing conditions of Portuguese and Italian problem drug users were one of the major concerns of the LDTS as the following statement shows:

> Newly arrived Portuguese and Italian drug users find it extremely difficult to access secure and suitable housing. They usually live in run-down, over-priced and over-crowded privately rented accommodation. *(Response to Question 2)*

Unstable accommodation is a known risk factor for drug users whose indulgence in drug use can become more chaotic and problematic under this circumstance. This is a situation to which a high number of the Portuguese clients in particular were exposed. A significant number of the clients in the Portuguese group had no fixed abode, as shown in *Table 5.1* above. They were mostly street homeless and had to sleep in places such as abandoned cars and garages, and in stairwells of council estates. Others lived in squats with little or none of the facilities required for creating a habitable environment. For the squatters, the constant threat of eviction they faced potentially paved the way to street homelessness. Amongst the Italian clients, the 'no fixed abode' accommodation status showed evidence of street homelessness. Although the majority of the Italian clients had permanent or temporary local authority housing, it is a situation that seems to be consistent with the fact that this sample had on average been in the UK longer than their Portuguese counterparts. As their housing history revealed, the Italian client group had a high incidence of homelessness in the past prior to presentation to the LDTS.

Unlike the Portuguese and Italian clients none of the white UK clients was shown to be street homeless; their housing status seemed more stable than that of their white minority counterparts. Even amongst the Portuguese and Italian clients who resided with friends, they were housed on a temporary basis and as such formed another group with shaky accommodation. The Portuguese clients in seemingly stable accommodation were permanently or temporarily housed by the local authority, or lived either in privately rented accommodation or with relatives. Securing local authority accommodation for the Portuguese clients seemed to have followed presentation to the LDTS. At the time of referral, most of the Portuguese clients who were to secure local authority housing rented privately. Despite what seemed to be a stable housing condition for significant numbers of Portuguese and Italian clients, many drug users from these ethnic communities are known to face problems of overcrowding. The LDTS identified this as a common problem particularly within the Portuguese drug using community where, for instance, a bedsit has been known to have been occupied by up to six people. In a sense, the issue of overcrowding for Portuguese drug users cannot be isolated from the economic circumstances of clients from this ethnic group. Not only was there a significantly high level of unemployment amongst this client group (see *Table 5.1* above), this situation was also worsened by the fact that over half of those unemployed were not in receipt of welfare benefits. Again, those in employment were not only lowly paid but also the temporary basis on which they were employed played a major influencing role in their housing situations, whereby the sharing of overcrowded accommodation became an inevitable consequence. Consequently there arose the possibility of homelessness in the event of a job loss. The negative outcomes of situations of homelessness and overcrowding as they apply to both Portuguese and Italian drug users are outlined in the following statement by the LDTS:

> A good number of Portuguese and Italian drug users have lost, or sold or had their ID [that is, national identity card] stolen in the first few months after arrival. This is due to the very precarious housing, financial situations and chaotic lifestyle. *(Response to Question 3)*

A national identity card provides nationals of member states of the European Economic Area the initial right to access the welfare system and the unavailability of this document precludes entitlements to welfare benefits including housing benefits. The process of replacing an identity card is not without its difficulties:

> If Italian drug users have unresolved legal issues in Italy they are not able to get any ID from the Italian Authority. If this is the case, they cannot access social housing and

> DSS benefits. Access to employment is usually not affected although they won't be able to apply for a National Insurance Number. A fake ID costs anything between £80 and £150. *(Response to Question 3)*

> Portuguese drug users are able to obtain IDs from the Portuguese Authority even though they may have unresolved legal issues. But generally they will only obtain new ID if they are supported in obtaining them from the Portuguese Consulate. *(Response to Question 3)*

Drug users' practical problems associated with their drug use play an influential role in their decision to seek help. According to Velleman and Rigby (1990: 25),

> [M]any of the problems presented to counselling agencies by problem drug users are concerned with aspects of their life that have been affected as a result of their drug use (e.g. housing, employment, relationships, etc.). The problem drug user may not, in fact, be seeking the agency's help in 'getting off' drugs, but instead may want advice on how to deal with the practical problems presented.

The significant numbers of self-directed referrals among the two minority ethnic groups of clients may be interpreted within the context of Velleman and Rigby's observation in the sense that it can be argued that the clients' practical needs may have forced them to self-direct their presentation to the LDTS. Information on referrals showed that 68 per cent of the Portuguese referrals (n=51) and 70 per cent of the Italian referrals (n=23) were self-directed. Other referrals were mostly initiated by a general practitioner or a friend, as was particularly the case with the Portuguese clients. In the case of white UK clients (n=54), self-directed referrals comprised 43 per cent of all known referrals.

CONCLUDING REMARKS

In Johnson and Carroll's (1995) Home Office paper *Dealing with Diversity*, cultural diversity is seen to include 'not only language but religion, diet, identity, history and family organization'; it is also found within the 'the white sector of society', which 'contains groups who may suffer discrimination or have particular cultural and linguistic needs' (ibid.: 2, 4). However, the tradition of viewing racial and cultural diversity largely in relation to people of south Asian and African-Caribbean origins is evident in Johnson and Carroll's paper, where also their concerns with regard to diversity in the white population are exemplified in explicit reference to UK minority white communities such as the Welsh and Irish.

Very little is known about non-UK white ethnic minority groups whose cultural and linguistic needs are probably more urgent than those of their UK white minority counterparts. As clearly shown in the observations made by the LDTS, these needs harbour their own dangers for problem drug use inasmuch as they can complicate and hamper intentions to abstain from a rather difficult habit. In prevention and treatment initiatives, the crucial role of the wider structural influences on drug use is undermined. Drug policy measures which are far removed from the broader structural context of drug use are open to difficulties in achieving positive results, especially in minority ethnic communities which by virtue of their racial or ethnic differences are subjected to high levels of social exclusion. 'Hard to reach' sections of the drug using population are more likely to be found within minority ethnic groups—both visible and invisible. Just as drug use research is beginning at least to question the drug using situations of visible minority ethnic groups, similar concerns need to be addressed in relation to non-UK white minority ethnic groups. The socio-cultural contexts of problematic drug use amongst Portuguese and Italian communities clearly attest to the need to integrate every spectrum of ethnic diversity as an essential component of both drug treatment and drug prevention strategies at local and national levels.

After all, the negative ingredients of problematic drug use – at the individual level – are not confined to the indigenous white population but are also evident in minority ethnic communities. At the societal level, the harmful impact of problematic drug use has its origins in the diverse ethnic communities and as such practising diversity is not just about attending to the drug-related needs of minority ethnic groups. It is also about prioritising the safety of society as a whole.

ENDNOTES for *Chapter 5*

1 Made-up of English, Scottish and Welsh.
2 Because of the statistical difference in the numbers of files studied for Portuguese, Italian and white UK clients, caution must be exercised in drawing conclusions from the quantitative data presented.
3 Employment data were missing on one Portuguese client and one white UK client.
4 Information on age at first heroin use was missing on nine Portuguese, nine Italian and ten white UK clients.
5 Data on method/s of heroin administration were missing on two Portuguese and five Italian clients.
6 Data on method/s of crack administration were missing on four Portuguese, one Italian and three white UK clients.

CHAPTER 6

The Drug Problem as a Global Phenomenon

A reading of the collective European policy and legislative agenda on drugs acknowledged in *Chapter 3* clearly signifies the international reach and parameters of the drug problem. Central to this problem has been a concern over the direct consequences of drug use, exemplified in its health and socio-legal ramifications. The severe threat which the resultant effects of widespread drug use pose to the social stability of drug-consuming nations in Europe is thus not restricted to Britain. According to the United Nations (UN) (2002: 67), 'the problem of drug use' in Europe 'appears to show no sign of abating' and the abuse of heroin 'in Europe as a whole exceeds the level reported by the US' (ibid.: 71). Contemporary drug problems in Europe seem to be impacting more on Central and Eastern European countries (CEECs) most of which started experiencing a drug problem in the 1990s. Heroin constitutes the major illicit drug used in the CEECs (European Monitoring Centre for Drugs and Drug Addiction (EMCDDA) 2002). Unlike the EU which generally reports a stable pattern of problem drug use and an ageing population of especially problem opiate users, 'the majority of candidate countries' according to the EMCDDA (ibid.: 16) 'are still situated in the rising part of the curve and problem drug users are younger, on average'. The UN (ibid.: 67) also adds:

> The abuse of heroin (by smoking or injecting) has become more common in Eastern Europe than in Western Europe. In Croatia, Latvia, Lithuania, Romania and the Russian Federation, heroin is the most widely abused drug among young persons aged 15-16. The number of registered drug abusers in the Russian Federation reached 496,000 in July 2002, up from 156,000 in 1995. The total number of drug abusers is estimated by Russian authorities to be between three million and four million.

The UN report further noted that HIV infection is one of the disturbing health consequences of heroin abuse in Central and Eastern countries where 'the widespread availability of heroin', the increase in youth intravenous drug use, the increase in HIV infection amongst intravenous drug users and 'the absence of effective treatment facilities for drug abusers' result in a rapid increase in the levels of HIV infection. Eighty thousand new cases of HIV infection were recorded in the Russian Federation in 2001; in Ukraine, the UN states 'one per cent of the population is already infected with HIV and that figure is expected to double by 2010'; and in Estonia, HIV infection was linked to intravenous drug use in over 1,500 cases (p.70). The other Baltic states, Latvia and Lithuania, are also experiencing a sharp increase in the spread of HIV among intravenous drug users (EMCDDA 2002).

On the other side of the Atlantic, the US has traditionally set the pace for assessing and measuring the nature, extent and consequences of illicit drug use in the West. Cannabis and cocaine consumption have presented the US with her greatest drug problem. According to the aforementioned UN report (2002), cannabis is so widely available that American teenagers find it easier to procure than they would both beer and cigarettes. Not only did the report show an increase in the rate of teenage cannabis use, but it also reported that there is also a higher likelihood of later dependency on cocaine and heroin among teenagers whose first use of cannabis occurred before the age of 15 than among adults who started abusing cannabis in their twenties. The rate of cocaine use fluctuates between an increase, decrease or stable trends, which nevertheless are problematic to the US. In her neighbouring countries, Canada and Mexico, cannabis is the most widely available drug and invariably the most commonly used.

Lessons learnt from the US' longstanding history of cannabis, cocaine and crack cocaine consumption in particular have informed policy and practical responses toward drugs in parts of Europe. This is clearly illustrated with regard to drug trafficking. In both Europe and the US the popular policy approach towards the sale and consumption of drugs is that which has relied upon what Taylor (1992) refers to as 'conventionalist and demonological presuppositions'. These presuppositions, Taylor elaborates, constitute a

> very partial and highly conventional theory of the exploding international trade in drugs which informs governmental and quasi-governmental initiatives with respect to the production, distribution, and consumption of such drugs....this conventionalist theory of the drug trade is in the nature of a demonological account, organized around some powerful and longstanding myths about 'foreigners', aliens', and corruption.

Secondly, he adds:

> [T]he continuing adoption and mobilization of this conventionalist and demonological account of the international drugs trade results in the constant restriction of debates with respect to the control of the drug trade to the issues of policing and detection, in the first instance, or to pre-emptive action, including military-style campaigns of 'crop eradication' conducted against foreigners, on the other hand. (p. 183)

This direction towards drugs law enforcement provides a central base for collaborative work in Europe's attack on its drug problem. Since the formation of the TREVI Group in 1975, European co-operation on issues of drug trafficking has blossomed into a wide range of drugs law enforcement policy and practical initiatives. In the US this strategy has exhibited relatively drastic measures toward drug producer and transit non-western nations. Following Ronald Reagan's announcement of a war on drugs in the early 1980s, the US drug war has not been contained within the country's borders but it has also been carried beyond her domain. US drug wars within and beyond have thus ranged from stringent immigration controls on certain non-western nations identified with drug production and distribution, military war against 'narcoterrorists' in Latin America, crop eradication raids including the use of chemical spray in drug producer countries to interference with Third-world drug producer governments to commit to the US war strategies against drugs (Taylor 1992; Sudbury 2002). As

Sudbury (2002: 65) argues, the use of US economic influence in US foreign policy decisions to push 'a US drug agenda on the global community' has since the mid-1980s played a key role in her drug war. And 'by the mid-1990s', countries in Central America and the Caribbean, North and South America, Oceania and Africa 'were fully fledged partners in the US-driven transnational war on drugs'. In Europe, the Americanised drug policy is also evident, as shown, for example in the 'British approach to criminalized drug use, trafficking and retail' (ibid.)

MARGINALISED SOCIETIES AND THE POLITICAL ECONOMY OF DRUGS

To relate to the global nature of drug consumption and trade also requires coming to terms with the political economy of not just the drug producer and transit countries but also the drug consuming nations of the West (Green 1998). Often discourses which locate the drug trade within its political and economic context have made drug producing and transit nations their focus area. In such discourses notions of the Third-world syndrome illustrated in 'corrupt government' and 'socio-economic deprivation and poverty' have served to explain the involvement of Third-world nationals in international drug trafficking, whether in terms of drug production or drug transportation. Drug-related financial assistance to drug producer and transit nations—geared towards controlling the influx of illicit drugs into the West—has been one of the western approaches to this form of Third-world syndrome, but with conditions designed by the West to serve her interest. Through US-led foreign policies, drug producing and drug transit countries have been overtly coerced into playing a significant role in addressing the West's drug problem, often depicted as an international drug problem (Kalunta-Crumpton 2001). An instance of such a coercive approach aimed at gaining compliance is shown in how international agreements between the West and drug producing/transit Third-world countries— as well as the West's economic assistance and drug-related financial aid to those countries—came to be balanced against their performance in fighting the West's drug war. For drug producer countries, their assigned responsibilities have included eradicating and replacing drug crops with alternative 'licit' crops, and for drug transit countries such as Nigeria and those in the Caribbean, their fundamental task is concerned with strengthening their domestic drugs law enforcement policy and practice (Kalunta-Crumpton ibid.).

Such western demands have exerted significant pressure on some of these countries to a point where drastic domestic wars on the international drugs trade have been waged to suit the West. Nigeria's history of drugs law enforcement exemplifies this. Sometime in the early 1980s, Nigeria's punitive response to Nigerians involved in the international drugs trade was the death penalty. The use of capital punishment for Nigerian drug traffickers was repealed following General Ibrahim Babangida's regime in 1985. Instead, a notable step taken under Babangida's regime in response to international calls to address Nigerian's participation in the drugs trade was to create the National Drug Law Enforcement Agency (NDLEA) in 1989. Modelled on the American Drug Law

Enforcement Agency, its task was to launch a domestic drugs war on international drug trafficking with a crucial objective to remedy Nigeria's tainted image abroad. Repressive strategies implemented by the NDLEA to achieve this key objective included imposing an additional prison sentence upon convicted Nigerian drug traffickers deported after serving a prison sentence abroad. A public naming and shaming tactic was also enforced, which involved publishing the names and photographs of Nigerians serving a prison sentence abroad for drug trafficking in the national press. This latter approach was premised on its deterrent effect at both individual and societal levels. In 2000, the NDLEA launched the West African Joint Operations, an initiative which underlines enhanced law enforcement cooperation amongst West African countries with the primary aim to attack drug traffickers and related criminals (UN 2002).

Notwithstanding the international pressures on drug producing and transit nations and the internal measures that individual countries concerned may have adopted to fight the drugs war, what occupies a relatively insignificant position in the West's war on drugs strategy is the political economy of the drugs trade. Whether the impoverished state of Third-world drug producing and transit countries is down to corruption and mismanagement at both political and economic levels (see, for instance, Green 1998), or/and to the huge inequalities in the international political economy, is not of concern to the West. Clearly economic factors underlie and sustain the global drugs trade. Aside from the lucrative nature of drugs supply which favours the international drug trafficker, particularly those at the upper reaches of the drugs economy, drugs production in producing countries can simply serve as a profitable means of subsistence for certain sections of society. Opium is a traditional cash crop in opium producing countries of Southeast and Southwest Asia and so is coca in drug producing parts of South America. For peasant farmers in these parts of the world drugs production has provided an attractive economic option given that they have very limited access to legitimate sources of income.

Whilst the economic value of drugs production has been paraded as a strong justification for its ongoing existence in drug producing countries, the UN (2002) has recently claimed that illicit drug production in drug producing countries hampers long-term economic development of such countries. In the report, comparisons are made between periods of a rise and fall in drug crop cultivation, and how these transitions impacted on economic development in countries in South America, Southeast and Southwest Asia. As the report states, Bolivia and Peru in the 1980s experienced an increase in coca leaf production, with no positive impact on their economic developments. But through most of the 1990s these countries' economic growth increased despite a fall in coca leaf production. During this latter period however, Colombia's economic development witnessed a downward spiral whilst the country gained an increase in coca leaf production. In Southwest Asia, Afghanistan's influential role in opium poppy cultivation is claimed to have made no positive impact on her social and economic wellbeing. In contrast Pakistan's 'strongest economic growth rate' was recorded in the 1980s during which she reported 'the strongest decline in opium production'. Reports on Southeast Asia present a positive image of her economic development following a fall in opium poppy production:

> Thailand was the first country in the region to drastically curtail illicit opium production (from 146 tons in the period 1965-1966 to less than 60 tons in 1982 and to six tons in 2000). As the levels of illicit opium production in Thailand fell in the 1980s, its GDP growth rate exceeded those of neighbouring countries, and today Thailand is one of the most developed countries in the region. Data for both the Lao People's Democratic Republic and Viet Nam show an increase in GDP growth rates in the 1990s compared with the 1980s. The increase in the GDP growth rate in both countries was accompanied by a decline in opium production in both of those countries in the 1990s. (UN 2002: 4)

The extent to which drug crop production impacts negatively on the overall economic growth of a country is a scenario which would be probably difficult to put across to those whose manual labour serves the drug production industry and whose limited education restricts them to such job opportunities in the face of high unemployment levels. As the UN report quite rightly states, the illicit drug production industry 'in the rural areas of many countries ... provides jobs in the agricultural sector to a large number of people with limited skills and education, such as small farmers and itinerant labourers' (ibid.: 1). To this extent the long-term negative consequences of illicit drug production which the UN report is concerned with are bound to be subservient to the short-term gains prioritised by the average manual worker in the industry. It is a situation tantamount to the fact that despite the array of international efforts and policies geared toward drugs supply reduction in the West, domestic circumstances specific to drug producing nations pattern their policies and practical responses toward the international drug problem. As such, attempts to control drug cultivation are less likely to receive a positive response from the masses due significantly to economic contingencies rather than the reality of the dangers embedded in drug use (Kalunta-Crumpton 1999). This situation creates variations in policies between drug consuming and drug producing nations and weakens international drug control strategies. Opportunities enhanced by contradictory drug policies and practices are exploited by the international drug trafficker.

In spite of the first and foremost huge contributions made at the point of drug production to the overall drugs trade, drug traffickers at various points in the trafficking business have stood as the main beneficiaries of the drugs economy. In developed countries of Western Europe and the US where the bulk of the drug trafficking profits are made, the financial gain from the activity amounts to 99 per cent of the 'global illicit drug income' according to the UN (2002). The remaining one per cent of the world illicit drug trade is 'earned as farm income' in drug producing developing countries (ibid.).

Like marginalised groups in drug producing countries for which drugs production offers an immediate economic getaway from impoverishment, drug dealing/trafficking is one of the illegitimate ways through which certain sectors in Western and non-western societies fight against their experiences of socio-economic deprivation, whether absolute or relative. This relationship invokes Robert Merton's (1938) concepts of 'strain' and 'anomie', which he applied to the US. Merton describes how pressures exerted by society on its members to aspire toward the prescribed culture goal of economic success creates strains on some sectors of society, given that access to prescribed legitimate means to material success is not equally distributed across the social structure. For many in Third-world countries, participation in the drugs trade is principally driven by socio-economic deprivation largely caused by what Green (1998) refers to as 'economic mismanagement' and 'corruption' by the 'ruling elite'. For western-based minority ethnic communities such as black people, this conflicting relationship between culture goals and legitimate means is compounded by obstacles, which racial discrimination presents in the way of access to legitimate means. This is a situation which worsens at times of economic recession, when the competitive embodiment of capitalism calls for economic restructuring resulting in high levels of redundancy and unemployment, limited job opportunities and low wages in marginalised communities (Taylor 1992; Hall *et al.* 1978). Yet there has also been a relatively limited effort on how to constructively address any relationships between socio-economic deprivation and drug trafficking amongst marginalised communities in western societies.

Whilst these analyses add to our understanding of drug trafficking within the frameworks of political economy, it would however be myopic to simply centralise the effects of economic and political conditions on socio-economically deprived drug producer and transit countries or marginalised minority groups in western societies in explanations of drug trafficking. This is principally because the lucrative nature of the drugs trade has rendered it an activity that operates within a global framework and networks of drug production, distribution and consumption. It cuts across nationality, race and class. But as Lewis (1985: 42) rightly noted, the media portrayal of drug trafficking fails to see the illicit drug trade in terms of 'an articulated world economy' which also incorporates networks of organized western drug traffickers. Rather, it is popularly perceived in the context of evil and unscrupulous foreigners who dump deadly substances on the West for financial gain. But like other marginalised communities in Third-world countries, minority ethnic communities, particularly the black community in western societies such as the US, Canada and the UK, have merely joined the bandwagon in the global capitalist drugs trade and its provision of economic opportunities otherwise denied them in the western-controlled global economy (Lusane 2000). Nevertheless, the contributions of the black community and similar minority ethnic communities in sustaining this highly profitable global business are relatively small given that they are often located at the lower end of the trade.

THE POLITICS OF DRUG CONTROL WITH REFERENCE TO WESTERN HISTORY

To date, the West's approach to its drug problem assigns priority to drugs supply. This approach, which found huge discursive and practical significance in the 1980s particularly in the US and the UK, has since wooed many into believing that the demand for drugs is primarily rooted in the drug trafficking activities of non-westerners who profit from the West's misery. An obvious conspiracy theory advanced in this strategy has not only been used to justify ongoing drug wars on foreigners within and outside the West but it has also thrived on depicting drug trafficking as a recent (late twentieth century) phenomenon. In essence debates on drug trafficking have ignored its historical depth and projected a distorted picture of its existence.

Drug trafficking has a very long history and a wide global reach. Likewise, drug wars are not unique to contemporary times. Whilst the twentieth- and twenty-first century drug wars underline attempts to control drug trafficking, pre-twentieth-century drug wars, in the form of the opium wars, were fought to facilitate drug trafficking. The opium wars were a result of British deep economic involvement in the opium trade from the early eighteenth century. During her long period of involvement in the trade, Britain through the British East India Company organized poppy cultivation in India for the Chinese market (Lindesmith 1965). Prior to this period, China—often associated with opium smoking—only grew poppy principally as an ornamental plant (Inciardi and Chambers 1974; Stimson and Oppenheimer 1982). In 1729, China had promulgated her first drug prohibition laws against the sale and use of opium but despite efforts to control the drug, the British East India Company facilitated extensive smuggling of it into China (Stimson and Oppenheimer 1982). Although international criticisms were levelled against all European powers (such as France) with interests in the Far East, much of the blame was placed on Britain for exporting opium to China and for causing Chinese misery from opium addiction (Lindesmith 1965; King 1974). However, the trade continued in light of the high demand for opium as well as the deep involvement of Chinese officials in the profit making illicit trade (Lindesmith 1965).

In the nineteenth century, the market in opium heightened in South Asia following, as Lewis (1985: 17) states, 'the emergence of modern capitalism and its emergent need for labour, profits and international markets'. As there grew international demands for Chinese items such as silk, tea and spices, so did Britain's involvement in opium smuggling into China. Continuous efforts by Chinese authorities to suppress the opium trade pursued by Britain and the latter's determination to maintain and advance her economic interest in the trade led to two opium wars between 1839 and 1858 (Willis 1969; Berridge and Edwards 1981). Those wars failed to stop the opium trade, which carried on throughout the nineteenth century.

'By the 1930s', Hooker (1996 cited in Barton 2003: 9) states,

> The English had become the major drug-trafficking criminal organization in the world; very few drug cartels of the twentieth century can even touch the England of the early nineteenth century in sheer size of criminality. This trade (in opium) had produced, quite literally, a country filled with drug addicts, as opium parlours proliferated all throughout China in the early part of the nineteenth century.

It was in the early twentieth century that the drug problem in the Far East began to attract formal international intervention. In 1909, an international opium conference was held in Shanghai to discuss anti-opium measures in the Far East (Hartnoll 1989). The conference, attended by major European powers, China, Japan and the US, was largely initiated by the US, which had no economic interest in the opium trade. Britain, as some claimed, only attended the conference following pressures from the US and her reluctance was linked to her economic benefits from the opium trade. However, there are claims that her reluctance to take part in the conference was due to an agreement that had already been reached in 1907 to end the opium trade and as such attendance was viewed by Britain as unnecessary (Berridge 1984).

The conference at Shanghai and its central focus on the Far East gave rise to three Hague conferences (1911-2, 1913 and 1914), which moved beyond the Far East to endorse an international framework for addressing drug use and drug trafficking. It was at the 1912 Hague Convention, to which Britain was one of the signatories, that the European policy of gradual suppression of drug use (agreed at the 1909 Shanghai Conference) was implemented (Bean 1974; Lindesmith 1965) thus placing international drug trafficking under regulation. It was also decided at the 1912 Hague Convention that morphine (at the time mainly manufactured by Britain), opium and cocaine be used only for legitimate medical reasons. China, which advocated immediate and complete prohibition, found this concession unfavourable as it was believed to result in European government monopolisation of the legal production and distribution of opium, which invariably sustained Europe's revenue-raising agenda and disinterest in the Far East's drug problem.

Meanwhile in Britain, international commitment to the Hague conference of 1912 motivated Britain's Dangerous Drugs Act 1920, which conformed to the Hague conference guidelines and extended controls to cover drugs addressed at the conference. This Act promulgated the criminalisation of drug use given its move towards penal reaction and also laid the foundation for subsequent legislation. Thus, when viewing how contemporary UK drug legislation and policies focus on and externalise drugs supply, it is worth remembering that they grew out of economic interest in the opium trade and later attempts in the nineteenth century to control the trade. Indeed as Pearson (1992: 280) observes:

> Nineteenth-century Britain was ... certainly not in a state of innocence about drug issues. Its notorious role in the Opium Wars and the promotion of opium markets in Southeast Asia is, in any case, legend.

To recognise Britain's 'notorious role' in the opium trade and the opium wars also means assigning recognition to the driving force of *economic interest* behind that role. This point begins to give greater importance to my observation above that the lucrative nature of drug trafficking is such that it has guaranteed it a comfortable position across the globe. Given that a government can fight an open drug war to sustain drug trafficking in order continually to reap the enormous profits made from the trade, regardless of the health and social consequences of this activity on the drug users and the wider community, it is therefore quite an easy task to understand why economic reasons can surpass any other concerns in individually or organizationally-based drug trafficking business.

Even indirectly, the economically driven ethos of drugs has historically and contemporarily generated and facilitated a variety of interests and benefits. Drug trafficking has served interests outside its direct and immediate economic profits.

Relating this latter point to historical times calls to mind the US undisputed initiating role in the 1909 Shanghai conference discussed above. There are claims that the US's intervention to suppress the opium trade in which she had no involvement was partly influenced by economic factors, albeit long-term. According to Berridge (1984: 19), the US lead role was

> partly inspired by the moral motives of the US missionaries in China and the Philippines, partly the result of a policy of extending American influence in the Pacific and increasing US economic importance in China.

In this sense it is inevitable to ask what really are the reasons behind the West's contemporary concerns about the drug problem. To address this question, it seems only logical to argue that the West's ongoing attack on drugs supply is consequent on the growing problems of illicit drug use in western societies, at least this is what *official* reasons embraced in political discursive and pragmatic representations of the problem lead us to believe. The context of 'official reasons', described by Emerson (1991) as those formal reasons that legitimate grounds for action and are geared towards official procedures and policies, is illustrated in that which projects a disturbing image of drug use, blames the problem of drug use on the drug trafficking role of non-westerners and uses these justifications to galvanise public support for stringent policy and law enforcement measures. In the US, this strategy is perhaps best exemplified in Reagan and Bush's crusade against drugs in the 1980s during and after which the war on drugs was voiced as imperative in the interest of the welfare of American people, and then put into law enforcement practice including military-style attacks in drug producing nations of Latin America. In the UK, successive governments have made the issue of drugs prominent in their law and order concerns and rhetoric, in which the UK's interest is presented as the priority in the justification to wage a war against drug trafficking, which itself is explicitly or implicitly alienated. In 1994, the then Conservative prime minister, John Major, described drugs as 'a menace to our society', which 'can wreck the lives of individuals and their families' and as such 'everyone's aim must be to put the drug barons out of business and protect our people from the misery and waste that drugs produce' (Home Office 1994a). The current prime minister, Tony Blair, holds a similar view as he states 'we must all work together to make sure there is no hiding place for the pushers at the school gate who peddle filth or the "Mr Bigs" who grow rich on the back of their vile trade' (*Sun* 14 June 1997).

But as Emerson (1991) also states, official reasons can be underlined by *real* reasons. 'Real reasons' according to Emerson (ibid.) are 'products of prior personal and institutional decision-making ...', which themselves are not transparent or simply self-evident. *Real* reasons transposed onto the drugs politics can be instanced by what O'Malley and Mugford (1991: 62) describe as the Left's interpretation of the US drug wars:

> The War on Drugs is depicted simply as a front or vehicle for the wider interests of the state or the capital. These interests are suggested to be twofold. Internationally, they center on the extension of American hegemony combined with anticommunism, especially in Central/South America. Nationally, they center on an extension of

> surveillance over and control of the workers, the poor, and the underclass ... Thus, it is often argued that the War on Drugs is 'really' a success, because it allows these latter aims to be successfully pursued under the 'guise' of something else.

Complementing this left-leaning interpretation are issues such as the exclusionary strategy of European drugs policy and practice, the hegemonic elements of the US drug-related foreign policy and the racialisation of drug trafficking in individual western societies, which have already received some attention in this book. While some may argue that such viewpoints from the Left present a biased scenario of the West's drug control systems, perhaps it is worth reflecting on Lusane's (2000) account of the ironical relationship between the US drug war and her past involvements in geopolitics against communism, before passing critical judgements on the Left. In the relationship, international drug trafficking activities of certain drug trafficking organizations were latently permitted by the US amidst her concerted interests in fighting communism. Controlling international drug trafficking both within and outside the US boundaries was at this point secondary to her key objective to rid the 'world' of communist ideologies and practices. In stating that 'official collaboration between US government entities and known drug traffickers dates back to at least the World War II era' Lusane (2000: 61-62) outlines instances of such cases of collaboration:

> The Office of Strategic Services (OSS), the predecessor to the CIA, made deals with the Corsican heroin drug traffickers as well as with gangster Lucky Luciano in the US effort to prevent communists from gaining a political foothold in postwar France and Italy. Luciano (and eventually other organized crime figures) had dealt heroin in the US since 1915. The OSS's Operation Underworld would negotiate a deal that would eventually free Luciano from prison in 1946 in exchange for his role in helping to secure the docks of New York from Nazi sabotage and using his mob contacts in Sicily to attack the Italian Communist Party. From 1924 to 1944, the US heroin addict population dropped from 200,000 to about 20,000. These numbers would begin to grow again after the war and after Luciano established a worldwide network of traffickers, distributors, and retailers for heroin.
>
> In Laos (Southeast Asia), beginning around 1960, the CIA created a secret army of 30,000 Hmong tribesmen to fight the Communists in charge of the nation, Hmong Gen. Vang Pao was allowed to use the CIA's Air America planes to traffic opium, the Hmong's major cash crop. This heroin would not only be used to addict thousands of US soldiers fighting in Vietnam, including a disproportionate number of African American soldiers, but it would eventually comprise about one-third of all heroin in the US by the end of the war in the mid-1970s. By 1989, 73 percent of the world's heroin was being produced in Southeast Asia.
>
> Beginning in the late 1970s, in Southwest Asia, in the area known as the Golden Crescent where Afghanistan, Pakistan, and Iran come together, the US supported the anti-Communist Mujahedeen guerrillas fighting to overthrow their Soviet-backed government. The covert activities of the CIA in the area would create trafficking lines that did not previously exist. A tremendous spurt in heroin production occurred that would have a direct impact on heroin use in the US.

> ...the Reagan administration made the decision to support anticommunist rebels in Central America. From Honduras to Costa Rica to Panama to Nicaragua, the CIA and other agencies would employ numerous drug traffickers to assist their covert wars against the Sandinistas in Nicaragua and guerrillas fighting to overthrow military and political dictatorships in El Salvador and Guatemala.

These instances of double standards illuminate some of the complexities surrounding the sustenance and growth of the global drug trade. Herein US political concerns in attacking communism following the creation of the Soviet Union in 1917 and other communist states thereafter, took precedence over the negative consequences of drug trafficking within and outside of her territory. The Cold War, which according to Lusane placed US drug policies in a subservient position, may be over, but nevertheless its drug-related political implications illustrated above are bound to force us to ask what other disguised political priorities are in place in the face of the contemporary war on drugs?

In Europe, the influential role of geopolitics, albeit economically driven, has been shown to render its domestic political and official concerns about drugs questionable. Green (1998: 36) narrates how despite Burma's lead role in the supply of opium and heroin in the 1990s, its 'appalling record of human rights violations and the economic misery the junta has heaped upon thousands of its inhabitants', Britain and France refused to back the trade sanctions imposed by the European Union against the junta in the mid-1990s. Economic reasons underlined their decision. To Britain, Burma presented a likely future trade route, which deserved to be protected. France was already in a business transaction with Burma. The junta had commissioned a $1.2 billion contract to France to erect a pipeline across Burma—a business deal, which France was not ready to jeopardise.

In sum, from its direct and indirect economic value to its political usefulness—be it domestic election campaigns that preach tough measures on drug trafficking or its purpose in providing an international platform for coercing Third-world compliance with the West and for waging war against opposing political leanings—drug trafficking (and the war on it) appear to be valuable economic and political entities, which can at some points render irrelevant the health and social wellbeing of those who are directly or indirectly affected by the trade. Critical questions can also be raised around the West's 'real' concerns about the harmful effects of drugs, when considerations are given to her direct economic gains from 'drugs' which despite their harmfulness are nevertheless legal and thus a legitimate source of profit. For example, the US makes enormous profits from tobacco, alcohol and pharmaceuticals, and as O'Malley and Mugford (1991) have noted, the US has been known to sell in the Third World many of her alcoholic beverages and pharmaceuticals 'in ways that would not be allowed within the US.' In cases where Third-world governments have tried to control the influx of US tobacco into their countries, the US has been known to respond by coupling 'the rhetoric of the war on drugs with economic pressure' on those governments (ibid.).

WHAT ABOUT DEMAND FOR DRUGS?

Relatively insignificant in western discourses of and policy on the international drug trade is the demand-oriented aspect of drug production and distribution. The popular arguments have been those which rest on supply. On the other hand, when demand for drugs features, it has primarily been addressed within a medical context in which treatment forms a reactive measure toward the disease found in drug addiction. On a secondary level, it is linked to prevention—a proactive drugs education strategy geared toward preventing the onset of illicit drug use. None of these approaches to drug demand is, in practice, sufficiently concerned with why there is a demand for drugs in the first place, especially in relation to the issue of socio-economic deprivation.

How the socio-economically marginalised sections of society are more predisposed to illicit drug use is a notion which holds a general consensus around the globe (UN 2002; EMCDDA 2002) but its place in policy intervention is limited. In the UK, the heroin epidemic of the 1980s pushed the drug debate to its height, initiating various explanations for drug use and whilst the relationship between socio-economic deprivation and heroin use was acknowledged in some political quarters, it was a concern that failed to impact on policy changes at the time. Although more recently, government-funded projects such as Positive Futures and Communities Against Drugs have aimed at diverting vulnerable young people from drugs, there is however the crucial question of how long such initiatives would last, and related to that, how effective they really are in addressing the relationship between socio-economic factors and drug demand. Across the Atlantic the relative neglect of drug demand in the political and policy attack on drugs is evident (UN 2002). In the US, the level of drug use is high amongst marginalised communities, and in particular the black community whose experience with crack cocaine is widely acknowledged.

That said, drug use is however not restricted to marginalised groups in either western or non-western societies. In a sense, the fact that illicit drug consumption cuts across different classes and groups in society may well disfavour the deprivation-drug use link both in theory and policy. Whatever the reasons for the relative silence on demand, it is however an aspect of the drugs economy that requires the same attention as that accorded to drugs supply. The importance of drug demand in the contextualisation of the drug problem is well narrated by O'Malley and Mugford (1991) in a particularly interesting and creative analysis of the US drug war—an analysis which I take pleasure in recognising in relative detail.

O'Malley and Mugford moved beyond highlighting the secondary location of demand in the order of the US drug control agenda, to prioritise the role of demand in the US drug problem. The authors argue that the US war on drugs is popularly justified on two discursive grounds: pathology and profit. While the former is that which views drug use as a medical issue, which can be addressed through drug treatment and education, the latter discourse thrives on blaming the US drug problem on drug trafficking activities of foreigners from Third-world nations. In explaining demand, the authors drew a distinction between what they referred to as 'deficit use' and 'leisure use' of drugs. Deficit-type drug use applies to people whose drug use is likely to be harmful and also is likely to bring them into contact with the criminal justice system and/or drug treatment services. This type of drug use according to the authors raises the main concern about the subject. Leisure drug use is recreational and pleasure oriented, and in this context revolves around a mixture of licit and illicit drugs commonly administered through smoking, snorting or swallowing rather than the injecting route frequently adopted by deficit users. Drugs which hold the interest of leisure drug users are those which have an upmarket social appeal such as cocaine and MDMA. The authors draw upon Robert Merton's retreatist and innovatory modes of deviant adaptation to distinguish further between drug demands by deficit users and leisure users. While deficit drug use is retreatist in nature given its problematic underpinnings, the pleasure and entertainment purpose of leisure drug use renders it innovatory. Within these frameworks, the authors argue that despite the dominant discursive conception of 'deficit-retreatism' as the major problem in US political and official concerns about drug use, it is the 'leisure-innovative' use which is more common.

This latter form of drug use is highly unreported and thus mostly unknown to official agencies, and whilst it is relatively insignificant to drug control priorities, it is 'essential to the large-scale demand that drives trades like cocaine' (p.56). Drug users who use drugs leisurely do so as part of their routine and normal lifestyle and, as the authors state, as part of 'a wider network of activities that are not dominated by use, but rather limit it' (p.55). O'Malley and Mugford explain these drug using characteristics of the leisure drug user in terms of the commodification and consumerist ethos underlying modern American society and culture:

> [M]odern society can be understood to contain a complex and possibly contradictory relationship between the production-centered ethic that constructs the self through discipline, control, work, 'clock time', deferred gratification, and calculative rationality, and a consumption-centered hedonist ethic that encourages the pursuit of selfhood through self-expression, leisure, consumer goods, and pleasure ... The former ethic is the production-oriented cultural component of a social system founded on a capitalist economy, industrial and post-industrial production systems, urban dwelling, and an international system made up of trade and, at the political level, nation-states. Its stress is upon calculation, economic cost-benefit rationality, purposive labor, and the related values commonly understood as the Protestant Ethic. The consumption ethic is the complementary component of the system. Powerfully constructed and reinforced by the mass media and youth culture (advertising, popular music etc.) it portrays and applauds a world of pleasure in commodities and commodified pleasures. (p56)

In the US capitalism thrives on the Protestant (work) ethic; it thrives on an ongoing creation of new commodities and markets, and it also thrives on ongoing new commodity consumption. These somewhat contradictory features of capitalism also complement each other in creating the leisure-innovative drug user who may use drugs leisurely as an escape mechanism from and/or a much needed coping mechanism for the work-related pressures and stress exerted by the work ethic of capitalism. Consumerism itself encourages pleasure, which commodification provides, and inherent in this capitalist process is people's continual search for new experiences of pleasure. It is in this context that drugs serve as a pleasurable commodity, creating an army of leisure-innovative users who are in the majority in comparison to problem drug users. Because of the inherent nature of what O'Malley and Mugford refer to as drug 'demand-in-general' in the modern culture of consumerism, drug policy which orients itself toward supply, control, treatment and education can only make insignificant impact on the reduction of 'demand-in-general'. They state that this is because 'since "demand-in-general" arises from deep-seated forces in the society and is not merely a result either of personal deficiency or of incorrect information, approaches that deal with the *symptoms* of demand cannot remove its cause' (p.60).

It is also from the demand angle that drug producer countries have levelled their criticisms against the West for the way drugs supply is represented in discourse, policy and practice as a non-western invention. Contrary to the West's popular representation of drug demand as a response to supply, the view from drug producer countries is that supply is demand-led and 'inspired by the insatiable markets of the industrialised, metropolitan world' (Henman *et al.*, 1985: 2). For example, during the 1980s heated political concerns in Britain about the influence of international drug trafficking on Britain's drug problem, Pakistan was one of the foreign countries blamed. In response, a letter to the *Guardian* (7 January 1984) from the Pakistan Embassy in London referred to 'the follies of the rich, heroin consuming West' and stated that 'if the demand for heroin and cocaine in Britain and the other countries of the West can be stamped out, there will be no supply'.

The externalisation tactic, which permeates the West's perceptions and interpretations of her drug problem, tends to undermine the fact that the problem of drug consumption and its consequences for the drug user and the wider community is a global experience which moves beyond the West and westerners:

> Contrary to expectations that drugs illicitly produced in a country would only be transported to illicit markets outside the country, experience has shown that most countries in which illicit drugs are produced and transit countries eventually face their own domestic drug abuse problems, as spillover is a common phenomenon. Local drug trafficking groups, which assist in the transit operations, are often paid in kind, and they sell their share of illicit [drugs] in order to generate income. As they rarely have access to foreign markets, they sell the drugs locally. (UN 2002: 8)

In effect, drug producing countries such as Pakistan, Colombia, Bolivia and Peru have their own share of domestic problematic drug misuse and its wider effects on their differing societies. Transit countries such as South Africa, Brazil, Mexico and in the Caribbean are not exceptions to this problem (ibid.). In other words, non-whites outside (and within) western countries directly and indirectly fall victim to the ramifications of drug use.

In the mid-1990s, as Lusane (2000: 54) states, drug use in the Caribbean made a significant contribution to the 'spread of AIDS' and registered 'the highest per capita prevalence of HIV in the world, 1.9 per cent, outside of sub-Saharan Africa'. Citing statistical information from the Caribbean Epidemiology Center, he notes that the number of AIDS cases 'grew by 13.5 percent in 1993 from the year before, by 19.2 percent in 1994, and 22.5 percent in 1995' (ibid. 55). Statistical data from the UN also showed that there were about 310,000 AIDS or HIV cases in the Caribbean (ibid.). The relationship between such cases and drug use lies very much in the link between sex and drugs, rather than intravenous drug use which has been central to drug-related HIV/AIDS infection in western societies. With the increase in crack cocaine and heroin use and addiction in the Caribbean, also came an increase in drug-related unprotected sex and prostitution, and related to this an increase in HIV/AIDS contamination.

This connection between unprotected sex and HIV/AIDS infection has taken its alarming toll on sub-Saharan Africa where the HIV/AIDS health situation is further compounded by the problem of drug use (Lusane 2000). Black communities in Central America have experienced problems of drug use. Lusane refers to the devastating effects that crack cocaine has had on 'the black and Indian populations of the Atlantic Coast' in Nicaragua, a country where crack cocaine addiction rates for black and Indian communities have been known to be significantly high. Recent years have seen an increase in the use of cocaine and crack cocaine in Central America and the Caribbean. The UN (2002: 41) states that the rise is 'mainly a spillover of the transit traffic', adding that in the Caribbean, an estimated two-thirds of those who consume cocaine do so in the form of crack. In transit areas in South America such as Argentina, Chile and Brazil, cocaine abuse is a problem. South Asian countries[1] also encounter the 'spillover effect of transit trafficking' involving 'consignments of heroin from South-West Asia, and to a lesser degree, from South-East Asia, mostly destined for European Countries and, to some extent, the US' (UN 2002: 56). One of the effects of this is an increase in heroin misuse in the region. In neighbouring regions of East and Southeast Asia,[2] and West Asia,[3] the increasing rate of HIV/AIDS infection via intravenous opiate or heroin use is indicated as a worrying problem in some countries in these regions. Many parts of the Asian regions encounter widespread use of cannabis and psychotropic drugs such as methamphetamine.

Drug abuse poses a threat to African societies, particularly those which are major transit points. For example, heroin and opiates are abused in the eastern and southern parts of Africa, and to lesser degrees in the western and northern parts; and cocaine is abused in 'almost all countries in the southern and western parts of Africa, in particular in Nigeria and South Africa' according to the UN (2002: 33). Cannabis however is the most popularly used drug in Africa and this is mainly influenced by the fact that cannabis cultivation is carried out in many parts of the region. Psychotropic drugs such as amphetamines and ecstasy are not unknown in Africa. The UN (2002) reports on the increase in ecstasy use in the South African white community. The likelihood of an increase in drug use in Africa, the UN (ibid.) adds, is high in light of the devastating effects of socio-economic deprivation experienced in many parts of the continent.

There is also a drug related health plight of non-whites in western societies. For example, in the US great numbers of African-Americans are affected by the health related problems of intravenous drug use. Lusane (2000) cited Day (1996) as reporting that over 12,600 new injection-related cases reported in 1995 concerned African-Americans and between 1990 and 1995, more than 70 per cent of all intravenous-related AIDS cases among African-Americans was reported. Lusane also referred to projections by Leigh (no date) that by the year 2001, African-Americans would have made up more than half of all AIDS cases in the US. Their neighbouring black communities in Canada have their own encounters with the drug problem (Lusane 2000). In Britain, despite the contradictory pieces of information regarding the extent and nature of problem drug use amongst visible minority ethnic groups (see *Chapters* 2 and 4 of this book), there is sufficient evidence that these groups are not immune to the drug problem, particularly in relation to crack cocaine and its effect on the black community.

THE BOUNDARIES OF DRUG TRAFFICKING?

Both international and domestic drug trafficking activities draw upon a global network of drug production and distribution. In this process, geographical, racial, ethnic and class boundaries are non-existent since these aspects need to co-exist to ensure the continuous functioning of one of the world's major global enterprises—the drug trade. According to the UN (2002) expenditures on cocaine and heroin in Western Europe and the US alone are estimated at $32 billion and $48 billion per annum respectively. These estimates were considered by the UN to be conservative, and clearly did not include expenditures on cannabis and psychotropic substances, or on drugs in other parts of the globe. The process through which various illicit drugs reach the consuming populations around the world is a complex but seemingly a traceable one. It is my intention here simply to link together some of the drug production, transit and distribution points with a view to highlighting further the limitless boundaries of the drug trade, primarily in relation to the major drugs.

The major source of cocaine and heroin smuggled into North America is Colombia, a country which also is a source of cocaine destined for Europe. Although illicit coca bush is grown in various parts of South America such as Bolivia and Peru, much of the world's coca leaf production and cocaine manufacturing is based in Colombia. Countries in Africa and the Caribbean provide transit points for South American cocaine destined for Europe and North America. Brazil and Venezuela are major routes through which cocaine is transported to Senegal and Cape Verde or through routes such as Nigeria and South Africa for transportation to the West. Other cocaine transit points in South America include Argentina, Paraguay and Chile. However, Jamaica in the Caribbean and Haiti in Central America are the main transit areas for cocaine smuggling into North America. Europe plays a significant role in cocaine trafficking. Western European transit areas for cocaine entering Europe include Spain, Italy, The Netherlands and Belgium (UN 2002). Central and Eastern European countries such as Albania, Bulgaria, Estonia and Poland are direct

routes as well as storage bases for cocaine shipped from South America destined for western Europe (EMCDDA 2002). Australia is also a major destination for South American cocaine, which is smuggled in via transit states on the Pacific island (UN 2002). These transit states are used for smuggling heroin and cannabis into Australia.

Illicit opium poppy cultivation and heroin manufacturing are a huge part of the South American drug production business, particularly in Colombia. A large proportion of the heroin produced in Colombia is smuggled into the US and Europe along the same transit routes used for cocaine smuggling. For heroin produced in Asia, notably Myanmar and Afghanistan, transit stations in the region for heroin heading for Europe in particular include China, India, Bangladesh and Sri Lanka. This route and others have developed alongside the traditional Balkan route used for smuggling drugs into the rest of Europe. Through the Balkan route along Bulgaria, Romania and Hungary heroin has been smuggled into Europe from Afghanistan, Pakistan, Iran and Turkey (EMCDDA 2002). This same route is also used 'in the opposite direction' to smuggle precursor chemicals used for processing heroin (ibid.). The Russian Federation is another primary route through which opiates and cannabis from Afghanistan are transported via central Asian countries (such as Iran and Pakistan) to other European countries. Not only are countries in central and Eastern Europe used as transit areas for heroin smuggling into countries in the EU, they are also storage bases for heroin meant for further distribution in the EU (ibid.). African countries such as Nigeria and South Africa also provide air routes for Southwest and Southeast Asian heroin heading for the West. In Europe there is evidence of clandestine production of opiates.

Africa is a major production base for cannabis, a large proportion of which is smuggled out for the European market. North African countries, especially Morocco, play a huge part in the cultivation of cannabis. Spain, France and Portugal are routes through which cannabis is transported from Morocco to other European countries. Morocco, the UN (ibid.: 33) states 'continues to be the source of 60-70 per cent of the cannabis resin seized in Europe'. A proportion of the cannabis grown in Africa is smuggled out the cannabis-cultivation countries to other parts of the region. The drug is also grown in most parts of the Caribbean for illicit drug markets in the region. Caribbean cannabis from Jamaica is largely smuggled out for the North American market. Cannabis is cultivated in Central and South American countries, and is widely used locally as well as smuggled into North America. In parts of East and Southeast Asia such as Cambodia, cannabis is cultivated and supplied regionally and globally. In West Asia, cannabis cultivation serves both regional and global demands. In all countries in South Asia, cannabis is cultivated and mostly smuggled within the region for domestic consumption. Hydroponic cannabis cultivation (where cannabis is grown in sand, gravel or liquid without soil) is widespread in Canada where according to the UN (ibid.: 44) 'companies continue to sell over the internet cannabis seeds and paraphernalia for growing cannabis'. Furthermore, a significant proportion of this hydroponically cultivated Canadian cannabis is smuggled into the US. Europe plays a significant part in the cultivation of cannabis, especially cannabis herb which is trafficked within Europe despite the

fact that the drug is also smuggled into Europe from non-western countries. In Australia, cannabis is cultivated both hydroponically and non-hydroponically.

Illicit amphetamines are manufactured in Western and Eastern Europe but mainly the latter (UN 2002) and are distributed within and outside European countries. European amphetamines are trafficked in Africa. Europe is also noted for illicit production of MDMA (ecstasy) for regional and global consumption. Much of ecstasy abused in the southern part of Africa is smuggled out of Europe, particularly the UK and The Netherlands. South Africa has been known to be a transit station for ecstasy heading for New Zealand where, like Australia, amphetamines are manufactured in clandestine laboratories. Proportions of ecstasy are smuggled into Asia, and also into the Caribbean and Central America from Western Europe to be transported mainly to the North American illicit markets through South America. Although ecstasy is manufactured in secret laboratories in both the US and Canada, much of the drug abused in these countries is smuggled out of Western Europe, where it is widely abused. Large-scale production of methamphetamine takes place in North America and this drug is smuggled into other countries such as in South America. Methamphetamine is also widely manufactured and abused illicitly in parts of Asia such as Japan, Thailand, the Republic of Korea and the Philippines.

These drug sources, routes of transportation and distribution, and destinations are by no means exhaustive. Yet they aim to provide a snapshot of the globe-trotting involved in the drugs trade. And it is a journeying that would require the collaborative work of westerners and non-westerners for it to be sustained and carried on the way it has. While the use of individual drug couriers is one of the modes of drug smuggling into western countries, most of the illegal drugs smuggled through transit points to their destinations are transported in container shipments. Herein the roles of drug traffickers at the upper and middle levels are crucial for the distribution and sale of drugs at street level in various parts of the world.

ENDNOTES for *Chapter 6*

1 Listed as Bangladesh, Bhutan, India, Sri Lanka, Nepal and Maldives (UN 2002).

2 Listed as Brunei Darussalam, Cambodia, China, Democratic People's Republic of Korea, Indonesia, Japan, Lao People's Democratic Republic, Malaysia, Mongolia, Myanmar, Philippines, Republic of Korea, Singapore, Thailand, Timor-Leste, and Viet Nam (UN 2002).

3 Listed as Afghanistan, Armenia, Azerbaijan, Bahrain, Georgia, Islamic Republic of Iran, Iraq, Israel, Jordan, Kazakhstan, Kuwait, Kyrgyzstan, Lebanon, Oman, Pakistan, Qatar, Saudi Arabia, Syrian Arab Republic, Tajikistan, Turkey, Turkmenistan, United Arab Emirates, Uzbekistan, and Yemen (UN 2002).

CHAPTER 7

Is There a Way Forward?

Many years of concerns over Britain's drug problem have expressed themselves via a drugs policy through which drug supply is primarily targeted via law enforcement. This is a response which has clearly marked a racial difference in the composition of those most likely to be arrested, convicted and imprisoned for drug trafficking offences (Kalunta-Crumpton 1999). Across the Atlantic, the evidence paints a similar picture (Bush-Baskette 1998; Lusane 2000; Sudbury 2002). But whilst the drug war has catapulted many black people of British and non-British nationalities into the prison system, this penal response has made no positive impact on the drug problem. A key reason for this is that the drug trafficking role of black people is hardly capable of sustaining the drug demand in the UK and elsewhere, principally because this racial group of people occupies the lower levels of the drugs distribution chain, which often operates at street level. In contrast their white counterparts are located at the top end of the drugs economy as suppliers and distributors with access to the lucrative parts of the drug trade (Ruggiero and South 1995). Since drugs policing has placed emphasis on street-level drug trafficking, focusing intensively on deprived inner-city areas, the lower-class and small-scale drug dealers at the retail level, it has always been easier to pick off black drug dealers at this level to demonstrate law enforcement success in this area amidst the huge problems of detecting and apprehending white drug traffickers at the upper reaches of the drugs economy. Invariably the spotlight is taken off the influential social categories that dominate the drug trafficking business. Indeed as Green (1998: 110) states:

> Class is central to understanding the dynamics of drug control strategies both against users and against traffickers. It is a truism that in the late twentieth century the cocaine users and their providers among Britain's rich and powerful are not policed or punished in the way that estate dwellers in Hackney, Brixton or Toxteth are policed and punished over illicit drugs.

What this argument aims to point out is that this pattern of discrimination in law enforcement strategy unless confronted will continue to be disruptive to law enforcement efforts to control drugs. Surely any drugs law enforcement measure is bound to be unsuccessful in practice if it fails to control the powerful forces at the top and middle levels of the market but thrives on making participants at the lower end of the trade vulnerable targets and ideal scapegoats for stringent drug trafficking control strategies. The role of HM Customs and Excise (now part of HM Revenue and Customs) in drug controls depicts a similar picture via its primary focus on stopping and searching certain ethnic groups of people popularised as potential drug traffickers. Often such interceptions involve drug 'mules' and relatively small amounts of drugs that can only make very little contribution to the drug market.

Although this is not to say that lower-level drug trafficking should be undermined, it is however to argue that since every level of the drug trafficking business has a vital role to play in ensuring that drug demand is met, they should also receive equal emphasis at the point of law enforcement. Instead upper-level drugs law enforcement has often been presented as problematic (see for instance Dorn *et al.* 1992), amidst complexities involved in intercepting the high fliers in the drugs trade, which renders it limited in its cost-effectiveness. A drastic consequence of this situation is the diversion of law enforcement endeavours to small-scale drug trafficking activities for which the lower-class, black people and visible foreign nationals are more likely to be arrested, convicted and imprisoned. Yet the financial costs of this journey from arrest through to incarceration may outweigh the social and economic costs associated with this level of drug trafficking. Furthermore, the temporary vacancies created by arrests, convictions and incarceration of drug traffickers at this level are quickly filled by others in the drugs trade (Bean 2004). As such Bean (ibid.: 172 states 'arresting key offenders may satisfy the requirements of justice but it does little to ease the drug problem, whether by assisting neighbourhood protection or reducing the amounts of drugs or numbers of drug users in the vicinity'.

In a society where drug misuse has continued to create adverse problems, i is only logical or even commonsensical to expect the application of reality tc every aspect of drug controls, including the implementation of unbiased and non-discriminatory law enforcement strategy. In *Chapter 3*, I noted the recen government recognition of the important role of middle-level drug trafficking that is, the supply link through which large-scale drugs imported into th country are made available to street retailers. According to the Home Offic (2002a: pp.4, 9) middle markets are targeted 'through new cross-regional teams involving joint partnerships between the 'police and other agencies ... to tackl one of the most profitable parts of the supply chain ...'. Whilst this new focus i considered a move in the right direction, I however raised issue with th practical implications of this drugs law enforcement transition for street-lev drugs policing given the noted evidence of inconsistency and discrepancy interpretations of middle-level drug trafficking by National Criminal Intelligen Service (NCIS) and National Crime Squad (NCS) agents and officers from pol force drug squads. How can it be assured that a sufficient degree of consiste is maintained across all levels of drugs law enforcement and that middle-l drug trafficking is not confused with low-level drug trafficking leading ba the same old drugs law enforcement tradition of arresting, convicting imprisoning small-scale drug traffickers?

Furthermore, where does the upper-level part of the drugs trade feat the sudden government awareness of the need to move beyond division drugs policing? The upper-level, which from a lay person's point of view understood to mean the importation of large-scale quantities (e.g. c shipments) of illicit drugs, is hardly mentioned in drug control agenda because of the familiar justification that this category, like its mi counterpart is difficult to detect and intercept. To compound this cor the lack of clarity surrounding its definition and what it involves in t pattern and nature of drug trafficking activities that underline

Literature Review on Upper Level Drug Trafficking, Dorn *et al.* (2005) acknowledge this limitation whilst aiming to provide an analytical tool for understanding—as well as develop a typology of—upper-level drug trafficking. They note that despite the existence of 'considerable activity aimed at reducing upper-level drug trafficking ... the impact of the activities of law enforcement agencies ... is not clear, partly because understanding of upper-level drug trafficking is still being developed' (p.1). However, Dorn *et al.* offer a description of upper-level drug trafficking as including

> source zone traders' relationships and transactions, including wholesale distribution within the source countries; export, international transit, and entry into Europe including the UK; and connections downwards to city level. (ibid.)

In this description of the international framework for comprehending the workings of upper-level drug trafficking, the authors further observe that this grade of drug trafficking has no 'linguistic, national, and cultural barriers between traffickers' (p.37). Rather, it benefits from a multinational and multicultural teamwork.

What has seemed to have suppressed attempts to detect participants in this grade of drug trafficking within the UK has been a focused interest in taking the drug war directly to the shores of drug producing and transit countries where, as popularly portrayed, the roots of the West's drug problems lie. Without assigning sufficient consideration to the fact that many of these countries experience their own share of the global drug problem, we nevertheless witness on the one hand the influence of the US global drug war through which the UK and the West have embraced elements of their drugs policies within their foreign policies and through which drug producing and transit nations are coerced into complying with the West's drug war agenda. On the other hand is the explicit and ongoing inclusion of 'international cooperation' in the UK's drugs policy (Home Office 1985, 1995, 1998). As stated in the *Updated Drug Strategy 2002*, this strategy has centralised 'increasing cooperation with countries on key supply routes so as to increase the quantities of heroin and cocaine taken out en route, at the border and within the UK', and has included 'providing training and equipment in places such as Afghanistan, the Balkans, Iran, Turkey, Central Asia, Pakistan, Latin America and the Caribbean' in order to disrupt drug trafficking activities in drug producing and transit regions (Home Office 2002a; see also Home Office 2004a.). Notwithstanding some evidence of interdictions of quantities of drugs in drug transit nations and crop eradication programmes in drug producing ones (see for example Home Office 2002a), the overall impact of international cooperation on the drug problem is limited. For one, the differing political, social and economic structures of the various nations concerned are crucial to how drug controls are enforced domestically and within an international framework. Invariably as Bean (2004: 155) states, 'policing at the international level has often been a hit-and-miss affair dominated by national interests, which seem rarely to be transcended to allow full cooperation to occur'.

Given such problems, it may be more realistic to target drugs law enforcement towards UK borders. By this I mean putting more resources into preventing the entry of drugs into the country by increasing the numbers of HM Customs officials with a defined responsibility to frequently and indiscriminately target drug smuggling at all levels. Their foci of attention should not simply be to pick out actual or supposed 'drug mules' from selected countries and nationalities but to diversify their intelligence to aim at frequent large-scale interdictions and also to view all airline passengers from various parts of the world as likely drug traffickers and all shipments at seaports entering the country as likely carriers of drugs. This strategy should also be extended to European railway links. *Chapter 6* has provided a snapshot of the globetrotting nature of international drug trafficking in order to demonstrate that the drugs trade has no geographical boundaries and it relies on western and non-western labour forces to meet the drug demand across the globe. More HM Customs officials at airports, seaports and other entry borders will for one deliver the message of a tightened security where no one is untouchable. Although one of the downsides of this measure could be an increase in the price of drugs and consequently an increase in acquisitive crime where heroin and crack cocaine in particular are concerned, price increase can however act as a deterrent to potential users, many of whom may fall under the category of 'leisure-innovative' drug use described in *Chapter 6*. Whatever the negative effects of a stepped-up law enforcement tactic are, they are less likely to override the positives that derive from a determined effort to prevent drug entry into the country.

Working alongside HM Customs in this approach are the police whose primary role is to detect and intercept drugs that missed the attention of customs officials. To reiterate, this does not merely mean concentrating drugs policing in deprived inner-city neighbourhoods where police practice towards low-level drug trafficking, despite its disruption of drug markets within given localities, has little effect on the overall problem. It is equally unhealthy for the sake of genuine drug controls to operate on the assumption that drug trafficking groups are principally foreigners. For example cracking down on crack has over the years amounted to a range of drugs policing operations (such as Operation Dalehouse and Operation Crackdown) targeted at black communities; and the creation of a Turkish Intelligence Unit within the National Criminal Intelligence Squad is self-evidently geared towards controlling Turkish heroin trafficking. Whilst emphatic references to 'Yardies', Turkish Mafia, Chinese Triads, Colombia cartels and so forth assign ethnic characteristics to drug trafficking in discourse, policy and practice, it is as if the British white community is so far detached from the supply angle of the drugs economy. It is hard to imagine that the drugs trade will cease to flourish if all the Jamaican, Turkish, Chinese, South American connections in Britain for example are removed from the country. Drugs policing ought to move beyond such racial/ethnic-oriented strategy to design promising ways to detect large-scale drugs trade, including synthetic drugs such as ecstasy and LSD which are also manufactured in Britain yet are relatively sidetracked in the drugs war and its focus on heroin, crack and cocaine.

As earlier noted the drugs trade is lucrative even at its lowest level and it is this fact that essentially precludes policy and practical efforts to control it in the face of an ongoing high demand for drugs. If we recall (see *Chapter 6*), Britain in the nineteenth century waged two wars against China when her huge economic gain from the opium trade was on the line as a result of attempts by the Chinese government to suppress the trade in order to control the widespread effects of opium addiction on the Chinese population. Within the law enforcement circle itself, the drug trade has produced its share of corrupt law enforcement officials whose responsibility has moved beyond controlling drugs supply to encompass supplying drugs and/or taking bribes from drug traffickers in order to protect them from arrest and prosecution. In a description of the key characteristics of a corrupt police officer, Bean (2004: 205) draws upon Clark's (2001) analysis to describe the corrupt officer thus:

> [H]e (it is very rarely a woman) will be a very active police officer, usually with a reputation for being successful, having 'done a number of good jobs' and continuing to work at that pace. He will have served as a police officer for about 12 years and will have reached a reasonably high or middle rank. He will be divorced, probably paying a heavy maintenance, or will have other similar monthly expenses. He will be working in one of the specialist detective units and will meet criminals who have ready access to large amounts of money.

Police corruption has been identified in studies as a notable limitation in drugs law enforcement. Green (1998) draws attention to Operation Jackpot launched in 1992 by the Scotland Yard's Central Investigation Branch to probe allegations of police corruption in Stoke Newington (North London) police station. This operation, which ran for three years, investigated 134 separate allegations against 46 police officers. Although the allegations included police engagement in drug dealing, drug planting, theft and assault, Green states that the 'central allegation investigated during Operation Jackpot was that an officer was receiving £1,000 per month from a woman who dealt in crack cocaine on his behalf' (ibid.: 143). Despite the lengthy period of investigation, there was very little disciplinary and prosecutorial response to the allegations. There are instances of press coverage of police corruption. For example, on 12 August 2000, the *Sun* newspaper reported on drug-related police corruption. Under the headline 'Crackdown on Bent Cops: Yard Pledge after Drug Scandal', it was reported that five police detectives who worked for an elite crime unit were involved in a drugs racket in which drugs that they seized were recycled 'back onto London's streets'. Although the officers were jailed at the Old Bailey, the role of law enforcement agents in the sustenance of drug markets is worrying. In non-western societies such as parts of South America and Africa where corruption in drugs law enforcement is relatively open, the negative implications for drug trafficking controls abound. In Britain, improving drugs law enforcement would also require fighting corruption by placing law enforcers under regular and effective scrutiny before we can even begin to wage a genuine war against drug trafficking.

Legislative and law enforcement attack on drugs supply forms one method of Britain's drug control strategy. And as it stands, assessing the extent of success at the level of law enforcement has remained superficial. Statistics on HM Customs and police drug seizures and recorded drug offences—like other official statistics—do not provide fully reliable data and as such are not wholly useful for accurate assessments of the level of illicit drug use and in particular their impact on drug demand. The direct influence of law enforcement on the demand for drugs is a process which needs to be monitored via a comprehensive and effective system in its own right. Instead, drug demand, which is the other aspect of the drug problem, has traditionally been located within the frameworks of drug treatment and drug prevention measures. Since the 1980s when the government began to make more explicit its drug control agendas, drug treatment and prevention mechanisms were for a long time subordinated by the emphasis on drug control through law enforcement. By the mid-1990s, these drug control measures had started to receive a new approach and emphasis which embraced joint partnerships. Arrest referral schemes and the drug treatment and testing orders (DTTOs) are instances of the multi-agency treatment approach. For drugs prevention, the transition was marked by the range of prevention projects set up and supported by the Home Office Drugs Prevention Initiative and later by the Drugs Prevention Advisory Service. Such drugs prevention programmes are aimed at young people and the agenda includes the provision of awareness education on the dangers of drugs as well as the setting up of initiatives such as sports in order to divert the most vulnerable young people from the drug scene. However what is unclear is the overall effectiveness of drugs prevention strategy in preventing the onset of drug misuse, particularly the misuse of class 'A' drugs.

We know that there are now many Home Office publications detailing one drugs prevention project after another. We also know that according to the British Crime Survey of 2001/2, the prevalence rate of the use of ecstasy, crack and cocaine amongst those aged 16-24 is on a slight increase (Aust *et al.* 2002). But what we do not know is how the various preventive measures collectively account for the seeming non-reduction in youth recreational drug use. Based on the findings of the 2001/2 BCS findings, the Home Office (2002a: 17) projected that 'around 1 million young people are at risk of becoming problematic drug users, and that around one in ten of these will go on to develop longer-term addiction or health problems'. This risk factor is arguably most likely to occur amongst the most vulnerable young people such as those from minority ethnic communities, who experience higher levels of socio-economic deprivation, and who invariably need the most drugs prevention intervention measures. However, as some have argued, the preventive strategies in place have not sufficiently addressed the needs of minority ethnic communities. For example, practical drugs prevention programmes which embrace young people from minority ethnic communities have tended to be short-lived. Evans (2002: 5) describes this problem thus:

> Although the CAD [Communities Against Drugs] resource has opened a window of hope on a bleak situation, its finite and time-limited nature poses problems for workers in the field. There is a danger of projects being set up and then collapsing when the time and the money have run out. This is why many DATs are putting an emphasis on community liaison and empowerment, so that projects can work towards becoming self-sufficient ... The last decade has seen the government close

one youth or community centre after another, and this has played a role in allowing delinquent or criminal behaviour to flourish.

Relating such problematic situations in drugs prevention work to a political agenda, Evans (ibid.) quotes Viv Ahmun (chair of the Federation of Black and Minority Ethnic Professionals in the drugs field) as stating:

> The Government is very target driven, even if the targets have little relevance to what we're trying to achieve. There is a lack of diligence and true professionalism in favour of a political agenda, objectives and timeframes. Extra-curricular activity for young people is key. Getting them into activities that will inform their sense of belonging to a collective. And initiatives for parents to learn parenting skills—a lot of parents out there now are not really adults themselves—are also very important.

The relative neglect of race and ethnicity in drugs prevention work is something which had been acknowledged by Johnson and Carroll (1995) in their Home Office paper, *Dealing with Diversity*. Therein, they viewed the gap in issues of racial and cultural diversity in prevention work as an obstacle, which can be tackled if the often culturally homogenous structuring of drugs prevention services begins fully to embrace the demands of diversity. This also requires moving beyond the traditional focus on African-Caribbeans and South Asians to look at other minority ethnic groups from Africa, Asia and Europe. As demonstrated in *Chapter 5*, the case studies of Italian and Portuguese problem drug users point out some problematic issues that can be specific to the drug using experiences of white minority ethnic communities.

It seems clear that what is desperately needed in the government's drugs prevention agenda is a dedicated and sustained statement of purpose demonstrated in practice and not simply in theory. This is a question of clearly defining what we aim to achieve, how we aim to achieve that and, very importantly, how we measure whether or not we have achieved that which we proposed. Setting up a range of drugs prevention programmes in parts of the country and evaluating them can only be sufficiently useful to the problem of illicit drug misuse if these programmes and their evaluation processes are geared towards assessing their impact on the onset of drug misuse within given geographical areas at least, and on the basis of findings assessing whether or not improvements are needed in existing drugs prevention strategies. For the most vulnerable sections of society, it is a major hindrance to any efforts to draw a relationship between drugs prevention and drug misuse when drugs prevention youth projects are set up and closed down in short periods of time.

The seeming lack of a systematic monitoring system also befalls drug treatment. Despite its very long history as a drug demand control mechanism, it is only recently that some useful information on treatment outcomes has been gained through the National Treatment Outcomes Research Study (Gossop *et al.* 2003). As already noted in *Chapter 2*, the study concluded that there are benefits in drug treatment, having followed the progress of 1,100 problem drug users for four to five years after their entry into treatment. Previous to this national study, the success or failure rates of treatment had been unclear. Before and after the 'British System' of maintenance prescribing, drug treatment success seemed to have been measured by the numbers of those registered with drug treatment agencies. This tradition of primarily assessing progress based on increasing figures of known drug users has been carried on and prioritised within ongoing developments in drug treatment strategy, which has since the 1980s prioritised a harm-reductionist approach (Home Office 2004a).

The DTTOs, arrest referral schemes and the CARAT programme are instances of recent channels to drug treatment juxtaposed alongside the conventional method of voluntary presentations to drug treatment services. Doubtless these developments, which are premised on the notion that 'treatment works' at least for the sake of harm reduction, are welcomed but they will be most welcomed if their effectiveness is frequently monitored, with abstinence as the main aim to achieve. The ultimate outcome of increasing the number of people in treatment ought to focus on getting problem drug users to lead a drug-free life and one of the key ways of measuring treatment progress in this sense is to open all drug treatment services—within and outside the community—to frequent, constructive and pragmatic scrutiny. These services are the final destination for problem drug users who may have volunteered for treatment or been coerced by the criminal justice system to undertake treatment. Regardless of how they got there or any professional disagreements that may occur in this partnership approach to treatment, data on how clients are responding to treatment are central to further developments in the drug treatment approach. Bearing this in mind, it would then mean that drug services are required to be thorough in recording client's profiles including their social profile and drug using characteristics, accurate data of source of referrals, closed and re-opened cases as well as withdrawals from treatment.

Such a defined and focused approach in the collection and collation of data would naturally uncover or illuminate gaps in knowledge particularly in relation to visible minority ethnic communities. It is also important to recognise the role of culturally-specific voluntary drug treatment agencies which many problem drug users from minority ethnic communities find more accessible. It may be the case that with a full government backing, such agencies can work collaboratively with mainstream drug treatment services towards a common goal to tackle minority ethnic community problem drug use. If drug treatment service provision is to address racial and cultural diversity, it is imperative firstly to acquire a comprehensive detail of the nature and patterns of problem drug use among various racial and ethnic groups. This could be achieved by tapping into varied sources of information. Complexities surrounding issues such as drug treatment provision and retention rates for problem drug users from minority ethnic communities can be untangled.

In all, an ongoing all-inclusive nationwide data collection process with a clear effect on purpose and outcome is first and foremost crucial to all aspects of the drug control strategy in order to move forward in addressing the drug situation which Bean (2004: 90) describes as 'a problem that is almost out of control'. Unless we are prepared to settle for the legalisation of all drugs as some have suggested, it is otherwise imperative that we re-demonstrate that drug prohibition is worthwhile.

Bibliography

Advisory Council on the Misuse of Drugs (1982) *Treatment and Rehabilitation.* London: HMSO.

______ (1988) *AIDS and Drug Misuse,* Part I. London: HMSO.

______ (1989) *AIDS and Drug Misuse,* Part II. London: HMSO.

______ (1994) *Drug Misusers and the Criminal Justice System.* London: HMSO.

______ (1998) *Drug Misuse and the Environment.* London: HMSO.

Ahmad, M. and Mwenda, L. (2004) 'Drug Seizure and Offender Statistics: United Kingdom, 2001 and 2002', 2nd edn., *Home Office Statistical Bulletin,* 08/04. London: Home Office.

Aust, R., Sharp, C. and Goulden, C. (2002) *Prevalence of Drug Use: Key Findings from the 2001/2002 British Crime Survey.* London: Home Office.

Aust, R. and Smith N. (2003) 'Ethnicity and Drug Use: Key Findings from the 2001/2002 British Crime Survey', *Findings 209.* London: Home Office.

Aviles, N., Barnard, M., Rhodes, T., Hariga, F., Weber, U., Coppel, A. and Fountain, J. (2000) 'Qualitative Research on the Health Risks Associated with Drug Injecting: Needle and Syringe Sharing', in European Monitoring Centre for Drugs and Drug Addiction, eds., *Understanding and Responding to Drug Use.* Luxembourg: Office for Official Publications of the European Communities.

Awiah, J., Butt, S. and Dorn, N. (1990) '"The Last Place I Would Go": Black People and Drug Services in Britain', *DrugLink,* vol. 5, issue 5.

______ (1992) *Race, Gender and Drug Services,* ISDD Research Monograph 6. London: Institute for the Study of Drug Dependence.

Bamford, T., Child, P., Drugscope and Measden, J. (2000) *Commissioning Tier 4 Drug Services for Young People,* Confidential Report for the Department of Health.

Barton, A. (1999) 'Breaking the Crime/Drugs Cycle: The Birth of a New Approach?', *Howard Journal of Criminal Justice,* vol. 38, no. 2.

______ (2003) *Illicit Drugs: Use and Control.* London: Routledge.

Bashford, J., Knight, M., Sheikh, N., Fountain, J. and Patel, K. (2000) *Substance Misuse and the Service Provision Needs of Young People in Shropshire,* Report to Shropshire Drug Action Team. Preston: Centre for Ethnicity and Health, Faculty of Health, University of Central Lancashire.

Bashford, J., Patel, K., Sheikh, N. and Winters, M. (2001) *A Review of Current Drug Service Provision for the South Asian Community in Calderdale, with a Particular Focus on Young People,* Report to Health Living Team. Preston: Centre for Ethnicity and Health, Faculty of Health, University of Central Lancashire.

Bean, P. (1974) *The Social Control of Drugs.* London: Martin Robertson.

______ (2002) *Drugs and Crime.* Devon: Willan Publishing.

______ (2004) *Drugs and Crime.* 2nd Edn. Devon: Willan Publishing

Becker, J. and Roe, S. (2005) 'Drug Use among Vulnerable Groups of Young People: Findings from the 2003 Crime and Justice Survey', *Findings 254.* London: Home Office.

Bennett, T. (1994) 'Drug Use and Criminal Behaviour', in I. Glass, ed., *The International Handbook of Addiction Behaviour.* London: Routledge.

Bennett, T. (1998) *Drugs and Crime: The Results of the Research on Drug Testing and Interviewing Arrestees,* Home Office Research Study 183. London: Home Office.

Bentley, C. and Hanton, A. (1997) *A Study to Investigate the Extent to which there is a Drug Problem amongst Young Asian People in Nottingham. How Effective are Drugs Services in Providing Assistance for such Minority Ethnic Groups?,* Report, ADAPT, Nottingham.

Berridge, V. (1984) 'Drugs and Social Policy: The Establishment of Social Control in Britain, 1900-1930', *British Journal of Addiction,* vol. 79, pp. 17-29.

______ (1988) 'The Origins of the English Drug "Scene" 1890-1930', *Medical History,* vol. 32, pp. 51-64.

Berridge, V. and Edwards, G. (1981) *Opium and the People: Opiate in Nineteenth-Century England.* London: Allen Lane.

Bewley, T. (1966) 'Recent Changes in Patterns of Drug Addiction in the United Kingdom', *Bulletin of Narcotics,* vol. 18, no. 4.

Box, S. (1981) *Deviance, Reality and Society,* 2nd edn. London: Holt, Rinehart and Winston.

Brain, K., Parker, H. and Bottomley, T. (1998) *Evolving Crack Cocaine Careers.* Manchester: University of Manchester.

Bramley-Harker, E. (2001) *Sizing the UK Market for Illicit Drugs*, RDS Occasional Paper 74. London: Home Office.

Burr (1987) 'Chasing the Dragon: Heroin Use, Delinquency and Crime in the Context of South London Culture', *British Journal of Criminology*, vol. 27, no. 4.

Bush-Baskette, S. (1998) 'The War on Drugs as a War against Women', in S. Miller, ed., *Crime Control and Women*. California: Sage.

Cashmore, E. and McLaughlin, E. (1991) 'Out of Order', in E. Cashmore and E. McLaughlin, eds., *Out of Order*. London: Routledge.

Cashmore, E. and Troyna, B. eds. (1982) *Black Youth in Crisis*. London: George Allen and Unwin.

Chantler, K. (1998) *An Analysis of Present Drug Service Delivery to Black Communities in Greater Manchester*, Project Report March 1998. Greater Manchester: Greater Manchester Drug Action Partnership and Black Drug Workers Forum.

Chaundery, M., Sherlock, K. and Patel, K. (1997) *Drugs and Ethnic Health Project: Oldham and Tameside 1997*, A Report to the West Pennine Drug Action Team. Manchester: Lifeline/Preston: University of Central Lancashire.

Clark, R. (2001) 'Informers and Corruption', in R. Billingsley *et al.*, eds., *Informers: Policing, Policy and Practice*. Cullompton: Willan Publishing.

Conrad, P. and Schneider, J. (1980) *Deviance and Medicalization: From Badness to Sickness*. St Louis: C.V. Mosby.

Cook, P. (1999) 'European Drug Policy on Supply and Demand Reduction', in C. Stark, B. Kidd and R. Sykes, eds., *Illegal Drug Use in the United Kingdom: Prevention, Treatment and Enforcement*. Aldershot: Ashgate.

Cooney, M. (1994) 'Evidence as Partisanship', *Law and Society Review*, vol. 28, no. 4.

Corkery, J. (1998) 'Statistics of Drugs Seizures and Offenders Dealt With, United Kingdom, 1996', *Home Office Statistical Bulletin*, 10/98. London: Home Office.

______ (1999) 'Drug Seizure and Offender Statistics, United Kingdom, 1997', *Home Office Statistical Bulletin*, 8/99. London: Home Office.

______ (2002) 'Drug Seizure and Offender Statistics, United Kingdom, 2000', *Home Office Statistical Bulletin*, 4/02. London: Home Office.

Corkery, J.M. and Airs, J. (2003) 'Seizure of Drugs in the UK 2001', *Findings 202*. London: Home Office.

Crowley, J. and Simmons, S. (1992) 'Mental Health, Race and Ethnicity: A Retrospective Study of the Care of Ethnic Minorities and Whites in a Psychiatric Unit', *Journal of Advanced Nursing*, vol. 17, pp. 1078-1087.

Cunningham, T. (1998) 'The Culture of Kat', *Nursing Standard*, vol. 13, no.12.

Dale-Perera, A. and Farrant, F. (1999) 'At Home with Diversity', *DrugLink*, vol. 14, issue 5.

Day, D. (1996) *Health Emergency 1997: The Spread of Drug-related AIDS among African Americans and Latinos*. Princeton, New Jersey: Dogwood Center.

Deedes, W. (1970) *The Drugs Epidemic*. London: Tom Stacey.

Department of Health (2001) *Statistics from the Regional Drug Misuse Databases for Six Months Ending September 2000*. London: Department of Health.

Department of Social Security (1998) *Your Social Security Insurance, Benefits and Health Care Rights in the European Community, and in Iceland, Liechtenstein and Norway*, Leaflet SA29. London: Department of Social Security.

______ (2000) *Benefits for People from Abroad*, Fact Sheets on Social Security. London: Department of Social Security.

Department of Sociology, City University (1997) *Race, Drugs, Europe: Specialist Drug services and Managing Change to Meet the Needs of Black and Other Visible Minority Drug Users*. London: Department of Sociology, City University.

Dodd (1978) 'Police and Thieves in London', *New Society*, 16 March.

Dorn, N. and South, N. (1985) *Helping Drug Users*. Hants: Gower.

Dorn, N. and South, N. eds. (1987) *A Land Fit for Heroin?* London: Macmillan.

Dorn, N., Ribbens, J. and South, N. (1987) *Coping with a Nightmare*. London: Institute for the Study of Drug Dependence.

Dorn, N. and Murji, K. (1992) *Drug Prevention: A Review of the English Language Literature*, Research Monograph 5. London: Institute for the Study of Drug Dependence.

Dorn, N., Murji, K. and South, N. (1992) *Traffickers: Drug Markets and Law Enforcement*. London: Routledge.

Dorn, N., Levi, M. and King, L (2005) *Literature Review on Upper Level Drug Trafficking,* Home Office Online Report 22/05. http://www.homeoffice.gov.uk/rds

DrugScope (2003) *Providing Information for Black and Minority Ethnic Groups.* London: DrugScope.

Drugs Prevention Initiative (1999) *Final Progress Report 1997-99.* London: Home Office.

Edmunds, M., Hough, M., Turnbull, P. and May, T. (1999) *Doing Justice to Treatment,* DPAS Paper 2. London: Home Office.

Emerson, R. (1991) 'Case Processing and Interorganizational Knowledge: Detecting the "Real Reasons" for Referrals', *Social Problems,* vol. 38, no. 2.

European Monitoring Centre for Drugs and Drug Addiction. ed. (2000) *Understanding and Responding to Drug Use.* Luxembourg: Office for Official Publications of the European Communities.

______ (2002) *Report on the Drug Situation in the Candidate CEECs.* Luxembourg: Office for Official Publications of the European Communities.

Evans, D. (2002) 'Drug Crime: What's the Colour of Money?', *Fed Express,* issue 2.

Federation, The (2002) 'Re-offending by Ex-prisoners Examined by Government Think Tank', *Fed Express,* issue 3.

Fountain, J., Bashford, J., Underwood, S., Khurana, J., Winters, M., Patel, K. and Carpenter, C. (2002) *Update and Complete the Analysis of Drug Use, Consequences and Correlates amongst Minorities,* unpublished report.

Foy, S. (1996) 'Getting a Grip', *Criminal Justice Matters,* 24, pp. 8-9.

Gay, P. (1989) *Getting Together: A Study of Self-help Groups for Drug Users' Families.* London: Policy Studies Institute.

Gilman (2000) 'A Qualitative View of Drugs Policing: Heroin Markets in Greater Manchester, UK', in European Monitoring Centre for Drugs and Drug Addiction, ed. *Understanding and Responding to Drug Use: The Role of Qualitative Research.* Luxembourg: Office for Official Publications of the European Communities.

Gilroy, P. (1987) *There Ain't No Black in the Union Jack.* London: Hutchinson.

Glatt, M. (1974) *A Guide to Addiction and its Treatment.* Lancaster, England: Medical and Technical Publishing Co.

Glover, S., Gott, C., Loizillon, A., Portes, J., Price, R., Spencer, S., Srinivasan, V. and Willis, C. (2001) *Migration: An Economic and Social Analysis,* RDS Occasional Paper 67. London: Home Office.

Godfrey, C., Eaton, G., McDougall, C. and Culyer, A. (2002) *The Economic and Social Costs of Class A Drug Use in England and Wales, 2000,* Home Office Research Study 249. London: Home Office.

Gooden, T. (1999) *Carers and Parents of African Caribbean and Asian Substance Users in Nottingham: A Needs Analysis,* Final Report. Nottingham: Organizational Change Innovation Development/Nottingham Black Initiative.

Gossop, M. (1993) *Living with Drugs.* Aldershot: Ashgate.

Gossop, M., Marsden, J., Stewart, D. and Kidd, T. (2003) 'The National Treatment Outcome Research Study (NTORS): 4-5 Year Follow-up Results', *Addiction,* vol. 98, pp. 291-303.

Graham, J. and Bowling, B. (1995) *Young People and Crime,* Home Office Research Study 145. London: Home Office.

Green, P. (1991) *Drug Couriers.* London: The Howard League for Penal Reform.

______ ed. (1996) *Drug Couriers: A New Perspective.* London: Quartet Books Ltd.

______ (1998) *Drugs, Trafficking and Criminal Policy: The Scapegoat Strategy.* Winchester: Waterside Press.

Groom, C., Davies, T. and Balchin, S. (1998) ' Developing a Methodology for Measuring Illegal Activity for the UK National Accounts', *Economic Trends,* no. 356, pp. 33-71.

Hall, S., Critcher, C., Clarke, J., Jefferson, T. and Roberts, B. (1978) *Policing the Crisis.* London: Macmillan.

Harper, R. and Murphy, R. (1999) *Drug Smuggling: An Analysis of the Traffickers 1991-1997.* Middlesex: Middlesex Probation Service.

Harrison, L., Sutton, M. and Gardiner, E. (1997) 'Ethnic Differences in Substance Use and Alcohol Use-Related Mortality among First Generation Migrants to England and Wales', *Substance Use and Misuse,* vol. 32, pp. 849-876.

Hartnoll, R. (1989) 'The International Context', in S. MacGregor, ed., *Drugs and British Society.* London: Routledge.

______ (1993) 'Heroin Maintenance and AIDS Prevention: Going the Whole Way?, *International Journal of Drug Policy,* vol. 1, pp. 36-41.

Haw, S. (1985). *Drug Problems in Greater Glasgow.* London: Chamelion.

Henderson, S. (1999) 'Drugs and Culture: The Question of Gender', in: N. South, ed., *Drugs: Cultures, Controls and Everyday Life*. London: Sage.

Henman, A., Lewis, R. and Malyon, T. (1985) 'Junkie Behaviour v. the Merchants of Death', in A. Henman, R. Lewis and T. Malyon, eds., *Big Deal: The Politics of Illicit Drug Business*. London: Pluto.

Hiro, D. (1992) *Black British White British*. London: Paladin.

HM Inspector of Prisons (1992) *Annual Report April 1991-March 1992*. London: HMSO.

HM Prison Service (1995) *Drug Misuse in Prison*. London: HMSO.

Holloway, K., Bennett, T. and Farrington, D. (2005) *The Effectiveness of Criminal Justice and Treatment Programmes in Reducing Drug-related Crime: A Systematic Review*, Home Office Online Report 26/05. http://www.homeoffice.gov.uk/rds

Holzner, B. (1972) *Reality Construction in Society*. Cambridge: Schenkman.

Home Office (1985) *Tackling Drug Misuse: A Summary of the Government's Strategy*, 1st edn. London: HMSO.

______ (1986) 'The Ethnic Origin of Prisoners: The Prison Population on 30 June 1985 and Persons Received, July 1984-March 1985', *Home Office Statistical Bulletin*, 22/84. London: Home Office.

______ (1989) 'The Ethnic Group of Those Proceeded Against by the Courts in the Metropolitan Police District in 1984 and 1985', *Home Office Statistical Bulletin*, 6/89, London: Home Office.

______ (1990) *UK Action Plan on Drug Misuse: The Government's Strategy*. London: HMSO.

______ (1993) 'The Prison Population in 1992', *Home Office Statistical Bulletin 7/93*. London: Home Office.

______ (1994a). *Tackling Drugs Together: A Consultation Document on a Strategy for England 1995-98*, Green Paper. London: HMSO.

______ (1994b) 'The Ethnic Origins of Prisoners: Ethnic Composition of Prison Population 1985-1993', *Home Office Statistical Bulletin*, 21/94. London: Home Office.

______ (1995) *Tackling Drugs Together: A Strategy for England 1995-98*, White Paper. London: HMSO.

______ (1996) 'Drug Misuse Declared in 1996: Latest Results of the 1994 British Crime Survey', *Home Office Research Study 151*. London: Home Office.

______ (1997). 'Drug Misuse Declared: Results of the 1994 British Crime Survey', *Home Office Research Study 172*. London: Home Office.

______ (1998) *Tackling Drugs to Build a Better Britain: The Government's Ten Year Strategy for Tackling Drug Misuse*. London: HMSO.

______ (1999) *Statistics on Race and the Criminal Justice System*. London: Home Office.

______ (2000) *Statistics on Race and the Criminal Justice System*. London: Home Office.

______ (2001) *United Kingdom Anti-Drugs Co-ordinator's Annual Report 2000/01*. London: Home Office.

______ (2002a) *Updated Drug Strategy 2002*. London: Home Office.

______ (2002b) *Tackling Crack: A National Plan*. London: Home Office.

______ (2002c) *Statistics on Women and the Criminal Justice System*. London: Home Office.

______ (2003) *The Substance Misuse Needs of Minority Prisoner Groups: Women, Young Offenders and Ethnic Minorities*. London: Home Office.

______ (2004a) *Tackling Drugs. Changing Lives: Keeping Communities Safe from Drugs*. London: Home Office.

______ (2004b) *Statistics on Race and the Criminal Justice System*. London: Home Office.

______ (2005a) *Drug Use among Vulnerable Groups of Young People: Findings from the 2003 Crime and Justice Survey*. London: Home Office.

______ (2005b) *Drug Misuse Declared: Findings from the 2003/04 British Crime Survey*. London: Home Office.

Hooker, P. (1996) *Chinese Cultural Studies – Opium Wars*. http://www.accc6.its.brocklyn.cuny.edu

Hough, M. (1996) *Drugs Misuse and the Criminal Justice System: A Review of the Literature*, DPI Paper 15. London: Home Office.

Hough, M., Clancy, C., McSweeney, T. and Turnbull, P. (2003) 'The Impact of Drug Testing and Treatment Orders on Offending: Two Year Reconviction Results', *Findings 184*. London: Home Office.

Howe, D. (1973) 'Fighting Back: West Indian Youth and the Police in Nottingham', *Race Today*, vol. 5, no. 1.

Hucklesby, A. and Wilkinson, C. (2001) 'Drug Misuse in Prisons: Some Comments on the Prison Service Drug Strategy', *Howard Journal of Criminal Justice*, vol. 40, no. 4.

Hughes, R. (2000) 'Drug Injectors and Prison Mandatory Drug Testing', *Howard Journal of Criminal Justice*, vol. 39, no. 1.

Humphrey, D. (1972) *Police Power and Black People*. London: Panther.

Humphrey, D. and John, G. (1971) *Because They're Black*. Harmondsworth: Penguin.

Inciardi, A.J. and Chambers, D. eds. (1974) *Drugs and the Criminal Justice System*. London: Sage.

Jamieson, A., Glanz, A. and MacGregor, S. (1984) *Dealing with Drug Misuse: Crisis Intervention in the City*. London: Tavistock.

Jarvis, G. and Parker, H. (1989) 'Young Heroin Users and Crime', *British Journal of Criminology*, vol. 29, no. 2.

John, G. (1981) *In the Service of Black Youth*. London: National Association of Youth Clubs.

Johnson, M. and Carroll, M. (1995) *Dealing with Diversity*, Home Office Paper 5. London: Home Office.

Kalunta-Crumpton, A. (1998) 'Drug Trafficking and Criminal Justice', *International Journal of the Sociology of Law*, 26, 321-338.

______ (1999) *Race and Drug Trials*, Aldershot: Ashgate.

______ (2001) Review of Green, P. (1998) *Drugs, Trafficking and Criminal Policy* (Winchester: Waterside Press), *British Journal of Criminology*, vol. 41, no. 2, pp. 400-402.

______ (2003a) 'Blacklisted: Race, Drugs and Crime', *DrugLink*, vol.18, issue 3.

______ (2003b) 'Race and Problem Drug Use in an English City', *International Journal of Offender Therapy and Comparative Criminology*, vol. 47, no.8, pp. 677-697.

Keith, M. (1991) "Policing a Perplexed Society?': No-go Areas and the Mystification of Police-black Conflict', in E. Cashmore and E. McLaughlin, eds., *Out of Order*. London: Routledge.

______ (1993) *Race, Riots and Policing*. London: UCL.

Khan, F. and Ditton, J. (1999) *Minority Ethnic Drug Use in Glasgow, Part 2: Special Problems Experienced and Possible Gaps in Service Provision*. Glasgow: Glasgow Drugs Prevention Team.

Khan, K. (1999) 'Plaster Over the Cracks', *DrugLink*, vol. 14, issue 5.

King, J. F. (1969) *Probation and After-care Service*. London: Butterworths.

King, M., Coker, E., Leavey, G., Hoare, A. and Johnson-Sabine, E. (1994) 'Incidence of Psychotic Illness in London: Comparison of Ethnic Group', *British Medical Journal*, vol. 309, pp. 1115-1119.

King, R. (1974) 'The American System: Legal Sanctions to Repress Drug Abuse', in J.A. Inciardi and D. Chambers, eds., *Drugs and the Criminal Justice System*. London: Sage.

Kushlick, D. (2004) 'Globalised Drugs Policy - One Size Does Not Fit All', *Howard League Magazine*, vol. 22, no. 3.

Leigh, W.A. (n.d) 'Health of African American Youth', *Joint Center Fact Sheet*. Washington D.C: Joint Center for Political and Economic Studies.

Leitner, M., Shapland, J. and Wiles, P. (1993) *Drug Usage and Drug Prevention*. London: Home Office.

Lewis, R. (1985) 'Serious Business: The Global Heroin Economy', in A. Henman, R. Lewis and T. Maylon, eds., *Big Deal: The Politics of Illicit Drug Business*. London: Pluto.

Lindesmith, A.R. (1965) *The Addict and the Law*. Bloomington: Indiana University Press.

Lindsell, H. (2003) *Crack: The New Pimp?* London: West London Mission.

Lusane, C. (2000) 'We Are the World: Race and the International War on Drugs', in C. Henry, ed., *Foreign Policy and the Black (Inter)National Interest*. Albany: State University of New York.

MacGregor, S. (1989a) 'Choices for Policy and Practice', in S. MacGregor, ed., *Drugs and British Society*, London: Routledge.

______ (1989b) 'The Public Debate in the 1980s', in S. MacGregor, ed., *Drugs and British Society*, London: Routledge.

______ ed. (1989c) *Drugs and British Society*, London: Routledge.

______ (2000). 'Social Exclusion: An Overview', in European Monitoring Centre for Drugs and Drug Addiction, ed., *Understanding and Responding to Drug Use*. Luxembourg: Office for Official Publications of the European Communities.

Mainliners (2003) *Sex for Sale: New Challenges for Women Working On and Off the Streets*. London: Mainliners.

Matthews, L. (2002) 'Back to the Future', *Fed Express*, issue 2.

May, C. (2005) 'The CARAT Drug Service in Prisons: Findings from the Research Database', *Findings 262*. London: Home Office.

Maynard, S. (1994) *A Unified Approach: The Response of Newham's African-Caribbean Community to Drug Misuse*. London: Newham Drugs Prevention Team.

Measham, F., Parker, H. and Aldridge, J. (1998) 'The Teenage Transition: From Adolescent Recreational Drug Use to the Young Adult Dance Culture in Britain in the Mid-1990s', *Journal of Drug Issues*, vol. 28, pp. 9-32.

Merton, R. (1938) 'Social Structure and Anomie', American Sociological Review, 3, pp. 672-82.

Mirza, H., Pearson, G. and Philips, S. (1991a) *Drugs, People and Services in Lewisham,* Final Report of the Drug Information Project. London: Goldsmiths College, University of London.
Mirza, H., Philips, S. and Pearson, G. (1991b) 'Drug Misuse in a South London Borough', in T. Bennett, ed., *Drug Misuse in Local Communities.* London: The Police Foundation.
Mott, J. and Mirrlees-Black, C. (1995) *Self Reported Drug Misuse in England and Wales: Findings from the 1992 British Crime Survey.* London: Home Office.
Murji, K. (1998) *Policing Drugs.* Aldershot: Ashgate.
National Audit Office (2004) *The Drug Treatment and Testing Order: Early Lessons.* London: The Stationery Office.
National Treatment Agency (NTA) (2002a) *Commissioning Cocaine/Crack Treatment.* London: NTA.
______ (2002b) *Treating Cocaine/Crack Dependence.* London: NTA.
______ (2002c) *Models of Care for Treatment of Adult Drug Misusers, Part 1: Summary for Commissioners and Managers Responsible for Implementation.* London: NTA.
______ (2003) *Update.* London: NTA.
______ (2005) *Provisional Statistics for the National Drug Treatment Monitoring System in England, 2003/04.* London: NTA.
Nefertari, M. and Ahmun, V. (1999) 'Black Drug Services Eclipsed', *DrugLink,* vol. 14, issue. 5.
Newcombe, R. (1987) 'High Time for Harm Reduction', *DrugLink,* vol, 2, issue, 1.
Nolan-Trainer, G. (1996) 'Black Women and Drugs: Setting the Agenda', *DrugLink,* vol. 11, issue 2.
North and South Thames Regional Database Managers (1995) *Problem Drug Use Reported by the Services of Greater London: A Report of the Data Collected between April 1991 and March 1994.* London: North and South Thames Regional Database.
O'Malley, P. and Mugford, S. (1991) 'The Demand for Intoxicating Commodities: Implications for the "War on Drugs"', *Social Justice,* vol. 18, pp. 49-75.
Parker, H., Bakx, K. and Newcombe, R. (1986) 'Heroin and the Young', *New Society,* 24 January.
Parker, H., Newcombe, R. and Bakx, K. (1988) *Living with Heroin.* Milton Keynes: Open University Press.
Parker, H., Aldridge, J. and Measham, F. (1998a) *Illegal Leisure: The Normalisation of Adolescent Recreational Drug Use.* London: Routledge.
Parker, H., Bury, C. and Egginton, R. (1998b) *New Heroin Outbreaks Amongst Young People in England and Wales,* Crime Detection and Prevention Series, Paper 92. London: Home Office.
Patel, K. (2000) 'Using Qualitative Research to Examine the Nature of Drug Use among Minority Ethnic Communities in the UK', in European Monitoring Centre for Drugs and Drug Addiction, ed., *Understanding and Responding to Drug Use.* Luxembourg: Office for Official Publications of the European Communities.
Patel, K., Sherlock, K., Chaudy, M. and Buffin, J. (1998) Drug Use amongst Asian Communities in Cheetham Hill. Manchester: Lifeline/Preston: University of Central Lancashire.
Patel, K., Wardle, I., Bashford, J. and Winters, M. (2001) *The Evaluation of Nafas – A Bangladeshi Drug Service.* Preston: Ethnicity and Health Unit, Faculty of Health, University of Central Lancashire.
Patel, K. and Wibberley, C. (2002) 'Young Asians and Drug Use', *Journal of Child Health Care,* vol. 5, no. 1, pp. 53-61.
Pearson, G. (1987a) *The New Heroin Users.* Oxford: Basil Blackwell.
______ (1987b) 'Social Deprivation, Unemployment and Patterns of Heroin Use', in N. Dorn and N. South, eds, *A Land Fit for Heroin?* London: Macmillan.
______ (1992) 'Drug Problems and Criminal Justice Policy', *Contemporary Drug Problems,* vol. 19, pp. 279-301.
Pearson, G., Gilman, M. and McLver, S. (1987) *Young People and Heroin.* Aldershot: Gower.
Pearson, G. and Patel, K. (1998) 'Drugs, Deprivation and Ethnicity: Outreach among Asian Drug Users in a Northern English City', *Journal of Drug Issues,* vol. 28, no. 1.
Pearson, G. and Hobbs, D. (2001) *Middle Market Drug Distribution,* Home Office Research Study 227. London: Home Office.
Pearson, Y. (1996) *A Report on the Work of the Crack Awareness Team with Crack Users in Nottingham from September 1994-August 1995 (CAT Progress Report Year 2).* Nottingham: CAT.
Peck, D. and Plant, M. (1986) 'Unemployment and Illegal Drug Use: Concordant Evidence from a Prospective Study and from National Trends', *British Medical Journal,* vol. 293, pp. 929-932.
Penfold, C., Turnbull, P. and Webster, R. (2005) *Tackling Prison Drug Markets: An Exploratory Qualitative Study,* Home Office Online Report 39/05. http://www.homeoffice.gov.uk/rds

Perera, J. (1996) *Drug Misuse in Bedfordshire: Preliminary Report to Inform Further Assessment Research*, Report to Public Health Specialist and DAT Coordinator. London: Action Research Consultancies.

Perera, J., Power, R. and Gibson, N. (1993) *Assessing the Needs of Black Drug Users in North Westminster*. London: The Hungerford Drug Project & The Centre for Research on Drugs and Health Behaviour.

Perera, J., Khalifah, A. and Ahmed, H. (1997) *Assessing the Needs of Black and Minority Ethnic Drug Users: A Preliminary Report*. Watford: Watford Drug Education Forum.

Plant, M. (1987) *Drugs in Perspective*. London: Hodder and Stoughton.

Ramsay, M. (2003) 'Prisoners' Drug Use and Treatment: Seven Studies', *Findings 186*. London: Home Office.

Ramsay, M. and Percy, A. (1996) *Drug Misuse Declared: Results of the 1994 British Crime Survey*, Home Office Research Study 151. London: Home Office.

Ramsay, M. and Spiller, J. (1997) *Drug Misuse Declared in 1996: Latest Results from the British Crime Survey*, Home Office Research Study 172. London: Home Office.

Ramsay, M., Baker, P., Goulden, C., Sharp, C. and Sondhi, A. (2001) *Drug Misuse Declared in 2000: Results from the British Crime Survey*, Home Office Research Study 224. London: Home Office.

Rex, J. (1982) 'West Indian and Asian Youth', in E. Cashmore and B. Troyna, eds., *Black Youth in Crisis*. London: George Allen and Unwin.

Richards, M., McWilliams, B., Batten, N., Cameron, C. and Cutler, J. (1995) 'Foreign Nationals in English Prisons: 11. Some Policy Issues', *Howard Journal of Criminal Justice*, vol. 34, no. 3.

Roach Family Support Committee (1989) *Policing in Hackney 1945-1984*. London: Karia/RFSC.

Ruggiero, V. (1992) *Perceptions of the Drug Prevention in Central Lambeth: A Report to Lambeth Drugs Prevention Team*. London: Home Office.

Ruggiero, V. and South, N. (1995) *Organised Crime and Drug Markets: Images of Illegal Drug Markets in the Late Modern City*, A Working Paper 1, BSA.

Sanders, A. (1994) 'From Suspect to Trial', in M. Maguire, R. Morgan and R. Reiner, eds., *The Oxford Handbook of Criminology*. Oxford: Clarendon Press.

Sangster, D., Shiner, M., Patel, K. and Sheikh, N. (2001) *Delivering Drug Services to Black and Minority Ethnic Communities*. London: Home Office.

Sheikh, N., Fountain, J., Bashford, J. and Patel, K. (2001) *A Review of Current Drug Service Provision for Black and Minority Ethnic Communities in Bedfordshire*, Final Report to Bedfordshire Drug Action Team. Preston: Centre for Ethnicity and Health, Faculty of Health, University of Central Lancashire.

Sheikh, N., Fountain, J., Khurana, J., Syed, A. and Patel, K. (2002) *Planning Drug and Alcohol Services for Adults from Black and Minority Ethnic Communities in Waltham Forest and Redbridge*, Final Report on a Needs Assessment for Waltham Forest and Redbridge Drug Action Teams. Preston: Centre for Ethnicity and Health, Faculty of Health, University of Central Lancashire.

Smith, D. and Gray, J. (1985) *Police and People in London*, The PSI Report. Gower: Aldershot.

Solomos, J. (1989) *Race and Racism in Contemporary Britain*. London: Macmillan.

______ (1993). *Race and Racism in Britain*. London: Macmillan.

Sondhi, A., O'Shea, J. and Williams, T. (2002) *Arrest Referral: Emerging Findings from the National Monitoring and Evaluation Programme*, DPAS Briefing Paper 18. London: Home Office.

South, N. (1994) 'Drugs: Control, Crime and Criminological Studies', in M. Maguire, R. Morgan and R. Reiner, eds., *The Oxford Handbook of Criminology*. Oxford: Clarendon Press.

Southwell, M. (1995) 'Shape Up or Pay Up', *DrugLink*, vol. 10, issue 1.

Spear, H. B. (1969) 'The Growth of Heroin Addiction in the United Kingdom', *British Journal of Addiction*, vol. 64, pp. 245-255.

Stein, S. (1985) *International Diplomacy, State Administration and Narcotics Control*. Aldershot: Gower.

Stimson, G. and Lart, R. (1991) 'HIV, Drugs, and Public Health in England: New Worlds, Old Tunes', *The International Journal of the Addictions*, vol. 26, pp. 1263-1277.

Stimson, G. and Oppenheimer, E. (1982) *Heroin Addiction: Treatment and Control in Britain*. London: Tavistock.

Sudbury, J. (2002) 'Celling Black Bodies: Black Women in the Global Prison Industrial Complex', *Feminist Review*, vol. 70.

Taylor, I. (1992) 'The International Drug Trade and Money-Laundering: Border Controls and Other Issues', *European Sociological Review*, vol. 8, no. 2.

Turnbull, P., Dolan, K. and Stimson, G. (1991) *Prisons, HIV and AIDS: Risks and Experiences in Custodial Care*. Horsham: AVERT.

Turnbull, P., Stimson, G. and Stillwell, G. (1994) *Drug Use in Prison*. Horsham: AVERT.

Turnbull, P., Webster, R. and Stillwell, G. (1996) *Get it While You Can: An Evaluation of an Early Intervention Project for Arrestees with Alcohol and Drug Problems*, Drugs DPI Paper 9. London: Home Office.

Turnbull, P., McSweeney, T., Webster, R., Edmunds, M. and Hough, M. (2000) *Drug Treatment and Testing Orders: Final Evaluation*, Home Office Research Study 212. London: Home Office.

Turning Point (2004) *Routes to Drug Treatment: Drugs and Crime*. London: Turning Point.

______ (2005) *The Crack Report*. London: Turning Point.

Turning Point/Home Office (2004) *Khat Use in Somali, Ethiopian and Yemeni Communities in England: Issues and Solutions*. London: Turning Point/Home Office.

Turning Point/Conference on Crack and Cocaine (COCA) (2005) *Protocols and Good Practice Guidelines for Working with Crack Users in Generic Substance Misuse Services*. London: Turning Point/COCA

Tyler, A. (1986) *Street Drugs*. Great Britain: New English Library.

United Nations (UN) (2002) *Report of the International Narcotics Control Board for 2002*. Vienna: United Nations.

Velleman, R. and Rigby, J. (1990) 'Harm-minimisation: Old Wine in New Bottles', *International Journal on Drug Policy*, vol. 1, pp. 24-27.

Webster, R. (2001) *An Assessment of the Substance Misuse Treatment Needs of Young People in Bedfordshire*, Report to Bedfordshire Health Authority. Bedford: Bedford Health Authority.

Weekes, G. (2002) 'Cracking the Problem', *Fed Express*, issue 3.

Whittington, D. (1999) Nang Tien Nan: Princess Opium in Deptford, *DrugLink*, September/October, pp. 13-14.

Willis, J. (1969) *Drug Dependence*. London: Faber and Faber.

______ (1973) *Addicts: Drugs and Alcohol Re-examined*. Nairobi: Pitman.

Wodak, A. (1994) AIDS and Drug Use: To Shun the Heaven that Leads Man to this Hell, in I. Glass, ed., *The International Handbook of Addiction Behaviour*. London: Routledge.

Young, J. (1971) *The Drug Takers*. London: Paladin

Index